Growth of Art in American Schools

Harper's Exploration Series in Education

Under the Advisory Editorship of John Guy Fowlkes

No. 50
G. A. C.

Notan Landscape Composition in Two
Tones. (From A. W. Dow, "Composition,"
J. M. Bowles, 1899.)

Visual Illusion of Size and Direction.
(From Gyorgy Kepes, "Language of Vision," Paul Theobald, 1944.)

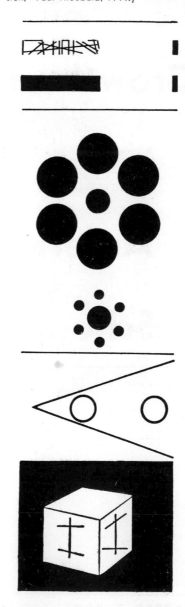

Growth of Art

in

American

Schools

FREDERICK M. LOGAN
UNIVERSITY OF WISCONSIN

HARPER & BROTHERS   PUBLISHERS   NEW YORK

Contents

V. Art, Education, and Modernism   116

Child Study in Art Forms—The Modernists in Art Reach America—"School" Arts—Art-Education Associations—Education in the Museum of Art—War and Postwar

VI. Progressive Education   152

Montessori and Cizek—"The Child" Arrives—What Develops "Art Appreciation"?—The Patrons of Progressive Education—Professional Stabilization: The 1920's—Depression Decade—Art Education in 1929: The Elementary School—High-School Art and Art Schools—Industrial Design and the Bauhaus—The Museum of Modern Art—Museum Education in the Depression—National Government in Art—The Owatonna Project—The Eight Year Study

VII. A Psychology and Philosophy for Art Education   201

Art as Experience—Creative Thought Comes of Age—1941: Before Pearl Harbor—Child as Artist—*Creative and Mental Growth*—Art in the High School—*Education Through Art* —Contemporary Relationships in the Arts—Two Forms of Aesthetic Judgment—Therapy and the Amateur—Tests and Measurements in Art—*Painting and Personality*—Psychology and Aesthetic Creation

VIII. Art Education: The Shape of Things to Come   248

"Communication" an Effort Toward Aesthetic Integration—Social Responsibility in Art—Three Ways to Personal Growth in Expression—Schools of Art and General Education—Anticipation—Anticipation: The Museum—Anticipation: The Art School-Independent, College, and University —Anticipation: Art in the Elementary Curriculum—Anticipation: The Art-Education Associations—What To Expect of Art Teachers?—What May the Art Student Expect? —In Conclusion

Figures

Figures

Editor's Introduction

The importance of the fine arts in contemporary life is evidenced in manifold ways and forms. Such factors as design, color, size, and shape, when harmoniously applied, are a source of high satisfaction and inspiration on the one hand, while on the other, when developed in conflict to aesthetic laws, they can become items of irritation and discomfort. Since the fine arts hold inestimable values in the emotional development of human beings, it is not surprising that increasing attention is being given to the arts in the preparation of teachers.

The School of Education at the University of Wisconsin is the academic home of the faculty group which is described as the Department of Art Education and Applied Art. This department is responsible for two major aspects of the fine arts program at the University—the one commonly found among institutions which are responsible for the preparation of teachers, namely, Art Education, and another often described as the Fine Arts.

The curriculum in Art Education has enrolled those who are preparing for the teaching of art in the local school systems, colleges, and universities. The curriculum entitled Applied Art has enrolled those who are preparing for the practice of the arts in industrial and commercial concerns with heavy emphasis upon the graphic and design arts. All members of the Department of Art Education and Applied Art teach courses both in art education and what are usually described as the studio courses in the various media such as painting, sculpture, serigraphy, and so forth.

It is my conviction that in the fine arts, as in all areas of scholarship, this close relationship between art education and the course dealing with the traditional disciplines must be maintained to achieve the maximum fulfillment of both. It seems clear that governing philosophies of teaching and parallel development in the media of creative expression in the fine arts are inevitably of mutual import and influence. In light of this belief, one of the courses offered to both the students who are preparing to teach art in schools and those who are preparing to direct their efforts more exclusively to the application and utilization of art media is a course which deals with the interplay between the growth of art education and the practice of the arts. The volume presented here represents a substantial segment of the material covered in the above-mentioned course.

It is my belief that the author herein has produced an important work—one in which he has shown the growth of the arts and art education as an indivisible process, although often described as "Art" and education.

JOHN GUY FOWLKES

Preface

Experience in art has been an important activity in many American schools for more than a century. The author of this book, like the majority of his contemporaries, did crayon drawings and cardboard constructions in grade-school days, and, with a smaller group of fellow students, went into an elective high-school art class, and thence into the art department of the teachers' college. This experience in elementary-school art, in high school, and in college was, I now realize, not as readily available in all parts of the country, but neither was it too uncommon.

The last years of college and the early years of teaching brought the associations which made it inevitable for me, first, to notice the lack of studies dealing with the background of art education, and then to attempt to write one. The confidence of my editor, John Guy Fowlkes, in the value of the work has been a major stimulus; more than that, his clear attitudes on educational improvement and educational responsibility have had much to do with the underlying approach to the job. My teachers have been people I am proud of, and they have contributed largely—of course, without specific responsibility—to the ideas presented. Especially am I indebted to Rebecca Chase, Gustave Moeller, Howard Thomas, Elsa Ulbricht, Maude Schafer, Frank E. Baker, John Frost, Albert Heckman, Emerson H. Swift, Victor D'Amico, and Arthur Young.

Victor D'Amico has read the manuscript, as have Robert Iglehart and Italo de Francesco. I value their comments and have, in my own judgment, made major improvements by acting upon the points they brought to my attention.

My interpretations of practices in art education have been clarified and enlarged by our visitors to the University of Wisconsin summer sessions, who have included—in addition to de Francesco, Iglehart, and D'Amico—Josef Albers, Thomas Munro, Ben Shahn, Charles Eames, Mervin Jules, and Buckminster Fuller. During my years of teaching I have been able to rely on the help of librarian colleagues, particularly Wilbert Beck, Maxine Reed, and Lola Pierstorff. Clarice Logan has been copy reader, style critic, and listener for the several stages of the manuscript.

FREDERICK M. LOGAN

Madison, Wisconsin
September, 1954

Growth of Art in American Schools

Figure 1. Drawing Done by the Author in Freshman Sketching and Composition Class, State Teachers College, Milwaukee, Wisconsin, 1928.

A Perspective on Art Education

Art education in the United States is growing in influence. A century and three-quarters of democracy has established the American people as mechanical innovators. We habitually think of our efforts as inventive, scientific, ingenious in nature. But we have made equally distinctive structures in fields which can be otherwise characterized. We have created a varied and flexible pattern of arts education which is no less significant than our educational system in the sciences and mechanical areas.

We have made an effort to domesticate the fine arts for the daily life, the emotional expansion, and the education of all citizens. The support of American art has never been more vigorous and concentrated than in the last two decades, despite a vast confusion in art practices, objectives, and products. Vigor and confusion often do meet, in the arts as in other affairs, and encourage attempts, such as this volume, to resolve some of the confusion.

Our first fifty years as a nation were cramped by warfare, financial problems, industrial shortcomings, and primitive communication and travel facilities. True, works of art were being produced, there were some art teachers, and the beginnings of some of our present art institutions trace to the five decades ending in 1825; but the interest was shared by a scant few, the achievements being scattered and not too encouraging to the artists. However, by the time the Civil War broke out, a much more tolerable environment for the arts existed through the combined work of writers, artists, teachers, and by an increasing number of citizens who were concerned that the home-grown arts should become vigorous and well supported. Ralph Waldo Emerson dreamed of the day when all Americans would understand the arts.

Emerson wrote, "Art should exhilarate and throw down the walls of circumstance on every side. . . ."[1] Horace Mann, writing in his reports on education of the values of teaching drawing, believed that drawing would be indispensable in achieving greater literacy and ability to express ideas. It seemed justifiable to conclude that if men of intellectual grasp and leadership thought art had a place in life, it should therefore be taught in the schools.

During a century of tax-supported school operation, the arts, frequently in small ways, have usually been a part of the school day. The educational objectives in art have shifted by the decade. Under the imported and widely heralded direction of Walter Smith, in the Boston schools of 1873, the emphasis was on drawing as an aid to developing manual skills. The teacher and student handbook was titled *Teachers Manual of Free Hand Drawing and Designing*,[2] and this book had been preceded by a lecture series, *Industrial*

---

[1] Ralph Waldo Emerson, *The Complete Essays and Other Writings of Ralph Waldo Emerson*, Modern Library, 1940, p. 312.

[2] Walter Smith, *Teachers Manual of Free Hand Drawing and Designing*, Boston, 1873.

Drawing in the Public Schools,[3] indicating precisely Smith's interests and vocational aims.

By 1890 the "appreciation of the beautiful" was standard equipment everywhere among serious art teachers. Timidly painted watercolors, clay modeling done under the dominating presence of casts from the antique, were counted upon as the nearest approach to productions of beauty possible to school children. The doing of these works was expected to form a lifelong devotion to the fine arts.

Often the most ardent advocates of general art education have acted as if they were promoting an overprecious commodity. This has given rise to slogans, timely in nature, adapted to some small aspect of the whole value of art. Certainly "appreciation of the beautiful" was one such slogan. Today we have another, no less narrow. For its present incarnation, art education is of primary importance in "providing an outlet for emotional tensions." We may hope that these rather fanatic, single-track enthusiasms can be discarded as art teachers themselves reach a more inclusive, mature understanding of the arts.

Meanwhile, diverse activities in architecture, painting, the design fields, and sculpture have been developing in America, and have influenced and been influenced by the restless aesthetic wanderings of the teachers of art. Disparate achievements like the building of the great suspension span of the Brooklyn Bridge, and the founding of the Metropolitan Museum of Art in New York City; the masterly, but long-unrecognized painting of Albert Pinkham Ryder; the ingenuity of nineteenth-century designers of plywood furniture, plumbing fixtures, and the makers of hand tools—all are now absorbed into the fabric of art theory and philosophy. The books and magazines which have recorded art accomplishment, the World's Fairs come and gone, the great museums of art established through the century and active in exhibition and education, have paralleled the work of the artists. This growth in art product and the broadening of art interpretation is reflected wherever art is being taught in the present day.

To trace the major shifts of base in this teaching of art; to perform evaluation and salvage operations on the important qualities of these

---

[3] Walter Smith, *Industrial Drawing in the Public Schools*, Prang, 1875.

movements, particularly the earlier ones; and to relate school developments to concurrent social and art movements often not adequately reckoned with by the schools are the aims of this volume.

HISTORIANS OF CULTURAL DEVELOPMENT

For fifty years and more our historians, novelists, and poets have been showing us how rich we are in human and physical resources. Long ago their emphasis shifted from the military-political narrative to the way people have acted in creating the cultural environment out of the materials at hand: the earth, the weather, the mixture of racial heritage, the European aesthetic forms and their subsequent adaptations to this soil and people.

Like too many of my fellow citizens, I cannot recall any school experience previous to my last year in high school, which gave me the kind of inspired interpretation of American history that seemed literally to crowd in upon many of us in the best of our college classrooms. Perhaps we must agree that young children will never get a true feeling for depth in historical time. Perhaps high-school classes are immeasurably better than they were in stimulating thought, in generating a critical judgment about our national past, and in forming a basis of respect for the constructive elements that form the future.

However these things may have been in the student life of my generation and are now twenty-five years later, it was my experience to begin an art-student career at the same time I encountered the work of Charles and Mary Beard on our American civilization, Lewis Mumford on our temporarily overlooked great artists of the post-Civil War period, and the robust, pessimistic, but positive character studies from American life of Edgar Lee Masters and Edwin Arlington Robinson. The result of this dual impact of art training and of a browsing in Americana of all sorts, with an emphasis on the arts, was the creation of a curiosity to find out for myself what might be the interrelationships of art and art education in the larger cultural pattern. During the years of my college course, and later while I was teaching art in the public schools, the work of Suzanne La Follette on American art was published,[4] and new editions of

[4] Suzanne La Follette, *Art in America,* Harper, 1929.

4

The Education of Henry Adams [5] and of Louis Sullivan's *The Auto-biography of an Idea* [6] became available. Ludwig Lewisohn's *Expression in America* [7] gave currency to the theory of the repressive influence of the Puritan in American art.

These books and others established a pattern of thought which this volume attempts to shape more clearly in the area of art activity. As I read the texts available on art education, carried on studio work in painting, drawing, and some crafts, did my practice teaching, and later suffered through the difficult processes of learning to teach, my interest in the history of this professional calling increased.

WHAT WAS TAUGHT AND WHAT WAS LEARNED

Searching for the usable past in the growth of art education, I found it could be interpreted best in two partly parallel frames of reference. One was the cultural history already referred to. The other was that of my own experience in art education in grade schools, high schools, in college, in an art school summer session, in a university art department, in my own teaching, and in my association with the artists of our community.

Most, if not all, of the materials that can be presented in the course of this work seemed to have some counterpart in the restricted field of this experience and the experiences of my teachers, which gave me, as they do most students, my first glimpses of the continuity and change in art interpretation.

A high-school art class of the mid-twenties in which I was enrolled displays in retrospect several qualities of the larger art movements with which our teacher must have had some contacts.

She was persistently at odds with the meticulous, all-embracing strictness of the administration. While the principal wished to achieve, and to a remarkable extent did achieve, a reliable knowledge of where each teacher and each student was each minute of the school day, the art teacher was contrarily imbued with the philosophy that creative work called for considerable freedom on the part of the individual. Even this modest a statement of that point of

[5] Henry Adams, *The Education of Henry Adams,* Modern Library, 1931.
[6] Louis Sullivan, *The Autobiography of an Idea,* American Institute of Architecture, Inc., 1924.
[7] Ludwig Lewisohn, *Expression in America,* Harper, 1932.

view she would believe too pompous. Her Parisian art studies in the first decade of the century inclined her to the doctrine of letting people have some leeway in getting work accomplished. If she was aware of the progressive-education movement and of the philosophy of John Dewey, she interpreted it brusquely and purposely in a more colloquial vein. The chances are that, like many of her generation of art teachers, she was trying to introduce to the high-school art room some of the freedom of the artist's studio.

What she taught her students of practice in the arts was not to prove in later years of any great value. What aesthetic and social convictions she instilled were infinitely more permanent. The arts were important and the artist a person of consequence. The routines of life, in her case the keeping and recording of grades, the establishment and maintenance of class order, were useful only as a means of stimulating student work. To the extent that they did not aid in reaching that goal, she made no secret of her impatience with rigid requirements.

The more transitory art influences to which we were subjected might best be described as impressionism in art, with tinctures of the post-impressionism of Gauguin particularly. The British poster makers and the architectural renderers made contributions to our aesthetic. Then, too, the posteresque work of a young Wisconsin artist, Carl Holty, was occasionally in evidence. He was a former student of the school and was doing work dominantly in low key, few color relationships, using the flat pattern of the Lautrec posters with timid gestures toward cubism in the squared-off forms.

In later years students from these classes may have wished that a more arduous, demanding program had been required. More discernment in art history might, for instance, have been possible. Just an acquaintance with some of the artists and work mentioned above would have given us insight into the sources of our own work at the time. But when we recall that the Museum of Modern Art had not been established, that the art work encouraged in the grades by the progressive-education movement was only in the first few years of its influence, that Dewey's definitive philosophy of the arts was still years from publication, that the Bauhaus approach to materials and the crafts was in its midyears in Germany, but virtually unknown to all but a handful of Americans—in the light of this time placement, we must consider the accomplishments of our high-school art teachers of the nineteen-twenties most favorably.

They were probably more successful with their students who developed a special aptitude for the arts and who went on to art schools or college art departments. For the others, those who did not again enroll in art courses of any sort after their last work in high school, the sentimental and precious approach to all the arts often seemed prevalent. The cheerful freedom of their hours in the art room, combined with the innocuous treatment of all themes, the accent on impressionistic, freely handled color and on superficially spirited drawing, when carried no farther, developed little stamina for encountering Picasso's paintings or even the designs of Aalto or Le Corbusier. An environment of accomplishment with enjoyable materials had been created, but the effort to comprehend Goya as well as Sargent, Cezanne as well as Joseph Pennell, was not to be found. Maybe we were not ready for such fare. Maybe the teachers were not, or else believed that course content of that intellectual a caliber must be deferred to college years. Whatever the reason, the general art student in high school seldom continued afterward to a mature grasp of art forms.

ART DEPARTMENT, COLLEGE, MIDWEST, 1930

Art schools and college departments in 1930, as at present, were too apt to take the view that high-school art classes could be counted upon to instill some poor habits of technical skills, and little or no other basis upon which to build professional competence. At the worst this is almost true, but more often the encouragement and activity of the high school has been important to the freshman art student. The art faculties err in discounting high-school work too greatly.

Our Midwestern college department had already gone through several phases of growth. Inquisitive students found the past well represented in old catalogues and files of student work. The rigidities of cast and anatomical drawing, carried out with nearly uniform precision, had been accompanied by *art nouveau* ornament in textiles, pottery, and metalcraft. Lettering had evolved from severe classical forms in an architectural style to highly "decorative" styles, and in the late twenties was groping back to the classical just before the popularity of the modern sans-serif form came in.

In the pictorial-composition class Cézanne's *Basket of Apples* in a color reproduction from the Chicago Art Institute was carefully studied for its organization of three-dimensional space and color. At the same time, and in some confusion, we strove for a flat patterning in strong value contrasts in the manner of Arthur W. Dow's *Composition* [8] text.

At the time, "art for art's sake" was a prevalent philosophy in American departments. It was not acknowledged and practiced under that banner, which was more often used to describe the art of England in the eighteen-nineties; but the most widely read critics were dispensing a similar gospel in various forms. Clive Bell's book, *Art,* [9] originally published in 1913, was a handbook quite popular among our students. (It was reprinted in 1949.) Bell wished to isolate a quality which he called "significant form" as the underlying element of all great works of art. This "significant" form was not determined by the literary aspects of the artist's work, or by the historical or sociological context in which it was placed. It could be apprehended only by a person who was constantly sharpening his sensitivity to the abstract elements of line and form and color. Herbert Read's article, "Farewell to Formalism," [10] is one of many indications of the movement away from Bell's position.

In the early thirties, however, men like the Chicago critic Bulliett reflected and strengthened the trend. His treatise, *Apples and Madonnas,* [11] was given over to the thesis that ". . . an apple by Cézanne is more important than a Madonna by Raphael."

Art students, among them the art teachers of the future, were producing landscape, still life, and figure painting in quantity, in which the only modernist quality evident was a tentative effort toward expressionistic form distortion and arbitrary color schemes following the Franz Marc treatment of the *Red Horses.* But they were being taught, they were reading, and they believed that the subject matter

[8] Arthur Wesley Dow, *Composition*, Doubleday Page, 1913.
[9] Clive Bell, *Art*, Stokes, 1913.
[10] Herbert Read, "Farewell to Formalism," *Art News*, Summer, 1952.
[11] C. J. Bulliett, *Apples and Madonnas*, Covici-Friede, 1930.

of a work of art was nothing; that color, form, the way it was painted, were important to the exclusion of all else. This we held to mystically and inexplicably, regardless of our easily apparent struggle with representational forms in three dimensions.

Critical insight of this sort, coming years after the experience, is slowly being accepted as natural growth for the individual artist and teacher, for the schools, and for society. Art is no more static than politics. What is remarkable is not the occasional shortcomings of our small art schools, but the degree to which they were and are alert to the current valuable elements of aesthetic development. If we, as teachers of art, fail to qualify the teachings of our undergraduate years, we fail to grow as we should. It is discouraging to realize that some art teachers are thoughtlessly repeating the litany of their student years, teaching the preëminence of compositional forms, the organization of visual elements, as the only distinguishing quality separating important art forms from trash.

Nothing is more irritating to the intelligent layman than to be told, of a Rouault painting in which the human form is twisted to a shape of ugliness and pain, that ". . . the subject is negligible; you should look at the abstract qualities, the interlocking forms, the rich pigmentation; see how exciting and pleasing it is in dark and light relationships." Nor is it possible to be much more inaccurate aesthetically. For in most Rouault paintings the artist had no intent to provide excitement in abstract qualities as the only reaction to his work.

The artist's social and emotional environment, his total education, and, as a work progresses, his personal "handwriting" with brush or tool—every one of these elements, with the media he is using and the subject attempted, are a part of the work the public sees.

As a device to correct the common blind spot of unawareness of the abstract structure of art objects, it is helpful to see a work for those elements alone momentarily. But simple human reactions demonstrate that few people will, without a conscious effort, ignore the "subject" of a painting, or for that matter look at a building as primarily an abstract pattern.

On this vexatious problem and on other issues, a historical survey and cross section of educational practice should help the teacher in shaping and leading public interest in art.

"ART IN EVERYDAY LIFE"

The thinking best known as "art in everyday life" has been offered as a better art approach for the schools than the generous use of the delights of the painting media or the experimental uses of three-dimensional materials. The book by the Goldsteins of that title [12] probably set up the phrase, but the authors of the volume do not subscribe to the use of the term in the narrow interpretation here criticized.

Many movements in art important to the design of our environment have flourished in the last century. William Morris's arts and crafts movement, the *art nouveau* period, the cubist painting influence on early modernist furniture, the still-widening circle of influence from the German Bauhaus—all of these in subtle measure have helped to create the "art in everyday life" of the nineteen-fifties. And not one of the leading artists of those movements ever supported a theory of dissimilarity between the work of the creative painter and the designer of furniture. There is a creative quality which is inseparable from any true art expression, whether it is a clay modeling by a child or the design of a Diesel locomotive by the Raymond Loewy Associates. It is a distinctive characteristic of the designers of the nineteenth and twentieth centuries that they have insisted on qualitative consistency in all things, printing, wall paper, jewelry, as well as the pictorial arts.

In many schools today, the attitude is present not only among the staff and administration, but even with some art teachers, that the individualist creative art work in several media is somewhat messy, a great deal overrated for its educational efficacy, and in other ways questionable. A little probing discloses an adult dislike of the housekeeping chore inevitable when thirty ten-year-olds are using paint and clay in crowded quarters. The belief has some popularity that neat, rigid exercises in color and drawing, illustrating arbitrary "art principles," childish renderings of interior decoration ideas cribbed from magazines, or all-over patterns in painstaking imitation of wall

[12] H. and V. Goldstein, *Art in Everyday Life,* Macmillan, 1925.

paper or linoleum may deal with art as we know it in the home, and for that reason may be more valuable to the child. Furthermore, the results are thought to be more respectable as display items because more easily understood by the parents.

Such an unimaginative school practice is as wide of the mark as the unregimented free expression where responsibility for materials and respect for classmates' work is left to chance, which often means it is ignored by the group.

A good school arts program can and should synthesize the values in these contrasted and frequently exclusive extremes. Because we have at hand so many of the parts needed for greater synthesis in art education, a survey of the past from which our present art curricula derive seems worth the doing.

SCOPE OF THE VOLUME

The intent is to start the project of grouping and evaluating major movements and influences in art education. Three fields must be covered. The first is that of general education in the arts in the elementary and secondary schools and in the colleges. General education is to be interpreted as education for the acquisition and growth of an art background for all citizens not expecting to be professionally engaged in art.

The second area is that of the art education available to students hoping to practice the arts and the teaching of the arts professionally. The third field of inquiry is that of the social influences contributing to, and frequently determining, the content of school work. The books and magazines, museums and galleries, the patronage offered the artists by private means and by government, and the impact of the heterogeneous character of European art create the world of art in this society, and make the social framework from which educational theory and practice are projected.

These three aspects of art and art education do not operate separately. Each exercises strong pressures on the other two, and not enough emphasis has been put on that fact. Professional art schools cannot improve radically until their faculties understand better the fine elements of education in the arts that have been so productive with young children. The broad acceptance of the old Bauhaus elementary course in experiment with materials is valuable if it is planned creatively, and inspires the enthusiastic participation of mature students that one expects to see in the art work of a good kindergarten.

The reverse of the attitude of the professional art schools in being unacquainted with educational methods is to be observed among some public-school art teachers. They are adept at "teaching the child, not a subject," but the devices they use permit child production of cheap stereotyped forms known as "school art." If a work in art is a valid expression from a student of any age, it must have a personal form. If it has not this form, it will instead perpetuate the monotonous shapes of the gift counter, the cuteness of the animated cartoon. When it is of this imitative ilk, "school art" is no art at all. Then the divorce of the public-school teacher from the qualitative preoccupation of the art faculties damages children's potentialities.

To deal with the several parts and periods of education in the arts, and to do so with an effort at qualitative judgment, will raise issues which can profitably be projected into the future. Whatever that future is to be, something can be gained and nothing lost by an appraisal of the past.

X

Ca C

Qc

Dc   Fb

Mb   Ld

Nb

IX

Eb

Db   Fb

Nb   Ba

II

Art in the New Schools of a New Country

The little red schoolhouse is a nostalgic symbol to millions of Americans who have never been inside one—it is an attractive image. The small agricultural village deep in its roadside elms, the New England meeting house facing a village common or square, and down the road the village school, also embowered in trees, a swing dangling from a horizontal branch, the bell clanging smartly in the

little tower, and teacher welcoming the children at the doorway—
all these evoke nostalgia.

In such schools, millions of Americans secured their education.
There have been excellent schools and fine teachers in that environment. But the sober history of elementary education must refer
more often to inadequacies, to uncertainties, to unequal distribution
of opportunity, especially in the first fifty years of national existence
when the one-room rural school was almost the only truly public
school available. Some historians recount the strong classical education offered in New England before 1776. These schools are in great
contrast to the district-school organization after the departure of the
British, but it must be remembered that institutions like the Boston
Latin School seldom educated any but the children of the well-to-do
commercial and professional families, and that the district schools,
however inadequate, were freely open to all children.

In any view, then, of the school of the early nineteenth century,
we discount the bucolic charm of the Currier and Ives print. Mostly,
schools were too few, students too many, teachers poorly prepared,
school buildings a disgrace, school grounds too small and uncared
for. It was this situation, as well as the rapidly growing emigration
from Europe, which forced attention upon school improvement in
the late twenties and thirties of the nineteenth century, when
Horace Mann and other leaders established the basis of our present
tax-supported school system in which general art education was
begun.

NATIONAL SYSTEMS OF EDUCATION FOR A DEMOCRACY

There were, in the period Merle Curti calls the Patrician Leadership [1] (before 1830), valuable papers written and speeches made on
the subject of national plans of education reaching all citizens regardless of the accidents of birth. Two plans were submitted to the
American Philosophical Society and, of these, the one by Samuel H.
Smith shares with the others certain general assumptions and in
addition provides a place for the arts.

Allen Oscar Hansen's [2] description of the proposals for national

[1] Merle Curti, *The Growth of American Thought*, Harper, 1943, pp. 213–292.
[2] Allen Oscar Hansen, *Liberalism and American Education*, Macmillan, 1926.

education states that all were the product of the intense enthusiasm for pure democracy generated by the Revolution. They advocated a minimum education for everyone and usually a system of selective scholarships based on merit for successive steps upward in the schools. Most of the theorists proposed nationally tax-supported schools at least on the secondary and collegiate level. The universal thought was that only by a strong central school system could the radical ideals of American democracy be preserved and extended into the future. The individual must learn a rational, scientific approach to his problems as a sovereign citizen. In these generalities the influence of Rousseau was strong. It was taken for granted that Rousseau was right in elevating the development of the individual to a preëminent place, though there was a recognition that his "natural" growth remote from current social influences was not possible and not wanted in a democracy.

References by Smith to the arts came in his proposal for a board of literature and science which was to control his whole educational scheme. There were to be ". . . fourteen persons skilled in the several branches of (1) languages; (2) mathematics; (3) geography and history; (4) natural philosophy in general; (5) moral philosophy; (6) English language, belles lettres, and criticism; (7) agriculture; (8) manufactures; (9) government and laws; (10) medicine; (11) theology; (12) elements of taste, including principles of music, architecture, gardening, drawing, etc.; (13) military tactics; and, in addition, (14) a person eminently skilled in science, who should be President of the Board." [3]

The board was thus representative of academic fields and professional fields. What place the "elements of taste" might have in the curriculum is stated in the seventeenth of twenty-two recommendations: "That an opportunity be furnished to those who have the ability, without interfering with the established studies, of acquiring a knowledge of modern languages, music, drawing, dancing and fencing. . . ." The recommendation applied to students in colleges only and obviously ranks the modern languages and the arts as a group of social skills desirable though not absolutely essential for leaders in community life.

[3] Ibid., p. 158

A national system of education was never to exist except on paper. Private colleges, nearly all sectarian, opposed the idea of a national university as the crowning institution of a scholastic organization. While many of the states before 1800 passed generous enabling laws making possible state school systems for elementary and secondary schooling, there were only slight and fitful efforts to follow up the legislation with appropriations. The bulk of public activity regarding education at that time seems to have been optimistic theorizing on the part of intellectual groups, and patriotic posturing on the political level. It took three more decades for the public to demand something like the kind of educational opportunities that had been predicted.

ART IN THE REVIVAL OF THE COMMON SCHOOL

During the 1820's elementary education became so bad that responsible citizens in many places took the initiative for improving the schools and for arranging better financial support. Massachusetts was a leader through this period, and many of the accomplishments of that state system under Horace Mann have formed the basis of present school organization nationally.

Some early aspects of art education appeared in the schools from the beginning of this revival movement. Horace Mann himself was interested in the uses of drawing in the schools, and after 1839 the *Common School Journal* under his editorship gave impetus to that interest.

A few years earlier Amos Bronson Alcott was in the midst of carrying on what we would now call experimental teaching. He had taught rural school in several New England districts, then took a private school in Pennsylvania, returned to take another private-school post in Boston in 1828, and finally ran his own Temple School in Boston from 1834 to 1839.

Alcott's methods created in some degree the "activity" school of his day, though there is reason to suspect that the activity was less than his program indicated. Nevertheless, each week, according to that program, drawing from nature was indulged in for half an hour.

Alcott was a follower of Pestalozzi in some of his methods, though certainly not whole-heartedly in philosophy. Pestalozzi died in 1827.

16

His work at Yverdon had been widely commented on and his publications had a limited but enthusiastic circulation in America, particularly in Boston. The Pestalozzi emphasis on example and the worth of pleasant school environment, his concern for an expanded curriculum based on social relationships, on greater use of concrete objects and reference to situations familiar to the children, and on the mastery of simple manual skills, were all known to Alcott. He was probably sympathetic to Pestalozzi's rule of love and coöperation supplanting classroom discipline through fear and tyranny.

In an atmosphere adapted somewhat to the capacities and interests of children, Alcott set up three areas of mental endeavor at the Temple School, the "rational," the "imaginative," and the "spiritual." As a contribution to the nurture of the spiritual powers, drawing was listed for its half hour weekly. Drawing subjects were to be taken from nature, which meant, in those days, drawing from real objects; it did not mean outdoor drawing and sketching. From what we know of Alcott's thinking it is likely that he hoped the children would be able to draw spontaneously and well enough to illustrate the forms of nature in a pretty fashion. Child pictures of flowers, birds, and bees would have been ideal texts for some of the daily "conversations" on moral and spiritual subjects. In all probability he would be disappointed in this hope. As there is little reference to drawing other than its schedule placement in Temple School literature, it can be assumed that drawing did not become very important. Probably, like the time allotted for recreation and music, Alcott treated the drawing period as one more of the rest periods the children needed for stimulating further intellectual zeal in the next conversation. Alcott's best service to art education was that of classing the drawing work as an exercise of the imagination.

Elizabeth Peabody was Alcott's assistant, and a daily record which she kept for the school year 1834–1835 was published as the *Record of a School*.[4] Two passages are revealing. The first deals with the younger children's efforts to shape letters. "But the practice of the eye in looking at forms, and that of the hand in imitating them, should be simultaneous. Mr. Alcott thinks the slate and pencil, the chalk and the blackboard, can hardly be given too early. The latter

[4] Elizabeth Peabody, *Record of a School*, Roberts, 1835, pp. 19, 270.

is even better than the former; for children should have free scope, as we find that their first shapings are usually gigantic. And is it not best that they should be so? Miniature, when it appears first in the order of development, seems to be always the effect of checked spirit or some artificial influence." Today, the application of this sensible note to forming alphabet letters is no longer questioned, but its importance in children's drawings is still being ignored.

The second quotation interesting in connection with drawing includes a footnote. "He surrounds them also with statuary and pictures in his school room; and he has drawing taught to all his scholars by a gentleman who probably possesses the spirit of art more completely than any instructor who has ever taught in this country." A footnote follows:

"Mr. Francis Graeter: who has in contemplation to publish a work developing the whole art of drawing, especially from nature, in the same way as he has often done orally to such pupils as have received the most benefit from him; and more completely than he could do in a course of desultory lessons—more completely than has ever been done in a book for learners. We hope nothing will prevent nor delay this great desideratum *to all* lovers of the pencil."

The phrase "desultory lessons," and the ardent hopes expressed for Mr. Graeter's book, indicate no great success in classroom teaching. As for the projected book, Carl Drepperd [5] lists dozens of similar texts of about that period of time addressed to children, and there is no indication that Graeter's approach was startlingly original.

A record Miss Peabody made of the start of one of the daily conversations is a good indication of the real business of the school. Alcott asks, "Why do you come to school? To learn, said several. Yes, said he, to learn words; to learn to word your thoughts; this is a word shop."

Alcott's individualist approach to religion finally caused the closing of the Temple School in 1839. Publication of his volume, *Conversations*,[6] alarmed the parents and the public when they saw that he was reasoning out religious beliefs with the children. He hoped they would emerge with strongly felt religious convictions in place

[5] Carl Drepperd, *American Pioneer Arts and Artists,* Pond-Ekberg, 1942.
[6] Amos Bronson Alcott, *Conversations with Children on the Gospels,* James Monroe & Co., 1837.

of socially acceptable, conventional religious practices. But few Boston people were ready to accept the convictions Alcott expressed on social and religious affairs.

As his legacy for art education, Alcott encouraged the use of words as an art in itself, and subsequent educational practice extends the principle to art of all kinds as a means of personal expression. He wished that children might learn from directed experience; if his interpretation of what this meant in art was limited, at least he pointed a direction for later exploration.

DRAWING IN THE PRUSSIAN SCHOOLS

In 1838, during the last year of Alcott's school, Horace Mann began his tenure in the office of secretary of the Massachusetts State Board of Education, and began also the years of his editorship of the *Common School Journal.* His leadership was sound and persuasive. Even the ideas he formulated which were not at once taken up had a way of entering the school organization in later years. On an official trip to Germany in 1839 he was fascinated by the observation that nearly all of the Prussian schoolmasters drew with ease on the blackboard in illustration of school subjects. The schoolmasters were also teaching drawing to their pupils by having them copy at their desks while the teacher did a drawing on the board. Mann remarked that the younger children were not discouraged from going on in drawing by too harsh a criticism of their "taste and accuracy." At the time, a Peter Schmidt was teaching in Berlin with a drawing system on which he had worked for more than sixteen years. So successfully had it been practiced in various places that Berlin had invited him to start teaching it in secondary and trade schools. On every hand it was praised for its gratifying results. All students following it learned to draw accurately and in "true" proportion. The art academies claimed to be especially pleased; they noticed that students were able to develop faster, and to go farther in the academic routine of the art school, when they had a preparatory course from Professor Schmidt.

It was this system that ran with engraved illustrations in the *Common School Journal* for 1844 and 1845,[7] complete with directions to

[7] Peter Schmidt, "Schmidt's Guide to Drawing," *Common School Journal,* Vol. V, pp. 241–243. The rest of the series is in Vols. VI and VII, 1848, 1845.

be followed by student and teacher. Since these were the only illustrations in the *Journal* for several years, and had to be printed on special paper stock from steel engravings, we see the importance Mann attached to the project. No acknowledgment of copyright, authorship, adaptation, or source of illustrative material anywhere appears in the *Journal*. What we would consider today an ironclad, disastrous routine was welcomed as the answer to the school's need for activity. The *Journal* introduction to the series was as follows: "The chief objections to the introduction of drawing into the common schools, are the want of instructors and want of patterns; but both of these objections would be done away, could Peter Schmidt's *Guide to Drawing* be widely diffused in this Commonwealth. It is a series of twenty-four lessons, upon nineteen rectilinear blocks, together with directions for drawing a niche, a cylinder, and a ball, in every possible perspective view."

The plates which follow in successive numbers of the magazine begin with one containing several rectangles, all of different proportions, placed horizontally or vertically on the page, with one exception—a rectangle diagonally placed bridging a space between a squat and a tall vertical. The directions for drawing are extensive. Proportions are to be rigorously observed, points located in space and connected, lines to be thin and precise, drawn with a sharply pointed, hard pencil. Each plate becomes more intricate than the last. Halfway through the first series the perspective projections of the rectangles are included. One finds it difficult to believe that these exercises were welcome diversions; or it may be supposed that the rest of the school day was such that any hand work proved a relaxation.

AMERICAN APPROVAL OF "DRAWING"

Widespread approval of this kind of drawing was based on its value in the manual training of a population whose chief occupations would be in industry and skilled crafts. Over a period of five years, which culminated in the Schmidt publication, various writers had expressed their views of the utility of drawing. Another commonly stated thesis was a repetition of Horace Mann's dictum in the 1839 volume, "Drawing is a form of writing and should be taught with it." [8] Both activities were the copying of forms; in this was seen their resemblance.

In recent years an enormous amateur picture production from the period before the Civil War has been rediscovered. From this quantity of pictorial folk art, scholars have assembled impressive bibliographies of pamphlets, textbooks, portfolio, and magazine articles written for the instruction and pleasure of unprofessional artists of that time. But the contributors to the *Common School Journal* did not foresee a time when picture making would become a part of school work. One of them wrote:

They [students] may not only be permitted to make angles and triangles, squares and circles, but also irregular ones . . . thus, he who draws a circle to represent the moon . . . will be very aptly led to notice the objects connected with the moon . . . and may easily be induced to represent them also.

Here it may be asked, whether exercises of this sort will not degenerate into mere play and picture-making. . . . There is no necessity of any such degeneracy. . . . In the first place, the use of the slate should not be countenanced too long, at any one time. In the second place, they should be taken away when they play with them.[9]

An unquestionable masterpiece of frank opinion on the place of the arts in the curriculum is found in the 1846 volume of Horace Mann's periodical. Discounting the quaint practices referred to on the part of the pupils, the author's hasty bow to drawing as an "accomplishment," and her truly heartfelt thanksgiving for drawing as "busy work," are distressingly familiar notes. Art is still for many teachers an "accomplishment" rather than an important means of expression.

If the art of Drawing, instead of being a most desirable accomplishment for everyone, were utterly without value as an attainment, still its benefits, as a means of occupying the attention of small children, and of keeping them from idleness and its attendant mischiefs, would commend it to the adoption of teachers generally, and especially to the teachers of primary schools. . . . How are they [young students] to spend the residue of a session three hours long? They are not to whisper. They are not to manufacture and to fillip spit balls. They are not to try the law of

---

[8] Horace Mann, "Schools in Prussia," *Common School Journal*, Vol. I, 1839, p. 68.
[9] *Ibid.*, Vol. II, 1840, pp. 171–172.

projectiles by a quill or an elastic bit of wood. . . . All experiments on chips or pebbles are forbidden. They must not make their fingers ride astride of each other, nor draw images in spittle upon their shoes. . . . What, then, is to be done? We answer, find them occupation, direct this activity instead of suppressing it. . . . For all these purposes, there is no other single resource so valuable as Drawing.[10]

With this matter-of-fact approach to drawing as of 1846, and with the other selected points of view already surveyed, how may the introduction of drawing into the elementary school before 1850 be best assessed?

Elementary education at this time was based on ability to read and write, and to do some figuring: the use of verbal, written, and mathematical symbols.

Secondary education was classical in nature, the acquisition of a mature use of the English language and a thorough grounding in Latin. Perhaps the study of Latin should be indicated as having educational precedence in 1850. For the two hundred years of the existence of the American school it had taught children from English-speaking homes, with a scattered few from other national groups. In 1850, the secondary school was still taking care of only a small minority of the children of the age group it served. The bulk of its students came from homes of some cultural interests. Practical arts and fine arts could be and really were encountered by such children in the home, community, and even as an occasional by-product of their fathers' professional pursuits. School was a necessity for such children to aid them in making use of cultural advantages their family environment provided.

But the tasks of the common school became greater early in the nineteenth century. Population increased in industrial centers, and immigration began to crowd eastern cities with other than English-speaking nationalities. Family life for much of the urban population was no longer as varied nor as rich educationally for children as had been true for even the poorest of families when the country was more sparsely settled and the largest cities were virtually country towns. The elementary school, as class sizes rose, as language differences began to be a problem, as more children came from poverty-

---

[10] *Ibid.,* Vol. VII, 1845, p. 25.

stricken homes, was pressed to offer a more diverse curriculum. Reading, writing, and arithmetic were no longer all the education students needed outside the home, and also schools teaching only these subjects were filled with restless children, difficult to handle. Horace Mann admired the drawing in Prussian schools because the teaching of this kind of drawing might answer the criticism that the schools did little for the future mechanic or industrial worker. Manual skill, accurate judgment of line and proportion, ought to be good background for a shipwright, a bookkeeper, a weaver, a carpenter, indeed for all tradesmen.

As an approach to the fine arts, drawing was important to Alcott, and for that matter to Horace Mann, though neither of these men nor any of their followers grasped the nature of an experience in art, whether for a child or for an adult. Completeness, satisfaction in a finished creation at any level of schooling, was not important in any school branch of learning. So there was no reason why a complete creation on a child level in drawing should even be considered as a desirable experience. More than that, experience itself was not stressed in school philosophy. Schools existed to impart knowledge. Knowledge and attitudes must be acquired for their importance in adult life, but the life experience of the child was only an incidental to this process of acquisition.

For schoolroom purposes, any field of knowledge or practice at the adult level was dissected and its simpler elements parceled out as exercise materials appropriate for the younger grades. Hence the reference to idle play or school activity "degenerating" into picture making. Grown-up artists spent years drawing from the figure before they started painting pictures in a serious vein. It followed that a child could not be permitted to paint a picture in school, for school work was a serious business and the child could not presume to do, as serious work, what the professional art student waited years to attempt. The young pupil could, and should, draw lines and common geometrical shapes, and judge proportions of shapes and lines to one another. For the child whose adult life might be spent in one of the professions or in business, the experience in drawing was hoped to create a love of "just" and "true" forms, an ability to identify "correct" proportions. The whole intellectual community looked upon pictorial art as accurately representational. And with such a conception, a rigorous training in copying linear forms appeared as a natural first step for an education in drawing. Pictorial art was an extension of literature: a natural error among a people whose chief cultural insight was derived from the printed page, and whose most important works of art were books.

Circuitous as the development was to be, a start had been made in building new schools, and a curriculum proposed which was to include some experience besides reading and writing. The practice of a manual skill, the control of a medium of expression not dependent on the alphabet or upon numerals, was approved. The means of approaching the expressive medium was poorly understood, but not less so than in other parts of the world. The nature of visual and plastic art was never less understood than it was in 1840, but the public schools in any event were going to have the children draw. The start of general art education in this country was the creation of good intentions. There must have been many students, however, who felt that Professor Schmidt's exercises were but good pavement for the devil's domain.

THE FOUNDING OF AMERICAN ACADEMIES

American professional education in the arts for the period 1800 to 1860 was a provincial affair, an energetic aping of Europe. This yearning after European models proceeded ignorant of the fact that art schools in England and on the Continent, after Napoleon, were rapidly losing their prestige of leadership among artists. The changes in art patronage resulting from the industrial and commercial revolutions, as well as from the political, were reflected in the content and directions of the arts. Each generation of painters reaching maturity of expression found it difficult to understand or to respect the work and the aesthetic objectives of their immediate successors. Such a process in some degree is always found in the arts, but in this period the break between generations was especially marked. As a consequence, teachers in art institutions were apt to be more rigid than ever in clinging to the values familiar to their youth. The static practices of the academy and the venturesome work of artist leaders were worlds apart.

Nevertheless, after the American Revolution, our foremost artists seized each opportunity to build up on this side of the Atlantic something like the art institutions they knew and admired in France, Italy, and England. A government newly emerged from revolution aided the growth of institutional framework in all kinds of activity. To American artists whose work was publicly lauded and feebly supported by cash purchases, an art organization commanding broad public support was believed to be an unquestionable necessity.

European academies served as a bulwark of conventional practice against which the great creative artists could develop their independent conceptions and sharpen their thinking. Both the creators of the academy point of view and the dissenters from it formed a basis for the art of the late nineteenth century and the early twentieth century. Jacques-Louis David, followed by his student, J. A. D. Ingres, perpetuated the standards of art-school practice which they had inherited, making them more than ever formalized. In opposition to David, his works and all his teachings, Delacroix in France, and Turner and Constable in England, were making important art history in the first third of the century.

American efforts to found an academy were necessarily on a more primitive level than the struggle of minds represented by David and Delacroix. The history of the Philadelphia organizations, those that split apart and the one that survived, and the record of hot-tempered warfare between rival academies in New York City, reveal little, if any, discussion or vital differences on aesthetic matters among the American artists. All their energies were devoted to the form their academies ought to take and to a means of perpetuating the existence of the proposed institution. During the period we are reviewing, any criticism of an academy as unimaginative artistically was quite improbable. The job at hand was to create an establishment. Later generations would have to provide the healthy rejection by students of some of its values and overdeveloped dogma. The beginning of professional art education could not transpose the advanced quality of European thought directly to these shores. There had to be a period in American art of lesser output in quantity and quality, while some place in society was being made for the visual and plastic arts.

BENJAMIN WEST: A ONE-MAN ACADEMY

For many years after the Revolution the art of any American who wished to be considered professionally competent had to be started with study in Europe, for only in Europe were there to be found enough artists of advanced professional training and activity to undertake the teaching of art students. Foremost among the artists of Europe, in the minds of American students, was the American Benjamin West.

We may regret the length of time his influence dominated American students when we think of men like David and Ingres in France and of the English artists Turner, Constable, or even Blake. American arts might have been much richer had some American students ventured to seek out other teachers than West.

Benjamin West, as a painter, is a forgotten man and his work is not likely to enjoy a renewal of aesthetic interest. As an historical personage he grows in importance, because of the legendary character of his life story and because West alone was responsible for creating American art as an appendage to the art of England; or more accurately, as a product of his own studio and teaching.

He was born in Pennsylvania in 1738. Stories of his youth are filled with such items as the homemade colors squeezed out of roadside berries, and the paintbrushes skillfully made from the hairs of the house cat's tail. Not all the stories can be true, but whatever art experiences he had as a boy must have been mostly of his own seeking, and his association with men working at art would have been with the traveling sign painters and "likeness-takers." Today we realize that among a thousand children several hundred will have some drawing ability and will want to make pictures if the opportunity and materials are available. Only a few will have a compelling urge to do so in preference to all other kinds of work or play. Benjamin West was of the latter group; the folk tales about his childhood assure us of that. As he grew older his eagerness to practice art and his obvious talent encouraged financially able citizens of Pennsylvania to bear the expense of a period of study for him in Italy.

On his arrival in Rome he became the fortunate object of enthusiasm inspired by novelty. To the aristocracy and the cultured people of Rome it appeared a miracle of human chance that a youth of such charm and talent could come from the transatlantic wilderness. It was not West's last encounter with an extremely favorable reaction to his personality and to his work; throughout his three years of study in Italy and for most of his life, he could take such a friendly environment for granted. The beginning of his professional career in the cities of Italy was, at that time, a typically English program for the artist, and was undertaken by West in that spirit. After the three years, he removed to London to test, by the reactions of the English public, the adequacy of his preparation as a proper artist. His welcome was more gratifying than he hoped for; commissions came easily and he made friends with people· of influence. Rather than carry out his plans of returning to Philadelphia to be married, he sent for the girl and they were married in London. The most rewarding and constant association of his long life followed shortly when one of his paintings of historical Biblical subject matter was seen and generously appreciated by King George III. This led to his receiving an annual retainer as a member of the King's household, to his early prominence in the Royal Academy, and was valuable in securing for him the presidency of the Academy which he held for the last twenty-eight years of his life.

Portraits were always a staple product, especially for the artist in England in West's day, but the higher aim in the estimation of the artist was that of doing large historical and allegorical canvases. Because of his uninterrupted financial support, West had the opportunity of doing more such works than was possible for most of his contemporaries. As long as the King's mental stability lasted, each one of West's new compositions was a matter of interest to the high-placed persons of the royal circle. These historical-educational-moral pictures, with an occasional, but wholly decorous and classical interest in the nude figure, became the evidence of King George's aesthetic interest and patronage. What stimulated the royal taste of 1800 today seems grandiose and empty, of slight value as works of art.

AMERICAN ART: THE PRODUCT OF WEST'S STUDENTS

West's American students, however, accepted the evaluation of King and Academy as to the eminence of their teacher. It was the easier to do because of his charm and never-failing helpfulness to aspiring young artists. Matthew Pratt was the first of West's fellow countrymen to come to London in 1764. For fifty years, one or more young Americans studied in West's studio. When we examine the life product in art and social achievement of Charles Willson Peale, Gilbert Stuart, John Trumbull, William Dunlap, Washington Allston, Ralph Earl, Thomas Sully, and Samuel F. B. Morse, we are looking at the work of the students of America's first "academy." It was a one-man academy, located appropriately in the mother country. The activities of West's students in the United States constituted the first efforts in two of the three principal cities to establish professional art education. Interestingly enough, none of them had the desire, the personal leadership, or sufficiently established position in the arts to create a lifelong student following as did West. It was not until close to the twentieth century that circumstances were favorable in this country to produce artist-teachers approaching his lengthy period of service and influence.

Charles Willson Peale was not West's first student chronologically, but he was the first of the group, on his return to America, to command a community-wide respect, not only in the arts but in all kinds of related enterprises.

Peale was favored, as his teacher had been before him, by an offer from the leading citizens of Annapolis and Maryland to send him to England for study. His experiences before his departure for England, which took place in February of 1767, had included apprenticeship in one craft and experiment in several other crafts, the last of which was painting. As a boy he started his six-year service in the saddlery and harness trade; then set himself up in that business on borrowed money, ventured into the sideline of watch repair, and quite by chance stumbled into picture making as another possible sideline trade. Even before his apprenticeship was completed, he had married.

The venture into art was the most lasting interest in his life, though it never became his only calling. After making his first unskillful oil painting, on a trip to Philadelphia he visited a color merchant and an artist of dubious abilities. From each of these he picked up a little technical advice and some materials rather better than the house paint he had been using. Later, after doing several cut-rate portraits, he hitchhiked by boat to Boston; his creditors were pressing him, political activities of a liberal sort had estranged him from the men who set him up in his shop, and the opportunity to leave home temporarily seemed a godsend as well as a necessity. In Boston his interest in art was forwarded by a talk with John Singleton Copley. A few months later, his credit more happily settled and his painting continuing to develop, came the offer to study abroad. He was reluctant to leave his wife and child for a year or more, but there was no reasonable alternative.

Arrived in London, Peale found West the most helpful of teachers. One story told of Peale's stay in the West studio was a forecast of much that was to come. West was talking to a visitor when a shop-like clatter of tools and metal was heard from the larger studio room. On being questioned, West observed that his student, a Mr. Peale from America, enjoyed doing the needful repair work on the bells and clocks of the household. Peale's love of gadgets and mechanical devices never failed him.[11]

As to his painting, his final piece while he was in London contrasts strangely with his prosaic pleasure in working with the tools of the craftsman. His portrait of Lord Pitt in the popular grandiose vein, clothed in toga and sandals, standing amidst the theatrical props of a pedestal with a votive flame, a pillar, the portion of a distantly seen classical building, and a hovering statuary figure, was planned with an eye to a triumphal reception for the artist on his return home. Lord Pitt, of all the British statesmen of that day, was most sympathetic to the American colonies' struggle for greater independence. And resounding rhetoric in paint, particularly if it honored a public figure or a great event, was the mode in Peale's student days.

Financially Peale was disappointed with the greeting accorded his Lord Pitt portrait. But within a year or two after his return in March, 1769, he was established as a fairly successful painter of portraits. If the career which followed has been much neglected in the annals of American art and art education, perhaps it has been adjudged too largely on the basis of his paintings.

[11] William Dunlap, *A History of the Rise and Progress of the Arts of Design in the United States,* Vol. I, Scott, 1834, p. 137.

CHARLES WILLSON PEALE: CITIZEN, ARTIST, DESIGNER, EDUCATOR

Charles Willson Peale, during all his fifty-one years as an artist, was a respected professional man and an active public figure in the affairs of his adopted city, Philadelphia.

As a painter, Peale was not possessed of the gifts either of John Singleton Copley or Gilbert Stuart. He is not today a "painter's" painter, one whose canvases are studied for sheer delight in their handling. There were many periods of time in his life when he gave up painting for months, even, though rarely, for a year or more at a time. Nevertheless, in the one art task he set for himself, that of portrait painting, he developed steadily. His paintings show the never failing enlargement of skill and personality characteristic of his life. Essentially a primitive, because he never mastered a complete ease in drawing outside the narrow limits of face and bust painting, he never faked a sophistication he did not possess. The picture he painted of the excavation works for his project of digging up a mastodon skeleton found in New York State is a childlike pictorial story, including what is doubtless an exact description of the huge water wheel needed for keeping ground water out of the pit. Around the edge of the hole, and watching the workmen, he painted his own figure in the most prominent spot on the crowded canvas, certainly the proper place for the guiding spirit and the financial backer of the works. Then, by way of populating the rest of the area, he painted most of his family group, including his first wife, then deceased, and his second wife with many of her children.

His absorbed interest in a variety of pursuits never left Peale. Some things he liked to do were looked down upon by professional people generally and by one of his sons-in-law in particular. His artist friends, too, laughed at Peale's outside activities, but he was never influenced beyond suffering a measure of irritation. One of his best contributions to our present-day thinking is this—he is one more exemplar of the artist-personality blessed with creative hands and mind who is willing to work; indeed, who will not be stopped from working wherever his interests or personal needs direct him.

It was by his hands, through his physical grasp of materials, that he developed creative ideas. Psychiatric research in the field of understanding what constitutes a satisfying experience, and the analyses made of learning as best achieved through all the sense channels of the organism—both of these areas of contemporary scholarship recognize the value to the individual of knowing the material of the earth in the way Peale worked with it every day of his life.

One of the associates Peale worked with intermittently over the years was Benjamin Franklin. They were much alike in this characteristic of physical activity and curiosity. Both Peale and Franklin designed stoves. Two of Peale's stoves were used in his museum; they were efficient. Peale, in collaboration with Thomas Jefferson, made improvements in a copying device, which was called the polygraph. Jefferson gave several of them to visiting dignitaries to the United States, and used the machine himself throughout his life. Exact copies of Jefferson's correspondence exist today because of the polygraph.

At still another time, Peale designed a bridge of interbraced thin pieces of wood. He patented it, thus attaining the first bridge patent issued in the United States. The drawing resembled the work of the British designer Telford, and suggests that Peale had an excellent sense of structure and of stress and strain. His dentistry, which he carried on most of his life as part of his surprisingly sensible ideas on health and medicine, was skillful. In the manufacture of false teeth, he was a pioneer; he made porcelain artificial teeth many years before the practice was generally known.

His productions as craftsman and designer in connection with his museum were actually innumerable. With his son Rubens, in 1816, he illuminated the museum with gaslights. The installation, as it has been described in his drawings, was incredibly risky; since the location of the museum at that time was Independence Hall, it is perhaps fortunate that we do not blame the Peale family for its destruction by fire.

Peale's Museum, with which were also exhibited Peale family works of art, was a project reflecting the breadth of interests of its founder and owner. Also it was a product of the intellectual curiosity characterizing America's leading citizens of the caliber of Jefferson and Franklin. These men interpreted democracy as an aid to the pursuit of knowledge and its interpretation; in a sense they were unselective in the quantity and direction of inquiries they followed or encouraged others to follow. For his museum collections Peale gathered animals, birds, stones, insects, and other natural objects. His background was not that of a trained scholar, though he accepted eagerly the help of his contemporaries who were studying more intensively in ornithology, geology, or zoology. These studies were literally at the beginning of their professional development in the United States, concurrently with the first years of the museum. Consequently there was little intellectual impatience manifested toward Peale by the professional men; they were, rather, inclined to be grateful for his collections and to add whatever specimens they could to them.

Taxidermy, approximating as nearly as possible natural animal positions, and the use of native-habitat settings for groups of animals and birds, form a contribution by Peale to present-day museum practice which can hardly be exaggerated. Peale's museum degenerated after his death. The P. T. Barnum type of museum and freak show took its place. But the spirit of inquiry and legitimate educational values was revived in the great museums founded in the United States after the Civil War. The practice of showing collections in re-created environmental backgrounds has become general in community and national museums. For this practice, though he was probably not the sole originator, Peale deserves recognition as an artist measurably advancing an important educational technique.

AN ART ACADEMY FOR PHILADELPHIA

Peale would never hold aloof from organized activity in an intellectual or professional field concerned with any of his many interests. He was naturally the focus of the first attempt to establish an academy of art in America, an attempt which failed in a year's time. But the will to form it, the original scheme of its organization, its proposed program of activity, and the cause of the split destroying it internally—these aspects of the Columbianum, or the American Academy of the Fine Arts, are important. Its problems were surprisingly similar to those met by artists' organizations and schools today.

The artists of Philadelphia met in December of 1794 to form the academy. Within a month eight dissenters had formed a "monarchical" separatist group. Their proposal to nominate George Washington as honorary president and a number of leading citizens as honorary members was opposed without compromise by the majority as being an unworthy, lickspittle performance on the part of Americans and artists. Such honorary titles and the pseudo-association of eminent lay citizens smacked too much of the European artists' dependence on the ruling nobility and royalty. The "monarchists" would not recant their suggestion and the majority could not accept it as an unimportant matter. The implied need for patronage felt by the minority, and the desire of the others to avoid all appearance of needing high-placed indulgence, these differences in various guises have plagued artists' organizations ever since.

The spring of 1795 was spent in writing proclamations of intent and of opposition by the two groups. The larger, in possession of the original organization, did prepare and hang in Independence Hall the first exhibit of the work of American artists. Not all the exhibitors were members of the Academy and not all Academy members exhibited, so it would seem to have been an open showing, not juried. A studio class group met occasionally during the same spring and drew from casts and from the figure. Despite these apparently successful arrangements for annual exhibit and for the beginning of a school of art, the Academy did not survive long after the fall of 1795; it could not exist without the enthusiasm of all those actively interested in art in the Philadelphia area.

It is important to remember that the first comprehensive exhibit of contemporary art was undertaken by a coöperating group of professional artists. Some of the most productive art activities since that time have been similarly initiated and carried out.

Twelve years later in 1807 Peale, completing his unusual record of participation in art affairs, served as one of the two artist members on the board of the newly organized Pennsylvania Academy of Fine Arts. This was organized by Philadelphia patrons of art. A building was erected, and as a first exhibit a collection of casts was secured. This was to become typical of the opening plans of many of the first American art institutions. The growing knowledge of the art of antique Greece and Rome which followed the excavation of Pompeii in 1738 and the publication of Winckelmann's *History of Art Among the Ancients* in 1763 was seized upon by the educated people of Europe and America. An art gallery was thought to be best equipped for educational purposes with replicas of the statues rediscovered from classical antiquity. The lasting quality of this concept of the arts is evidenced by the fact that as late as 1914 the most precious gift that could be made to an American high school was a set of casts from the British Museum's Elgin marbles.

The Pennsylvania Academy has lasted and prospered. A Society of Artists of the United States was formed in 1810, and in 1811, under the auspices of the Pennsylvania Academy, the first of several annual exhibits was held; but this artists' society collapsed as had the Columbianum, though not too soon for its membership to complain to the Academy because the lay governors of that institution treated the artists as being privileged to show their work. The artists, then as now, wished to reverse the obligation, to have the art institution assume that the public was fortunate to be allowed to see their paintings.

Peale's personal activities in the arts outlasted any effectiveness shown by this second artists' organization. He died in 1827. The museum continued under the direction of one of his sons, but gradually declined in appeal and in actual worth as it was forced into the side-show-freak program of its competitors in New York as well as in Philadelphia. We cannot point to present-day institutions founded by Peale. We can only reflect upon the fact that his creative ingenuity in many things is a quality we admire, realizing how much of the emphasis of present-day art education is upon a freely ranging creative approach to all materials and problems. We remark upon the continued practice of great museums to think in the same educational terms as did Peale. And we note, too, that his unquenchable belief in the importance of artists' organized direction of art activities in the community is still a live issue, and has been vindicated by several noteworthy events promoted by artists in the last fifty years.

THE NEW YORK ACADEMY OF THE FINE ARTS

In New York City the New York Academy of the Fine Arts was founded in 1802 and chartered in 1808. A cast collection was brought together and viewed with interest for the first year of its assemblage. In 1816 Governeur Morris, as president of the New York Academy, made a lengthy, learned, and sympathetic address about the arts, in which he reviewed his support of the Academy, the great interest which the social and financial leaders of the city ought to have in the arts, and the fact that the Academy did not seem able to enlist any broad public interest or support. He also referred to a "lack of complete cooperation with our artists, and a consequent indisposition of our artists to countenance it." [12] During the next ten years the practices of the art institution organized by laymen, and the kind of art institution desired by an active artists' group, were to be more publicly discussed and disputed than has ever happened before or since in this country.

William Dunlap, in his *History of the Rise and Progress of the Arts of Design,* wrote in reference to the New York Academy, "We had then gentlemen of every profession, but that of an artist, constituted by law an Academy of Art." [13] Some years later, and as if to moderate Dunlap's scornful statement, the Academy did include one or two artist members on its board. But by 1820 John Trumbull was not only the only artist concerned with the organization; he was also its President.

Trumbull had studied with Benjamin West, as had Peale before him, and as Morse and Dunlap were to do after his stay. Early upon his return to the United States, he prepared small studies of possible large historical works, and with the planning of the Capitol at Washington he proposed ambitious mural panels for its rotunda. Because he was among the first on the scene, in part through the well-placed connections he had been able to cultivate among the membership of the board of the Academy, he was successful in his bidding and was awarded four of the eight rotunda spaces. To this point of Trumbull's progress, there is nothing which his fellow artists would need to question, however much they might envy him. Other circumstances created by him at the Academy, and activities attributed to him, did, however, provoke a bitter war of personalities all but obscuring the more important issues raised.

[12] Thomas S. Cummings, *Historic Annals of the National Academy of Design,* New York Drawing Association, etc., Childs, 1865, p. 8.
[13] Dunlap, *op. cit.,* Vol. I, p. 419.

For one thing the Academy occupied a building made available to it by the city. The building was devoted to the housing of the cast collection and to the accommodation of its president, Colonel John Trumbull, for his personal studio quarters. While this rent-free convenience might be questioned under any conditions by artists not so well located, Trumbull's arrogant personality and his method of carrying out the supposed services of the Academy to the public and to art students seemed insupportable to the artist group.

The cast gallery was scheduled to be open and heated, the casts to be available to students during regular periods of time each week. An incident occurred when Samuel F. B. Morse, recently returned from his tour of study with West, observed the quality of hospitality offered students by the Academy. Shortly after eight o'clock one morning, two young men approached the building as Morse stood on the steps. They explained to Morse that the student hours were from six to nine, but that the caretaker was never about until eight or after. As they chatted, the caretaker arrived; he refused the students permission to draw that day because they would have to finish their work well after the closing hour of nine. T. S. Cummings was one of the two young men turned away that morning. For years he was to serve as treasurer of the new academy which, in a way, was born of the disappointment suffered that morning.[14]

Similar incidents mounted up. The cast gallery was unheated when it was open to students, though the Trumbull studio was always well serviced. While Trumbull officially resented any inference that the New York Academy was uninterested in students, the actual facilities were available irregularly, without any courtesies extended or sense of concern shown for the student.

YOUNGSTERS FOUND THE NATIONAL ACADEMY

The Society for the Improvement of Drawing was formed on November 8, 1825. The young men composing the group had no unusual program, no Bohemian declaration of principles, like those common in Europe and in America later in the century. Neither was their educational aim opposed to the practices that would have been urged by Benjamin West or even by the irascible Trumbull. They wanted only to be able to draw regularly from casts. To this end

[14] Cummings, op. cit., p. 20.

they gathered casts from among the older members of the group, and one or two were included which were borrowed from the collection of the New York Academy. The rent of a room was prorated, as was the cost of oil for a central lamp lighting the casts. In addition to the large lamp, each student brought a small oil lamp to light his own board. By the close of two hours of drawing one evening a week, as T. S. Cummings writes, the smoke was thick and it was hard to see the casts. This provided an arbitrary limit of drawing time.[15]

The story is told by several observers of how, on one of the drawing nights, Colonel Trumbull entered the studio room and demanded that all present sign a register which he provided, indicating that they were officially students of the New York Academy of Fine Arts. He threatened immediate action if they did not do so. No one signed. As nearly as could be determined by those present, Trumbull's strange request was animated by no other claim on the group than the fact that some of the casts they were using came from the Academy gallery. A meeting was called at once. It was agreed to return all property of the Academy to Trumbull, and then the discussion turned in the direction of a real artists' academy. By the close of the meeting the National Academy of Design was launched; the date was January 19, 1826. The president elected was Samuel Finley Breese Morse.

A battle was on. To begin with the National Academy group was attacked as presumptuous. How was it possible for a small group, half of whom professed to be students, to identify itself as a "National" academy? The system of membership decided upon for incorporation purposes had divided the membership into a student unit and a "charter member" classification. Added to these were the names of ten other artists who, at the vote of the whole body, were extended invitations to become members. Some of the artists on this list were residents of Boston or Philadelphia. Resulting directly from this phase of the attack, one or two artists close to the New York Academy declined their invitations publicly and with heat, or simply ignored them. The rest of the list accepted the honor as it was offered.

Then the likelihood was suggested that two art academies would

15 *Ibid.*, p. 22.

perish where one might better serve all art purposes. For more than a year a committee from the National Academy, after the New York Academy urged the need for consolidation, pursued this line of thought, drawing up a document stating the bases on which the National Academy would be willing to consider such a union. From the records available, it would seem that Trumbull was responsible for the evasive and noncommittal way in which the New York Academy responded to the overtures of Morse and his colleagues. Members of Trumbull's board who were not artists were not as uninterested in meeting with Morse as Trumbull inferred. Finally, all efforts at negotiation were broken off when it was evident that Trumbull wanted one academy, to be sure, but he wanted it on his terms, and he did not want any fellow artists on the board of directors. Considering the established convictions of the two major participants, it is unlikely that an agreement would have been reached.

Trumbull stood upon his earned prerogatives; earned, as he felt, by seniority, by his service to his country in the Revolution, by his official position as president of the oldest art institution in the city. He believed that he deserved more than any other the great boon of the Capitol rotunda commission. He believed not only that the artist gained greatly in well-paid commissions and in prestige from relying on the good will and patronage of industrial leaders and men in the government, but that that was the only avenue to artistic eminence, and that he was obviously the best choice because of his access to these groups. In short, he was willing to accept the evaluation of his patrons as his right to claim aesthetic and academic leadership of all his artist colleagues.

The followers of Morse in the National Academy of Design favored a more open field. They wanted the opportunity to study and to work professionally in the arts open to as many young people as proved desirous and capable of an art career.

How this broadening of art professionalism was to be achieved they did not know; and in the lifetime of most of the charter members of the National Academy, discouragement and doubt succeeded the mood of enterprise in which the National Academy was begun. At any rate, theirs was the more popular cause in the public mind. Most of the artists, too, supported the National Academy, and the belief that art and art training should be democratically organized in American society was fairly established.

Morse wrote at length for the public press on the aims and objectives of the National Academy and on the merits of its position in the altercation with the New York Academy. The published version of his address on the occasion of the first anniversary of the National Academy forms an admirable summing up of his grasp of the situation faced by student and artist alike. He opened with this statement: "Every profession in society knows best what measures are necessary for its own improvement." [16]

Today, what with frequent criticism reaching all those professions which do organize their larger professional policies, namely, law, medicine, and education, there might be some quarrel with Morse on his statement. Yet, the right of the public to criticize the goals and decisions of a professional group has not interfered with a large measure of initiative and control of professional education and of the practice of that profession. Morse at least urged the measure of professional awareness and group activity that these other professions enjoy today. By no means all artists would welcome such professional unity now, but, lacking it, they must abide by the resultant individuality compounded, the lack of professional status, and the widely differentiated professional education in the arts.

Morse went on to outline four major requirements for the continued vigor of an academy of art. He held that an academy of art in America must be organized by artists, its voting members must be artists, and its business management and moneys, from whatever sources or endowments, must be controlled by the membership. On this point, whether he knew it or not, he agreed with Peale's interpretation of the British Royal Academy.

Second, but not of secondary importance, an artists' academy must establish a school of the arts. The third requirement reads somewhat strangely today and hardly appears to deserve the emphasis given it. Premiums or awards must annually be given to the outstanding students of the school. Fourth on his list of necessities was that the academy must regularly organize and present exhibitions of the work of contemporary artists.

[16] *Ibid.*, p. 37.

To his task of proposing objectives for the National Academy, Morse brought a study of scholarly completeness on the art academies of Europe, England, and even of South America, since 1750. He noted the fact that the rapid growth of all these institutions stemmed from Colbert's support of the French Royal Academy from the year 1672, which was planned to contribute to the enlargement of French international trade in textiles, jewelry, clothing, and furniture, as well as sculpture and painting. He was well acquainted with the school curricula common to all the early and more lately established academies overseas. Drawing from whatever drawings of masters or near masters the school possessed was followed by the inevitable drawing from casts, and that in turn was the prerequisite for entering the class drawing from the human figure. Even by 1827 there was no variation on this pattern, regardless of whether the student in these European schools was preparing for the practice of the fine arts or for the designing of textiles. Morse neither mentioned any promising deviations from this educational pattern nor did he propose any innovations in curriculum for the National Academy school. What was apparent, though, in Morse's address was that the National Academy group wanted and meant to have a school offering an orderly schedule of classes, in adequate quarters, with casts from which to work, heat when necessary, and the proper accompanying lectures on perspective and anatomy. As in the European schools, these aids to drawing were to be presented separately. No longer would art students have to depend on the caprice or the digestion of the caretaker at the New York Academy. Only instruction was lacking; professional academicians were expected to do the teaching on a volunteer basis, and after the first few months of enthusiasm this scheme of faculty organization became less and less satisfactory. Generally, the only faithful teachers were those who had offered to perform the lecture series.

The Royal Academy of Great Britain, as Morse and many others of the group had known it under West, was the inspiration not only for the artist control of the Academy but also for the regular exhibition of the work of living artists. The Royal Academy had begun annual exhibits in 1761 before the granting of its royal charter in 1768. These exhibits were highly successful and provided the funds for most of the other operations, including the school classes of the organization.

New York responded to the exhibition program of the National Academy reasonably well. Early in the history of the shows a member was lost by resignation because of the poor placement of his work, but other than that the committee did not meet the problems now involved in painting exhibitions. The enormous pressure of numbers of artists and the lack of sufficient wall space were unknown. Opening the gallery at night, under a carefully planned lighting arrangement, proved valuable in attendance increases.

The National Academy gradually settled into a routine pattern of school affairs and of planning for its major annual event, the exhibition. Having made a break from a confusing situation, and having created an organization more responsive to the artists' needs, the members were unable to maintain a high level of growth and achievement.

The decline of leadership, of influence exerted, was partly caused by the difficulty artist members experienced in earning a living by their art.

Though histories have been written, and the names of the unpatronized and frustrated artists of that first half of the nineteeth century are better known than their work, the whole of their activity, in the context of its time, was unimpressive. The huge historical canvases endearing West to his patron, George III, became the highest aim in art for West's many students. This was unfortunate, since the emphasis on moral, literary, and patriotic qualities reduced the artists' concern for growth in aesthetic power. Furthermore, though the artists fondly believed that the historical record was to become their great contribution to democratic society, they seemed to be alone in that conviction. Except for a few federal commissions reluctantly granted by Congress, there was no lively demand for pictorial history, either from individuals or from local, state, or national government. The artists were forced to portraiture, which was not too rewarding or steady as an income producer; or to barnstorming with a large canvas of spectacular subject, charging admission to see it in a circuit trip from city to city. Only an occasional picture was popular enough to make this kind of venture profitable. Morse spent a year and a half, off and on, doing a large piece depicting the entire House of Representatives in action. It did not prove to be of popular interest.

After years of experiences like that, Morse, who might have been expected to furnish intellectual leadership of a caliber to prevent the dry rot of the school and academy, became involved, almost against his will, in mechanical invention, resulting in the telegraph. Unlike Peale's many experiences in this direction, Morse hit upon a phenomenally successful thing in the telegraph, at a time when industrial exploitation was possible. It absorbed most of its inventor's energies and creative zest for the rest of his life. Though he was Academy president from 1826, the year of founding, to 1845, and was president again in 1861, there is no indication that he ever again devoted the time and consideration to the problems of art and art education which he did in the years 1826 to 1830. Intellectual leadership was lost and diffused, and with this the likelihood of continued development toward a more vigorous art education. Professional art education was to remain dormant until Thomas Eakins started his work at the Pennsylvania Academy after the Civil War.

PIONEERS IN A PHILOSOPHY OF ART

The teaching of drawing in the elementary schools, and the art academies which were founded, were based on European examples but took on a distinctive American coloration. A similar history characterizes American philosophizing in aesthetics, or in what might be called general art education for the reading or lecture-going public. The structure of the arts, the meanings to be gleaned from picture, statue, and building, was a serious preoccupation in the United States early in the nineteenth century. Not much humor or human flexibility was manifested in the interpretation of art to this new country.

Many of the essays written were close to absurdity, but there was no lack of trying. Not to make the generalization too exclusive, there was a plentiful quantity of sentimental nonsense written about art in England and Europe during the same period of time. The industrial disruption of handicrafts, the political bombardment of the royal courts and consequently of the arts of the courts, upset and confused the artists. These also set a host of philosophers and literary men to attempt to recognize and describe what there was in art for the newly enlarged circle of claimants to a share in the life of culture. The chief difference between Europe and America was the number and proportion of people here who believed they had a vested interest in the good things of life. If the visual and plastic arts were valuable, then everyone here assumed that they, or anyone especially interested, should have access to them.

Ralph Waldo Emerson and his respected friend, the American sculptor Horatio Greenough, did valuable pioneering in their aesthetic writing, which was in answer to the question, "What are works of art good for in our lives?"

Much of the life experience of the two men negates what they put down in words. There is a prophetic feel to the insight each possessed which neither was able to demonstrate fully in works of art, in personal collections, in stone sculptured, or by their specific examination of individual art works. However, the thoughts they left for us have retained a contemporary note; the several generations following them have, each in its own way, found them worth-while guides.

Emerson's essay, "Art," was included in his *Essays* issued in 1841. There are other references to the arts in Emerson, but this piece, part of his early and most vigorous work, is of nearly the same vintage as the work and writing of Mann and Alcott. Emerson's profundity was bound to affect his countrymen's thinking, but it was also bound to take time to sink in. At a time when classes of schoolchildren were copying their teachers' blackboard drawings line by line, Emerson was writing the following: "Because the soul is progressive, it never quite repeats itself, but in every act attempts the production of a new and fairer whole. . . . Thus in our fine arts, not imitation but creation is the aim. . . . The artist must employ the symbols in use in his day and nation to convey his enlarged sense to his fellow-men. Art is the need to create. . . . Art should exhilarate, and throw down the walls of circumstance on every side, awakening in the beholder the same sense of universal relation and power which the work evinced in the artist. . . ."

Finally: "Beauty must come back to the useful arts and the distinction between the fine and useful arts be forgotten." [17]

No American writer or artist in the nineteenth century ever clothed the last sentence from Emerson more specifically than did Horatio Greenough a few years later. Van Wyck Brooks in his *Flowering of New England,* published in 1936, revived Greenough's writings; in January of 1939, Nancy Wynne and Beaumont Newhall published excerpts from Greenough in the *Magazine of Art;* and in 1947, Harold A. Small edited the volume, *Horatio Greenough: Form and Function, Remarks on Art.*

Greenough deserves this latter-day attention. As a sculptor he worked in the manner of Italy, that is, in a second-hand interpretation of a classical mode. His half-nude *General and President George Washington* has been one of the favored targets of twentieth-century writers on nineteenth-century art. Even when Greenough was alive to defend the statue, Washington, stripped to the waist, legs swathed to the hips in a toga, with mace in hand, was not joyfully received by the Congress of the United States which had granted the commission.

Yet the same man, returned to America in the midst of the classic revival in architecture, made some of the most penetrating observations ever printed on the arts and the functional designs to be seen in American life.

These are some of his statements: "The men who have reduced locomotion to its simplest elements, in the trotting wagon and the yacht, *America,* are nearer to Athens at this moment than they who would bend the Greek temple to every use. I contend for Greek principles, not Greek things." [18] Other quotations from Greenough, of equally pertinent application, can be found in plenty. It is a matter of regret, though not perhaps of wonder, that the sculptor was unable in the few years left to him to apply the same keen insight to his own craft. Some men can see far beyond their own power to perform. Greenough must have been such a man.

Later, at the close of the nineteenth and the beginning of the

[17] Ralph Waldo Emerson, *The Complete Essays and Other Writings of Ralph Waldo Emerson,* Modern Library, 1940, p. 314.
[18] Horatio Greenough, *Form and Function: Remarks on Art,* ed. by Harold Small, University of California, 1947.

twentieth century, men and women teaching in professional art schools, teachers in the elementary and high schools, and professional artists in painting, sculpture, architecture, and design were only beginning to apply in their day-to-day work something of the vision of Emerson and Greenough.

The revelations from rare and gifted artists take time, first to be genuinely understood, and then to enter into daily usage. The practices of art education today are not as distant from, nor as independent of, the decades from 1800 to 1850 as we may think.

Bibliography

Alcott, Amos Bronson, *Observations on the Principles and Methods of Infant Instruction*, Carter and Hendee, 1830.

Beard, Charles A. and Mary R., *The Rise of American Civilization*, Macmillan, 1927.

Brooks, Van Wyck, *The Flowering of New England, 1815–1865*, Dutton, 1936.

Brooks, Van Wyck, *The World of Washington Irving*, Blakiston, 1945.

Common School Journal, Horace Mann, ed., Vol. I, 1839.

Curti, Merle, *The Growth of American Thought*, Harper, 1943.

Drepperd, Carl W., *American Pioneer Arts and Artists*, Pond-Ekberg, 1942.

Dunlap, William, *Address to the Students of the National Academy of Design at the Delivery of Premiums, April 18, 1831*, Clayton and Van Norden, 1831.

Dunlap, William, *A History of the Rise and Progress of the Arts of Design in the United States*, Scott, 1834.

Flagg, Jared B., *The Life and Letters of Washington Allston*, Bentley, 1893.

Flexner, James Thomas, *America's Old Masters*, Viking, 1939.

Greenough, Horatio, *Form and Function: Remarks on Art*, ed. by Harold Small, University of California, 1947.

Haefner, George E., *Critical Estimate of the Educational Theories and Practices of A. Bronson Alcott*, Columbia University, 1937.

Hansen, Allen Oscar, *Liberalism and American Education*, Macmillan, 1926.

Hogarth, William, *The Analysis of Beauty*, 1st pub., 1753, reprinted by Silver Lotus, Pittsfield, Mass., 1909.

Larkin, Oliver W., *Art and Life in America*, Rinehart, 1949.

McCuskey, Dorothy, *Bronson Alcott, Teacher*, Macmillan, 1940.

Martin, George H., *The Evolution of the Massachusetts Public School System,* Appleton, 1894.

Mumford, Lewis, *The Condition of Man,* Harcourt, Brace, 1944.

Pach, Walter, *The Art Museum in America,* Pantheon, 1948.

Parrington, Vernon Louis, *Main Currents in American Thought,* Harcourt, Brace, 1927–1930.

Peabody, Elizabeth, *Record of a School,* 3rd ed., Roberts, 1874, recorder's preface, 1835.

Peale, Rembrandt, *Graphics, a Manual of Drawing and Writing for the Use of Schools and Families,* Peaslee, 1835.

Peale, Rembrandt, *Graphics, the Art of Accurate Delineation,* Biddle, 1850.

Pevsner, Nikolaus, *Academies of Art: Past and Present,* Macmillan, 1940.

Reisner, Edward H., *Evolution of the Common School,* Macmillan, 1930.

Sellers, Charles Coleman, *Charles Willson Peale,* American Philosophical Society, 1947.

Swan, Mabel Munson, *The Boston Athenaeum as an Early Patron of Art,* Boston Athenaeum, 1940.

Figure 3. The Ninth Gift, The Disconnected Slat. (From Elizabeth Peabody, "Guide to the Kindergarten," 1860, 1877.)

III

Intellectual Imports from Europe: Artistic Plunder for America

There was a difference between the stanch New England which was Horatio Greenough's home and the world known to the American artists, critics, teachers, and collectors of art in the decades after the Civil War. Even after 1850 the interpretation of the arts, the relationships seen between the arts of Europe and the potentialities in America, were broader but perhaps not as sound as in earlier decades; a greater degree of aesthetic sophistication entered American life while a simpler grasp of principle was partly lost to view.

Emerson and Greenough were absorbed in studying the art of Europe, as were their contemporaries. But their absorption was profoundly aimed at the definition of basic principles. They believed that American artists in possession of fundamental aims in the arts could discover what was sound in their own society, even as Greenough identified the functional beauty of the unpretentious clapboard house and the clipper ship. From such vantage points of understanding, native arts might grow, securely rooted in quality of concept and form.

A small part of American art development after 1850 bore out such hopes. We are today seeking out, almost feverishly, the work and the personal philosophy of the artists whose aim was that of creating a strongly felt personal art, for which they sought little help from European painting movements.

On the whole, however, a less immediately productive psychology gained control of our arts activity. A greater glory was attached to Europe and all its works than to native and contemporary arts. As the rawness of life in America was emphasized in factory growth, in the phenomenal westward expansion, in the brutal thrust of the Northeast and Midwest economic and industrial domination, the vision of art in America on home-grown terms faded from public interest almost completely.

That vision was replaced for years with something infinitely weaker, with a vague sentimental contention that Europe knew how to live, that only Europe had created forms of art, and that only in Europe could one find an environment sympathetic to art.

Inasmuch as only rarely do individuals feel that they want to quit their native land forever, there was a great commerce in importing to the United States portions of the aesthetic background which seemed so attractive to the American abroad. The traffic which gathered impetus from this collective desire was by no means as philosophical, nor as devoted to a natural and slow development of contemporary art, as were the intellectual and critical European journeys and writings on Europe by Emerson, Morse, and Greenough.

JAMES JACKSON JARVES

James Jackson Jarves serves us as the best example and the most aesthetically reliable of the men who literally raided Europe to bring across the Atlantic art treasures of the past three thousand years.

Even as we use the life and accomplishments of Jarves as symbolic of all the "collectors" of art masterpieces, we must preface a review of his work by acknowledging that his writing shows a sensitive mind wholly opposed to the shallowness, the extremes of pseudo-culture collecting, which imitated his work without understanding.

Jarves was a nineteenth-century internationalist by birth and by residence. His well-to-do New England family found it possible and apparently quite natural to send him away at the age of nineteen to improve his health in the Hawaiian Islands. He stayed there eleven years and began his writing career with a *History of the Hawaiian or Sandwich Islands* and *Scenes and Scenery in the Sandwich Islands*. In 1851, after a two-year period spent back in the States, he left for his first trip to Europe. His occupation was ostensibly that of a purchasing agent for a Boston merchant. But, as sales of the books on the Hawaiian Islands were excellent, he turned soon to more writing, this time for *Harper's Magazine* and on the subject of his impressions of Paris.

He took his first trip through the art collections of the Louvre and was enthralled with what he saw there. Other Americans before Jarves, and literally thousands of travelers who were to take European tours after the Civil War, were properly and often sincerely impressed by their first encounter with the magnificence of European art. But it was the quality and discrimination of Jarves' reaction which was so significant to America; for Jarves was one whose life prior to that time had prepared him to see pictures more purely than was possible to most of his contemporaries. The high renaissance of Raphael was not automatically his point of departure for all qualitative evaluations of paintings and painters. He responded deeply to the simpler work of the Tuscan painters, and to the enthusiasms of Ruskin and other writers for the early Christian art of Giotto and his predecessors.

His money and such of his father's money as he could get was spent for a great collection of these works. While he enjoyed, frankly and with remarkable aesthetic insight, the works on their own merits, he was equally intent on the paintings as a record of an earlier era

49

of Christian culture. The first and greatest of his collections was largely complete in 1859; its subsequent history could cause anyone to doubt that his fellow countrymen had any art interests or any impulse to develop them.

He exhibited his pictures in New York City in 1859–1860, where critical comment was surprisingly controversial and on a plane of quarrelsome chitchat concerning religious virtues, the "crudeness" and "primitiveness" of the artists' rendering, and the dubious value of even showing the work of the "untalented" forerunners of the Renaissance.

As Jarves' original aim had been the assembling of a collection to be acquired by an American institution, it was both a disappointment to him and a financial blow. Almost ten years after the first exhibit, Yale University in 1868 loaned Jarves $20,000 on the pictures, and hung them in its newly built art school. In 1871 Jarves could not redeem his property; the pictures were put up at auction, without takers, and the university itself paid Jarves an additional $2,000 for full ownership.[1] Now, of course, it is generally conceded that the Jarves Collection is one of the finest owned by any institution in the country.

Although the history of Jarves' struggles to interest Americans in the pictures was unhappy and unsuccessful in securing a generous and willing sponsor, nonetheless Jarves continued to be tremendously influential in subsequent American cultural history.

His kind of thinking, expressed in many widely circulated books, turned the cultural activities of most wealthy Americans toward collecting the historical art of Europe. The discrimination practiced by Jarves was, however, too often absent from the purchases made both personally and by the agents of American millionaires. The result of all this collecting was to channel public education in the arts into a museum orbit. The more gradual creation of our own art background by our own living artists was handicapped and retarded perhaps for decades by this emphasis.

It is easier to see now what we have gained from the freebooting collectors of that era than it is to guess at what cost, in terms of

[1] Francis Steegmuller, "James Jackson Jarves: Thumbnail Sketch of a Collector," *Magazine of Art,* April, 1948, p. 132.

native development, it was accomplished. The Metropolitan Museum of Art in New York City was established in 1871. Other museums followed in Boston, Philadelphia, Pittsburgh, Cincinnati, Cleveland, Chicago, St. Louis, Kansas City, Detroit, Milwaukee, Minneapolis, and other places. All the founders and benefactors of these galleries participated in buying up the old masters of Europe; so that most European countries have now legally forbidden further trade, even by private owners, involving removal of an important work of art beyond their national borders.

The great American collections now so important a part of our educational facilities vary somewhat on the basis of the taste and interests of the original donors, but show a still wider range of art values, dependent upon the amounts of money spent for them. The great family fortunes—Mellon, Morgan, Frick, Bache, Kress, and others—have provided us with a large group of costly and irreplaceable art objects, largely European paintings of the period from 1000 B.C. to the nineteenth century.

Collectors of lesser fortune were frequently less fortunate also in their judgment, or perhaps in their advisers. Sometimes the institutions they created have come to deplore this flaw in their founders' benevolence. Especially to be regretted are the numerous copies of the great Renaissance paintings and the mass of paintings which were purchased from the late-nineteenth-century Parisian Salon painters.

By the close of the nineteenth century, there came into public prominence some of the first of the members of wealthy families to begin the present great collections of more contemporary art. Many of the individuals of this group later founded independent galleries or endowments for purchase of contemporary work.

It is as if the dominant social and financial element of the country willfully decided that there could be no great art among us until we procured part of the art wealth of the past. And such a point of view was exactly the one expressed not only by James Jackson Jarves but by many of his artist contemporaries. The art professionals, both painters and educators, are finally responsible for the era of masterpiece collecting.

The psychology of admiration for the art of the past, and for the

51

art of other nations above that of our native artists, is by no means extinct. It is still, and inescapably, the largest part of the conscious and unconscious background of the American artist and art student. There is reason to hope that the artists are now well advanced in assimilating the riches of our galleries and that an adult independence is not far off.

Jarves was one of the earliest and best intellectual middlemen engaged in the transplantation, on a scale unmatched in history, of cultural objects from an old society to a new one. But, in spite of his emotional reliance on Europe for aesthetic satisfaction, Jarves also provided encouragement, most of it healthy, for American growth in other aspects of the arts.

His writings, which were very popular, planted some of the seeds for a later interest in architectural functionalism and for certain of the more vigorous approaches to painting in the art schools and among the artists. In 1864, on the subject of New York City, he wrote: "They live and move by blocks and squares, are rectangular by compulsion, have lost the sense of the picturesque, or see beauty only in geometrical plots bounded by tall iron fences, flower-bed bastilles, from which dogs and people are remorselessly warned off, always excepting Central Park, the idea of which is so grand and universal that it seems like a protest for the beautiful wrung from the soul of famishing millions." [2]

Elaborating on this wrathy introduction, Jarves writes about the satisfying quality of cities where the original topography—the hills, streams, valleys, and wooded areas—is the very foundation of civic beauty. He shows his awareness of the urge to improve urban landscape which resulted in the building of the Parisian boulevards and new parks, and in America in the plans for suburbs with winding roadways and wooded publicly owned areas. The point is that Jarves, in many of his casual observations, was very much a leader of aesthetic thinking in our country, and easily abreast of ideas current among the artists and architects of Europe.

In defense of his interest in the collection of European masterworks, and concerning the eventual development of American art, he wrote: "It is a duty to vindicate art, not to foster national conceit,

[2] James Jackson Jarves, *The Art Idea,* Hurd and Houghton, 1864, p. 334.

stimulate personal vanity, or pander to individual interests." [3] And he continues: "To this loss of what may be termed a floating aesthetic capital [referring to the lack of great art collections] must be added the almost equal destitution of institutions for instruction in the science of art, except in a crude and elementary way. Academies and schools of design are few, and but imperfectly established. Public galleries exist only in idea."

He had some definite ideas, too, about the need for educational missionary work by the artist: "Studios would effect much for the development of taste and knowledge were they freely visited, by bringing our public into more cordial relations with artists, who do not yet exercise their legitimate influence. In a nation of lyceums and lecturers, every topic except art is heard." [4] Jarves' complaint sounds a familiar note if we recall Bronson Alcott's self-satisfied description of his school as a "word shop."

Jarves wrote in this vein in 1864. The book reached its fourth edition in 1877. Every chapter of this widely read book contains discerning observations on the arts in American life. While he approved of and stimulated the admiration for all things European, he did so intelligently, drawing attention more often to fundamental values than to superficialities. The gawking American tourist soon became the butt of well-earned ridicule, and the affectation of many American "art lovers" was rightly distrusted by their fellow citizens. But Jarves represents the best, not the worst, of what we imported from Europe after the Civil War.

EARLY PROFESSIONAL ART INSTRUCTION

The serious professionalism in American art schools which Jarves longed for, and probably hastened by his writing, was to be realized before he died in 1888. By that time the Pennsylvania Academy in Philadelphia and the Cooper Union and the Art Students League in New York City were all striving for high professional standards, and many other schools in Boston, Chicago, Pittsburgh, Cleveland, and Cincinnati were growing and improving.

Pioneer artist-teachers, including William Morris Hunt, Thomas Eakins, William Merritt Chase, and Frank Duveneck, were creating

[3] *Ibid.*, pp. 173, 176.
[4] *Ibid.*, p. 176.

a more serious professional art education in these institutions. They brought to their teaching a quite different art background from that of the founders of the National Academy. Their European training had been better, much broader, and at the same time sounder than the tight and timid scholasticism of Benjamin West's studio. They experienced in Europe, and insisted on bringing to America, an occasionally dramatic and stubbornly unconventional way of life. They returned from their European study to an America materially richer, crowded with newly arrived immigrants, alive with the hasty growth of the West, less disciplined by prim New England, and much more inclined to accept and even to enjoy a growing artist and art-student group.

William Morris Hunt's family was comfortable financially, and raised him and his brothers and sisters in a home where cultural interests were taken for granted. After William studied briefly at Harvard, the mother took the family on a trip to Italy and France. Hunt studied in academies in Düsseldorf and in Paris, and later, with greater interest, in the studios of Couture and, finally, Millet. He exhibited in the Paris Salons of 1852–1853 and 1855. That year he returned to Boston, set up a studio in Newport, and started on the first of his portrait commissions.

He began the first of his many private classes; most of the students were women and few of them intended to study as art professionals. Hunt's interest in the class was by no means abated by that fact. From the day of his return to Boston he proclaimed the artist's duty to educate the public in the arts. The lavish number of memoirs written by Bostonians include many recollections of Hunt's exciting personality and of his power in teaching the arts to all kinds of people in his classes or over the dinner table.

Young John La Farge came to the Newport studio class, after studying with Hunt's teacher, Couture, in Paris. He wanted to study with the artist who, he believed, would help him to work in Couture's way. In this hope he was disappointed, for Hunt had turned much more to Millet as a source of inspiration than to the study he had completed with Couture. Nevertheless, La Farge stayed on for some time, painting quite independently and enjoying his frequent discussions on the arts, specifically painting, which were so important a part of Hunt's teaching. La Farge was to become one of the most influential of America's artists. His home background, like that of Hunt, had been excellent; had helped him to be a ready and intelligent conversationalist and to be at ease in any sort of situation. In the arts he was to be remembered for his revival of the making of stained-glass windows and of large mural paintings. He lectured frequently to art-school students in cities as far west as Chicago. He was an intimate friend of Henry Adams and had a great influence on Adams' aesthetic point of view.

Hunt's other well-known students were not to make their fame in painting, but as a philosopher-teacher and writer, respectively. They were the brothers William and Henry James. Here, too, while Hunt's influence was probably not dominant, it turned both men to an interested and favorable attitude toward the visual and plastic arts.

Hunt moved his residence and studio into Boston in 1862. He was energetic in aiding the plans for the Boston Museum. He possessed a large number of paintings by Millet and interested other Bostonians in buying works from that artist. He was the leading member of an art group which he persuaded to buy a painting by Courbet, the first of his work to come to America. Just as the impressionists were doing in Paris, by 1864 Hunt was looking eagerly for Japanese prints, was beginning to study them for their dissimilarity from Western pictorial composition, and was arousing an enthusiasm for the Oriental arts which was to become a sort of special characteristic of Boston. One of the largest collections of Oriental arts is that of the Boston Museum. The Courbet and many of the Millets eventually were added to the museum collection as well.

The impact of such a man as Hunt was evident to all of Boston and to men and women of cultural interests who visited that city. He believed that the best in art from all over the world should be collected and publicly exhibited. And he was not uncertain or unwilling to commit himself on the work of contemporary artists; it may be that something of his spirit explains why Boston was generally recognized as a better market for living American artists' work, at least until 1900, than was New York.

He held the belief, and acted upon it, that the most important duty of the American artist was to teach the public, not only the potential artist. Not alone did he devote the work in his studio classes to this goal, but also he gave a series of "Talks on Art" in which he tried to improve the public level of art understanding.

William Morris Hunt, the teacher and public figure in the arts, was better known and has proved more of a lasting influence than Hunt, the artist. He would himself acknowledge that fact somewhat ruefully with the observation that his energies turned to public education seemed more necessary at the time.

PROFESSIONAL ART EDUCATION: POST-CIVIL WAR

Only a few years later, three other men were to dominate the teaching of the arts professionally in this country and to introduce qualities of instruction of lasting influence. Thomas Eakins was the first of the group in point of time. He began studying in the studio of Gérôme in Paris in the year 1866. In 1869 he spent a year working independently in Spain and in 1870 he returned to his native Philadelphia.

Hunt and La Farge were, in a sense, cosmopolites, as interested in people and movements, in a large flow of events, as in their own art. Eakins, though he always demonstrated as much intellectual ability as any man in American arts then or since, did show a greater reliance upon his art alone as his public expression.

In his teaching, Eakins began to instruct at the Pennsylvania Academy in 1876. In 1879 he was made director of the school; in 1882 a tuition fee was established for the first time because the school was becoming more demanding in its need for equipment and materials. Under Eakins, as the serious students became increasingly pleased with his teaching and curriculum, the larger group of more casually interested students, which by custom meant the girls, began to grow doubtful and unhappy about their work.

Eakins had himself studied anatomy at a medical school even before he left for Paris. He had been doing some drawing as a beginning student at the Pennsylvania Academy, and at the same time he studied with the anatomy class for medical students in a local school. Obviously, Eakins was convinced of the artist's absolute need for the most thorough anatomical knowledge. To attain such knowledge, he felt that the student must be required at least to attend dissection lectures, and preferably to have some direct experience in dissection in a medical-school class.

As to classroom procedures, Eakins used casts but little; in his regime cast drawings were merely a casual introductory stint for the beginner. Life drawing was begun quickly for all able students, and most were soon alternating painting from the model with drawing. These changes were less likely to be objected to since they delivered students from the most boring of routine work and speeded up the day they could start painting.

In the uses of the nude model, as in his emphasis on anatomical study, Eakins was at cross-purposes with many of the parents of women students, and finally with influential members of the Academy board. Such a practice as the use of a male and a female nude model together for the purpose of comparative anatomical study was often criticized heartily. Finally, in 1886, he was requested to give up the directorship and to agree to continue some teaching under a new director, with the understanding that he would agree with less complete approaches to the study of the human figure. He refused this offer without any hesitation. The incident which precipitated his departure from the school of the Academy was his removal of the loincloth from a male model who was posing in a women's class so that the leg muscles could be properly studied in relation to the pelvis.

Today this "teapot tempest" strikes us as unwarranted. Since Eakins' departure from his full-time teaching post, there has even been a period of time in some art schools when any extended study of the human figure was held as relatively unimportant to the professional student. Fortunately, the reaction to that has already arrived and the ability to draw freely and well is more than ever a major part of the artist's equipment. It is probably true that Eakins' insistence on dissection is not likely ever to be widely revived.

For the rest of his life Eakins was sought after by most of the important schools in Boston, New York, and finally in Philadelphia as descriptive lecturer in anatomy.

Of greater importance than the relative merits of more or less life study is the fact that Eakins established for the first time in Philadelphia, and quite likely for the United States, a determinedly professional art school. The large group of ambitious students who left the Academy with Eakins, and finished a year or two more of study with him in an independent studio, gives evidence of the respect he had earned as artist and teacher. The content of his teaching was recorded by one of his students in the independent class which he taught without salary as long as the group was able to raise the funds to rent a studio. What he taught was not too dissimilar from some contemporary practices which are considered distinctively modern. He is quoted as suggesting, "Take an egg or an orange, a piece of black cloth, and a piece of white paper, and try to get the light and color." "A chair is constructed with a great deal of common-sense. It has been arrived at by long experience." [5] In these and other bits of advice to students, he dwelt constantly on the need to feel and represent the qualities of light, of color, and, above all, of texture. He was concerned, too, with a clear grasp of essential form.

We add to the rest of our knowledge about Eakins the facts that he was a first-rate craftsman in wood, and that he was among the most advanced experimenters who were trying to analyze motion through the use of photography. In all his teaching and independent study, we find him allied with those nineteenth- and twentieth-century teachers of art who insisted on knowing their craft and profession thoroughly, and extending its practice as much as they could. Eakins did not push himself into much civic activity, as did Charles Willson Peale or William Morris Hunt, but his intensive practice of painting and his related teaching have been of inestimable value to our art traditions.

ART STUDENTS LEAGUE

The Art Students League was organized in New York City in 1875, under the prod of unsatisfactory conditions at the school of the National Academy. The Academy had reached a period of perfunctory and uninspiring offerings to its student group. There was even some question in the spring of 1875 as to whether or not the Academy classes would reopen until as late as December of that year.

The name of the new group, Art Students League, was to be an exact description of the organization. Students had initiated the or-

[5] Charles Bregler, "Thomas Eakins as a Teacher," Parts I and II, *The Arts*, March, October, 1931.

ganization meetings and the constitution provided for a board of directors to be composed of student and alumni members of the League. It was hoped that this administrative arrangement might avoid the gradual decline and lack of interest in student problems which the National Academy displayed. For three years the League functioned with Professor Lemuel Wilmarth as president and teacher. Wilmarth then returned to the Academy school, and the League's Board of Control nominated William Merritt Chase for its leading teacher. As in the case of Eakins in Philadelphia, this appointment proved to be the beginning of a period of exciting growth, of increasing seriousness and sophistication in studio class work. The example of the League was observed and in varying degree followed by other New York City art schools.

Chase was ideal as a choice for teacher at the League in 1878. He and Frank Duveneck, Walter Shirlaw, and other American students had left their native Midwest to study in Munich. It is easy to explain their selection of Munich in preference to Paris. In cities like Cincinnati, Indianapolis, and St. Louis every itinerant painter of church murals or skilled craftsman in woodcarving that a young artist was likely to meet was German or Austrian. Chase, from St. Louis, and Duveneck, from Covington, Kentucky, went to Munich through the influence of emigrant German artists.

Both Chase and Duveneck were rated as superior students within a short time after their enrollment in the Munich academy. For their entire European sojourn they were leaders artistically and socially among all the men, European and American, of their student group. Anecdotes abound of their art-student days, lived close to literal poverty, but nearly always with the saving grace of enthusiasm for their work and the moral support of everyone in the group for one another.

Upon their eventual return to America as teachers, it was not only their great facility and personal interpretation as painters and teachers that caused Merritt and later Duveneck to be so welcome to their new students. Undoubtedly, their absolute insistence on living by their art and with art; their love of colorful and rich surroundings in their semipublic studios; and, certainly in Chase, a more aggressive and assured Bohemianism of manner than New York had previously experienced—all these characteristics proved attractive and set them up in the public mind as important artists.

When Chase established himself in New York City, he came to the old studio building in Washington Square which had been occupied by countless artists, including Winslow Homer. Many of the rooms available were small and ill-lighted, except only the large general-exhibition gallery. Typically, Chase rented the gallery and adjoining rooms for his private studio and living quarters. Here he held the well-attended Saturday afternoon teas which began his dramatic public career. Many artists think of men like Chase as close to being charlatans. It would be more valuable all around to accept the self-dramatization of Chase, the sound scholarship of Eakins, the skill in community education of Hunt, as contributing each in its own special way to growth in American art.

At the League, Chase at once freed the curriculum from a dependence upon the duller academic routines of uninteresting draftsmanship. Figure drawing was directed in the Munich manner toward an understanding of mass and light and shade, as well as line quality and muscle structure. Also, painting from the figure, freely and with a heavily loaded brush, was introduced early. For a few years a feud developed between the "Munich School" and the classicist draftsmen.

The resolution of the disagreement was arrived at by a compromise firmly establishing the individualist nature of the League school. Teachers of both approaches were kept on the staff. Consistently since, the League has maintained the policy of offering instruction from teachers of the most diverse practices and philosophies.

Duveneck did not return to America permanently for many years, but instead started an American class of painters under his guidance in Europe. He taught three such groups, the first of which he suggested should disband when he wanted to spend some months in Italy. Instead, most of the students packed up and went on with him to paint in Italy.

Duveneck's first one-man show in America was held in 1875, in Boston. William Morris Hunt was of course helpful in the recognition extended to Duveneck, then an unknown artist whose style of work was quite different from the paintings already well known to the Bostonian public. It was in 1878 that Duveneck conducted his first European class. In 1886 he married Elizabeth Boott, and not until she died in Italy two years later did Duveneck return permanently to the United States and begin his teaching career at the Cincinnati Museum. It was somewhat later that Chase followed Duveneck's lead by teaching annual summer classes for American students in Europe. Chase, too, was one of the first important American artists to popularize the resort-style, seacoast-painting class held in the summer.

Several elements of the educational influence wielded by Chase and Duveneck, and in slightly different fashion by Eakins, have been underestimated or underemphasized. As artist-teachers, they were grateful to Europe for their training. Chase and Duveneck were devoted to Europe as providing a charming way of life; this attitude was not apparently shared to the same extent by Eakins, who enjoyed his stay in France and in Spain but who cut off the associations of his art-student days almost completely on his return to Philadelphia. But not one of these three men felt in the least apologetic about his work or inferior in all-round quality to his European contemporaries. They breathed an air of professional competence which was of great value to their young American students.

Then there is the attitude these teachers showed in their daily lives: intense enthusiasm for all the arts, their own constant production of work in which students could see the mature growth they must try to reach. The very way in which the artists' households were conducted, with the more conventional aspects of home life pleasingly dominated by the aesthetic interests still rare in America, cannot rightly be disregarded as part of the atmosphere in which their teaching was done. This was especially notable in Chase's large and impressive studio. His love of collecting beautiful and often costly bric-a-brac in metal, enamels, textiles, ceramics, etc., was more than once far beyond the limit of his income. His home as well as his person expressed richness and color in keeping with his interpretation of the arts. The details of furnishings, the design of objects in common use, have changed greatly in the last sixty years, but Chase's paintings of interiors and of people posed in such a way as to emphasize their place in a fine room demonstrate his ability to design with grace and elegance the rooms he occupied.

Finally, it is important to realize how many of the students these men taught were frankly amateurs, painters for personal enjoyment, for recreation. The really large quantity of "how-to-do-it" art books printed all through the nineteenth century has already been referred to. Very likely, the private teacher of art, similar to the private teacher of music, continued to thrive during most of the century. But it has not been acknowledged often enough that, from the very beginning of professional art academies in the United States, the majority of students would have to fall in the category of amateurs, if we mean by that term people who do not finally earn their livelihood in the arts.

Hunt was aware of and welcomed the nonvocational interest of most of his students, and certainly Eakins, Chase, Duveneck, and others were not blind to this fact. Particularly in the summer classes at the seashore and the later classes organized as vacation excursions to Europe, the general cultural interest on the part of most of the students must have been readily apparent. To be sure, we know that all artist-teachers welcome the occasional student with exceptional ability, and are frequently overeager to see that he travels in their own direction, but this rare student only serves as a contrast to the great majority.

Thus the new professionalism of the art schools, the increase in the numbers of such schools, the work of their outstanding teachers, must be counted in part as a great expansion of liberal education for the general student. This was true in the post-Civil War period and is probably even more true today. It is a significant aspect of the present immense growth of art education in colleges and universities, to which more consideration must be given.

EAKINS, HOMER, RYDER

Thomas Eakins, as a painter, joins a different galaxy of talent and impact on the art of America than he does as a teacher. His paintings were not liked by most of his contemporaries; neither did the same people like the work of Albert Pinkham Ryder. There were more buyers for the paintings of Winslow Homer than for either Ryder or Eakins. But Homer, with the other two, shares the distinction of being overwhelmed during his lifetime by the public reputation of artists whose work is no longer of any great interest.

Ryder, Eakins, and Homer were not gregarious among their fellow artists. Nor were they reliant upon Europe for inspiration, for subject matter, or for technical practices. Eakins was the only one educated abroad, Homer traveled to France and to England without ever referring to the works of art he had seen there, and Ryder never left America. They did not do what might be called brilliant paintings. Little of the artists' self-dramatization was evident either in their personalities or in their works; the swashbuckling bravado of the Munich School or of the John Singer Sargent portraits was lacking in all that they did.

Critics have since identified the work of all three as intrinsically native. Ryder is the romantic, the alone but not lonely individualist. Interestingly enough, the same description would serve for Homer, but Homer's work is matter-of-fact and easily identifiable in subject. Ryder's paintings are of no particular place and intensely poetic in mood.

As for Eakins, he simply returned to Philadelphia and painted pictures of the people and sports and other activities which made the life he knew. The plain honesty of his record, the keenness of his emotional grasp, the modest satisfaction he had in his ordinary interests, appeared beneath the talents of an artist to the average citizen. An artist, it was felt, was in this world, but should not be so closely a part of it. A painting should be grand or wistful or awe-inspiring in subject—a requirement not possible to meet in depicting a home-town prize fight.

What arts and artists we might now possess, had most painters and teachers behaved in so independent a fashion, we cannot know. The richness of Europe was being imported in the actualities of canvas and marble and in the teachings of the schools. The American arts in the twentieth century will have achieved whatever distinction they can through a complete absorption of the European traditions, and not only through the slower processes of Eakins, Homer, and Ryder.

The very growth of museums, of collections of art, of historical scholarship, from which these three artists stood apart, has been the chief instrument in recalling their work to public notice. Museum exhibitions, scholarly researches, originally turned toward European art, directed attention to their basic aesthetic qualities. This shift in values showed a willingness to recognize and to use what is good in art qualities wherever it is found—even when it is a native product.

ART IN COLLEGE AND UNIVERSITY

College and university students during this period of time could not dream of sharing with art students the excitement, the quest of the wonderful, which American art students in Paris and Munich experienced. Even American students in Europe who were enrolled in the academic university courses envied the dedication and sense of accomplishment of the art students. College life, here and abroad, when it was adventurous, was so on the extracurricular level. The classroom maintained professional calm and detachment. Art was being taught not in the studio, but as a course in cultural history, notably by Charles Eliot Norton at Harvard.

Some of Norton's lectures were preserved by two of his students, H. F. Brown and Wm. H. Wiggin, Jr.[6] They were decidedly of the "survey of art" nature, planned to aid in developing an appreciation of art among unspecialized students. Obviously, the history-of-art courses were begun in American colleges to broaden and enrich the background of the liberal-arts student.

The present highly competent and professional art-history departments have sometimes found it difficult, and sometimes downright irksome, to perform this basic chore for the general college student. Norton's teaching in that area engendered lifelong enthusiasm among his students. Many colleges today with larger faculties in art history and with infinitely superior facilities are not reaching the same proportion of students Norton did, nor are they making as pronounced an impression.

Partly, this may be traced to the increase of technical and vocational collegiate education. Many, indeed most, of the technical curricula, as well as the pre-professional curricula, have no time for courses in the arts. What little work is done in the humanities is selected for its direct bearing on the professional work to follow. This same tendency inevitably affects the art-history faculty, which in its turn wishes to become a small professional school on its own. Em-

[6] Charles Eliot Norton, *History of Ancient Art* (prepared by H. F. Brown and Wm. H. Wiggin, Jr., from lectures), Mudge, 1891.

phasis on advanced courses and students can make introductory courses dull and uninspired.

Norton was eager to define the arts, to create in the students' thinking a place for the arts as a historical record. He wanted to direct an interest in the arts in such fashion as to be acceptable to the most academically minded. Definitions from his lectures stated that:

In its broadest sense, art may perhaps be defined as any habitual labor requiring skill, discipline, and intelligence. We can speak as properly of the art of building a nest as of the art of sculpture or painting.

The arts of expression are the chosen modes of transmitting and perpetuating the gains of civilization. This is what makes them important at all times, and gives to the study of them a peculiar interest.

The limitations of Harvard's first professor of art were several. He was essentially literary and historical in his views of the arts. It was his habit to think of the arts as a refinement of a culture, an evidence of periods of relative perfection in the history of mankind. He looked upon America, most of it outside of Cambridge at any rate, as a dismal aesthetic desert. There was no beauty, no subtlety, no real craftsmanship, literally no true society in America, hence nothing of a refined nature for the arts to express. As a consequence of this line of thought, he knew relatively few artists outside the field of literature.

What is more, the idea of considering the arts as a direct expression of the moment, of seeking out whatever art does exist for interpretation and encouragement, was not a part of Norton's thinking. Great art and the past were synonymous to him. Possibly, by educating students to recognize these art forms, art might again exist at some future date. As he saw it, there was little or no art worthy of the name in America in his time. America was so big and boorish that all men of sensitivity could do was to withdraw as much as possible from the rush of business and to make private islands of culture within their homes.

His best-known students were Mrs. Jack Gardner, who became "the" great art collector in Boston, where art collections were common, and Bernard Berenson, the scholar of Renaissance art. Like most of the students Norton interested so deeply, they tended to dwell upon the need of importing other standards of life and art to America.

The effort to help the arts to grow in nostalgic imitation of Europe seemed to be Norton's most immediate contribution. Nevertheless, some of the sanest, most constructive art activity and interpretation of our day is found in the art faculties of the letters and science colleges, and it was Norton and his followers who supplied the original impulse for the growth of art in the colleges.

REQUIRED DRAWINGS IN MASSACHUSETTS SCHOOLS

An English development in the teaching of drawing caught the eye of American schoolmen after the Civil War. Ever since Horace Mann started to edit the *Common School Journal*, there had been agreement upon the desirability and merit of teaching drawing. Few teachers did so, however, with the exception of such original and creatively minded schoolteachers as Mary Mann, Horace Mann's wife and Elizabeth Peabody's sister, who describes having drawing periods in her classroom just to see how well the children could express an idea in drawing. She lamented her incapacities, for without her shortcomings she felt that some of her students might have turned out to be gifted artists.[7]

For that matter, such drawing as Mary Mann mentions was not what school boards had been encouraged to seek by her husband. The schools of Massachusetts had been persuaded that industrial drawing was an essential element in training a child population which was largely the sons and daughters of manual laborers. Drawing could increase skill and improve physical judgment of distances and proportions. England was already training teachers of such drawing skills.

Walter Smith was brought over from the South Kensington School of Industrial Drawing and Crafts in 1872 to become State Director of Art Education, Scholastic and Industrial, for the State of Massachusetts. Soon after his arrival he began a series of lectures to the teachers of Boston, which he later prepared as a printed manual.

[7] Elizabeth Peabody and Mary Mann, *Guide to the Kindergarten and Intermediate Class,* orig. pub., E. Steiger, 1860, rev., 1877.

Also he became principal of a newly formed Massachusetts Normal Art School. The nature of the work which he came over to start in Massachusetts is clearly and logically set forth in his book of lectures. In the Introduction he states:

The author . . . desires to emphasize . . . that any person capable of learning any branch of study can learn to draw, so as to be able to represent general forms with as much ease and certainty as he can speak or write. To do this, however, he must first learn the alphabet of the study, and know by name and at sight any feature of form from the dot to the most subtle compound curve, and from the simplest geometric form to the last problem in perspective.

In presenting this course of instruction to others, he is not therefore offering simply his own work, but also an adaptation for American schools of such features of the English and continental systems as his own experience teaches him are best suited to the necessity of American Art Education.[8]

Most of the *Manual* is given over to the publication of the plates of the Exercises. These are at the same time more numerous and a little less dull-looking and difficult than the Professor Schmidt course appearing in the *Common School Journal* of the 1840's (page 13). The first exercise deals with the judgment of distances on lines. This is followed by a series of squares in which the student is to master drawing parallel lines vertically, horizontally, and obliquely.

To present something of the entire nature and content of Smith's drawing course, one must list the major types of work called for in the rest of the *Manual*. After the squares filled with line patterns came drawings of triangles and polygons. On the next page is the Greek cross, the Maltese cross, and a silver cup; then simple and compound curves. In order followed flat molding, wave scrolls; vases; historical ornaments, rosettes; toy house; silver spoon, key, water bottle; page of square rosettes; objects based on simple division of the central vertical line (vase, hourglass); conventional ornament; conventionalized leaves; letters and figures; designs from natural foliage; horizontal, vertical, central repetition; ornament from medieval manuscript; drawing from nature (tomato leaf); designing, horizontal molding, maple leaf; symmetry, botanical analy-

[8] Walter Smith, *Teachers Manual of Freehand Drawing and Designing*, Boston, 1873, Introduction.

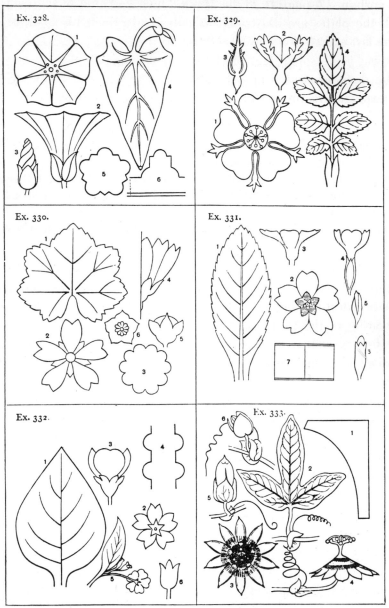

Figure 4. A Page of Advanced Exercises.
(From Walter Smith, "Teachers Manual
of Freehand Drawing and Designing and
Guide to Self-Instruction," 1873.)

sis; monograms and rosettes; a page of snow crystals; a design for a lace curtain. (A page from the *Manual* is reproduced as Figure 4.)

All the plates are illustrated in a thin, unaccented line. In a few of the last exercises a gray was introduced in background areas. The gray was just a solid block of closely drawn parallel lines.

The demand made upon the student, and the atmosphere which was expected to prevail in the classroom, are suggested in the author's Preface:

> Having said this much upon the proper value of the geometric exercises in drawing, and deprecated too stringent and arbitrary regulations concerning its practice, perhaps it would be proper the author should say that the opposite mistake of undue laxity is as much to be avoided . . . thus, sharp points to pencils, and clean hands and rubber, and a book neither dogs-eared, defiled, nor crumpled, should be absolutely insisted on; and incorrigibles should be made to draw upon slates only until they can be trusted in contact with white paper without defiling it.[9]

Emphasis upon precise, clean craftsmanship and on the exact performance of an exactly defined and limited problem is in itself not necessarily a poor practice. At the present time we are witnessing a rebirth of problems having that quality among others, and aiming at the acquisition of a broader set of skills and an understanding of the quality of line, texture, color, and the visual manipulation of forms.

Usually, this kind of work stems from the German Bauhaus, from the curriculum later established by Josef Albers at Black Mountain College in North Carolina, and from the work of the Institute of Design under Moholy-Nagy in Chicago. Usually, too, such precisely formulated work is addressed to mature students—not children of the youngest elementary grades.

Granted that there is only a slight correspondence between the actual exercises in Smith's manual and the infinitely inventive problems of the Bauhaus, there is some comparison to be made in the kind of experience each outlines: in the step-by-step progression with each problem based on the one preceding, in the craftsmanship required, in the use of forms abstracted from individualized picture-making symbols.

Smith visualized his dogmatically presented problems as suitable

[9] *Ibid.*, Preface.

for the very young. In this insistence he is found to be wrong by the child study and psychology already being developed in 1872. As a consequence, there has grown in American art education a tendency to minimize the value of craftsmanship and precise workmanship, only because Smith and his successors were wrong in expecting to begin with work of that sort at too early an age.

A would-be jocular reference, apparently to his own daughter at the age of three, makes us aware of the trial teachers must have had with the Smith Drawing Curriculum. We can wonder to what extent the drawing master later succeeded with his own child. Smith writes:

. . . a young lady of the mature age of three . . . [with] the advantage of being quite unprejudiced in the matter of style of execution and perfectly fearless in the expression of what she believes to be the truth, whilst the firmness of her natural touch is something tremendous. . . . Her mental disadvantages arise from an altogether too exalted opinion of her own works causing a self-satisfaction which hinders her progress and blinds her to defects in style, and her imperfect execution; and she is wildly indignant with me at any faults I point out, and simply turns round and thrashes me if I point out a faulty line.[10]

When an experienced art teacher of today considers how welcome is a student's feeling of self-satisfaction at any age or level of development, he cannot avoid a feeling of disbelief in reading of Walter Smith's criticism of a three-year-old's "defects in style" and "imperfect execution."

Smith was also the first principal of the Massachusetts Normal Art School, which was started in 1873. At the beginning of the academic year 1875–1876, the curriculum was established much as it was to remain until the addition of teacher-training courses in 1889–1890. The statement of purpose in the catalogue of 1875–1876 defines the school's self-imposed limitations:

This school is intended as a training school for the purpose of qualifying teachers and masters of industrial drawing.

In the future it may be necessary to provide for high skill in technical drawing and art-culture, but the immediate pressing demand is for teachers who know the elementary subjects thoroughly.

The work of Class A (first year) is devoted to Elementary Drawing; of Class B to Form, Color, and Industrial Design; of Class C to Con-

[10] Walter Smith, *Industrial Drawing in Public Schools*, Prang, 1875, p. 6.

structive Arts; and of Class D to Sculpture and Design in the round. These groups of subjects can be studied in any order after Class A has been passed through, subject only to an examination as to the fitness of the student.[11]

The whole of the first year's work consisted of painstaking drawing of geometrical problems, of perspective, of orthographic projection, of machines, building construction details, shadow projection, cast ornaments, human and animal forms from the cast, furniture details, designs to be derived from plant forms, and historical ornament. Toward the close of the year, the student was required to do a specimen lesson in blackboard drawing, and finally to hand in all his drawings in numbered order.

Sheer technical skill and neatness appear to have been the first consideration. An emphasis on drawings of some use in the building crafts is to be noted, and in the last half of the year time was spent on cast drawings like those usually done in the preliminary months of the professional-art-school courses.

Whatever additional work the student did after the first year could be done in any order. The first year was looked upon as a minimal preparation for teaching, and the additional years were planned as special fields. At first only a few people took all four years of work. The Class B diploma of the second year was earned by work in painting, from head studies or from the draped figure and in water color, tempera, and oil. Also required were four designs drawn from a list of such items as sculptural ornament, encaustic tile, lace curtains, etc. The student was required to make one of these designs.

Constructive arts was listed for the Class C diploma. This meant a good deal of architectural and building-construction drawings, drawings of mechanical details, elevations of objects such as locomotives, and finally descriptive geometrical and topographical drawings.

The fourth diploma available was awarded for sculpture and design in the round. Work done for it was that of modeling flowers in relief, and doing medallion portrait heads and anatomical renderings of antique figures. Designs were required and at least one piece was

[11] Massachusetts Normal Art School, *Third Annual Catalogue,* 1875–1876.

to be made of furniture, of a chandelier in metal, or of a pitcher enriched by medallions.

Not only was the Massachusetts Normal Art School important because so many of its graduates initiated public-school drawing and art programs all over the country by the year 1900, but we cannot fail to notice that its curriculum has served as the dominant pattern for teacher training in the arts up to the present time. Certainly the detailed descriptions of course work have a slightly archaic flavor. Nevertheless, the scheme of doing some drawing and painting similar to that of the art school, some industrial and crafts designing, some actual construction of craft objects, and some work in sculpture has prevailed ever since in the training of teachers of art for the elementary and secondary school.

As instruction in art schools changed, so has the drawing and painting work in art-teacher training. As the quality of design in industry and in sculpture has been reinterpreted, somewhat more slowly the art-teacher training centers have accepted the new direction.

Most art-education curricula, then, have been based on the theory that the prospective art teacher needs a little training in many art activities. Where instruction has been kept at a high level, the briefer time spent by student teachers in their art classes has been somewhat compensated for by a greater breadth of art activities. The least valuable teacher-training schools in art have assumed that the very quality of art work done by the students need not be kept high since their actual teaching to younger people may not call for a high degree of skill or understanding.

Perhaps the most important direction taken by the founders of the Massachusetts Normal Art School was one which was gradually supplanted as the growing division of subject-matter fields took possession of the American public schools. The entire curriculum of the first quarter of a century obviously considered drawing and art education generally, and the beginnings of what we now call manual training and shop work, as basically a united study. Even when the *School Arts Book* was started in 1901 by Henry Turner Bailey, its contents indicate that furniture making and metalwork, basketry, mechanical drawing, and other lesser crafts were still being taught by the same teachers who were teaching drawing and art work.

A slow growth in the understanding of the arts as a creative expression pictorially apparently led to the unfortunate assumption that "art" was better taught separately from at least some of the crafts, and even quite differently. The separation was accepted by shop and mechanical-drawing teachers as excluding their teaching from the necessity or the desirability of being creative in their approach to the design of objects made in the shops.

Every trend in industrial and furniture design, in professional art education, in educational philosophy, indicates the need for a reunion of the teaching of the arts and the shop crafts in our school systems. Here is an area where the Massachusetts Normal Art School was doing a better job for its time than we are doing today.

KINDERGARTEN

The kindergarten of Friedrich Wilhelm August Froebel is a nineteenth-century development of great significance for the growth of art education. There is a scant literature on the relationship of the arts to the history of education, and consequently not many art teachers are aware of the kindergarten's place in education or of the fact that it created precisely the environment needed for art as a part of the curriculum.

Friedrich Froebel in 1852, after forty-seven years of teaching, addressed the Teachers Convention at Gotha on the subject of his kindergarten and its operation. His invitation to this meeting was one of the first signs of official interest in the work of Froebel and his devoted associates. In June of the same year Froebel died.

Froebel's first kindergarten was established in 1837 in Blankenburg, Germany. The American, Elizabeth Peabody, established an infants' school in Boston in 1860–1861 and at that time wrote the first edition of her *Guide to the Kindergarten and Intermediate Class*. However, after her trip to Germany in 1867, she revised the book, withdrew her claims for the earlier school on the basis that it was not a true kindergarten, and became a whole-hearted Froebel disciple. The years 1869 to 1873 saw, in America, the establishment of several kindergartens as well as normal schools for kindergartner training by Froebel students. In the practice of that brilliantly conceived institution, during the years of its most rapid growth, the children's activities and the teachers' philosophy bear an amazing relationship to contemporary arts and art education.

Froebel was the great leader. He was one of those men who inspired great loyalties and high idealism. Wilhelm Middendorf and Johannes Barop married sisters of Froebel and, together with their wives, devoted themselves and whatever small fortunes they had to the realization of Froebel's dreams. In return for this whole-hearted devotion they were often rewarded by displays of impatience, mistrust, and jealousy; for Froebel was apparently a creative genius who, while demanding absolute loyalty and unlimited effort from his colleagues, at the same time vented his own small animosities on them and displayed utter ruthlessness in seeking to realize his vision of the true education for young children.

The kindergarten was indeed a work of art with Froebel. He planned it with all the intensity and passion of the true artist and lived for nothing else. He dreamed of kindergarten education as the savior of the generations to come, as the guide to proper motherhood, even as the means of improving the world through the adults who had been in kindergarten and who would be superior as citizens to all the millions of people whose education in early childhood had been blighted and misdirected.

That the kindergarten has not, after more than a century of existence, accomplished all the miracles he foresaw is no criticism of Froebel's efforts. It has never been organized on as large a scale as he expected, and it has never reached more than a small fraction of the children, even in the countries where it is common. Meanwhile, Froebel's primary doctrine, that of the importance of the first years of a child's life, has been repeatedly and completely validated with the passing of the years and the piling up of data on the subject. Were this Froebel's only contribution to education, it would still be considerable; but there is another in the field of the arts.

In certain aspects of the kindergarten, particularly as its American enthusiasts interpreted it after 1870, we find great significance for the future of art education. No better statement of intent can be found than that made by Elizabeth Peabody in a paper published in 1870, "A Plea for Froebel's Kindergarten as the First Grade of Primary Art Education":

Froebel's Kindergarten is a primary art school; for it employs the prodigious but originally blind activity and easily trained hand of childhood, from the age of three years, in intelligent production of things within the childish sphere of affection and fancy; giving thereby a harmonious play of heart and mind in actively educating—without straining the brain—even to the point of developing invention, while it keeps the temper sweet and spirits joyous with the pleasure of success. Childish play has all the main characteristics of art, inasmuch as it is the endeavor "to conform the outward show of things to the desires of the mind." Every child at play is histrionic and plastic. He personates character with mimic gesture and costume, and represents whatever fancy interests him by an embodiment of it,—perhaps in mud or as a row of footstools and chairs, which become a railroad train to him at his "own sweet will." [12]

A single sentence sums up Miss Peabody's view of the art of the kindergarten: "The divine impulse of activity is never directly opposed in the Kindergarten, but accepted and guided into beautiful *production* according to the laws of creative order." [13]

Activity guided and directed was obviously the foundation for kindergarten education. The games and the singing, the small gardens planted, the stories told and the stories invented together, and the physical exercise for indoors and out were all part of the active program for each day and week.

It is the Froebel "Gifts" and "Occupations" that the twentieth-century art teacher will find fascinating and provocative.

Two great artists who used the kindergarten Gifts as children were Frank Lloyd Wright, the American architect, and Wassily Kandinsky, the Russian painter. It will be worth while to return to the influence of the nineteenth-century kindergarten upon the art forms of the twentieth century; but first we must list and describe briefly the Gifts which these two internationally known artists, among thousands of other children, knew and remembered from their childhood.

The First Gift was six worsted yarn balls of the colors of the rain-

[12] Elizabeth Peabody, "A Plea for Froebel's Kindergarten as the First Grade of Primary Art Education," 1870, *Kindergarten and Child Culture Papers,* Barnard's American Journal of Education, 1890, p. 601.

[13] *Ibid.,* p. 675.

bow. As with all the Gifts, these balls were not meant to be played with idly, but were expected to help the child, through direct manipulation and play, to form concepts of color, of texture, of size, of number, and of creative arrangements.

The Second Gift consisted of a set of pieces of wood, including a solid sphere, a cube, and a cylinder.

The Third Gift was a two-inch cube divided equally once in each direction, producing eight small cubes.

The Fourth Gift was a two-inch cube divided by one vertical and two horizontal cuts into eight rectangular parallelepipeds. Each of the parallelepipeds was two inches long, one inch broad, and half an inch thick. These descriptions in proper solid geometrical terms were important to the kindergartner and were always given in this way. The effort to understand geometrical forms and relationships was firmly insisted upon. Play was expected and encouraged, but it was always to be directed toward the grasp of what seem to us startlingly abstract concepts for young children.

The Fifth Gift was a three-inch cube divided equally twice in each dimension into twenty-seven small cubes. Three of these were in turn divided by one diagonal, cut into two triangular parts, and three by two diagonal cuts into four triangular parts.

The Sixth Gift was a cube of three inches divided into twenty-seven parallelepipeds of the same dimensions as those of the Fourth Gift. Three of these were divided lengthwise into square prisms two inches long, half an inch wide, and half an inch thick; and six were divided crosswise into square tablets an inch square and half an inch thick. There were thus thirty-six pieces in the set.

The Seventh Gift was a group of square and triangular tablets, including four different triangles: equilateral, right, obtuse isosceles, and right scalene.

The Eighth Gift was a group of connected slats. The Ninth Gift was a set of disconnected slats. (See Figure 3, page 47.)

The Tenth Gift was a set of wooden sticks of several lengths. The Eleventh Gift was a set of whole and half wire rings of several diameters.[14]

[14] Wichard Lange, "Reminiscences of Froebel," *Kindergarten and Child Culture Papers*, Barnard's American Journal of Education, 1890, p. 85.

One of the early American kindergartners, Miss Susan E. Blow of St. Louis, describes the importance of the Gifts in such a way that we are forcibly reminded of the writings of Le Corbusier and Gropius, of painters like Feininger, and of the approach to design in almost any field of the present day. She writes:

. . . we see at once that their [the Gifts] basis is mathematical, and we notice that they illustrate successively the solid, the plane, and the line. We perceive, too, that they progress from undivided to divided wholes, and from these to separate and independent elements. Finally we observe that there is a suggestiveness in the earlier Gifts which the later ones lack, while on the other hand the range of the latter far exceeds that of the former. The meaning of these distinctions and connections will grow clear to us as we study the common objects of the varied Gifts. These objects are:

I. To aid the mind to abstract the essential qualities of objects by the representation of striking contrasts.

II. To lead to the classification of external objects by the presentation of typical forms.

III. To illustrate fundamental truths through simple applications.

IV. To stimulate creative activity.[15]

The European creators of the kindergarten, and the great propagandists and organizers who spread the gospel of Froebel in Europe and America, were generally well-educated people actively interested in the arts and sciences. Their great work for the kindergarten and their faith in it were based on the belief that young children could best be started on an education through sense experience and by learning basic abstract relationships through the handling of objects and materials.

The Kindergarten "Occupations" reinforced this approach. They were perforating, sewing, drawing, intertwining, weaving, folding, cutting, peas work, cardboard, and clay modeling. The perforating was done with a sharp pointed tool into paper, producing figures and pictures. The sewing was done from hole to hole on these perforated pictures. The drawing was first a copy of the perforated and sewn figures; this was followed by the drawing of simple geometrical forms possible to do with vertical and horizontal lines. Intertwining was done with paper strips of different colors. Folding and cutting

---

[15] Susan Blow, "Some Aspects of the Kindergarten," *Kindergarten and Child Culture Papers,* Barnard's American Journal of Education, 1890, p. 601.

of paper taught children to make certain standard constructions and then to try variations and combinations in the colored papers, inventing form constructions of their own. The peas work, done at that time with pointed sticks stuck into soaked peas, has since developed into the ever-popular Tinker Toy. Cardboard cutting and shaping and clay modeling were, again, used to form the simple geometrical shapes.[16]

All of this kindergarten work was deliberately planned to occupy constructively children's inevitable and incessant activity. Rousseau and Pestalozzi had early recognized and allowed for activity in young children. They had urged the importance of physical exercise in making students more alert for mental exercise. Pestalozzi welcomed the value of comradeship formed in play and in working together in school gardens.

But the kindergarten went beyond the idea of activity as a release of energy to be alternated with the restraint of book learning. Kindergartners determined to create the base even for book learning upon learning from activity. Activity was planned to occur in such a manner, in the Occupations, and with such materials, the Gifts, as to help children to understand the relationships of materials and the physical abstractions of the whole culture. What has been variously described as the activity curriculum, or sensory education, was from the beginning the essence of kindergarten work.

Many of the urban centers in America were quick to want the kindergarten and what it could do for children as a method of beginning their education. After almost a century of kindergartens in America, we find that one of the services which reorganization of rural schools and federal aid to schools are expected to offer is the extension of the kindergarten beyond the limits of the more prosperous areas of the nation.

During that century of school growth there has been a slow change of attitude concerning all levels of school work. At first, even the most enthusiastic of school superintendents, like William T. Harris of St. Louis, lauded the kindergarten because it offered manual activity and training at a time of life when the child was not ripe for more intellectual fare. Harris was of the belief that the child's

[16] Baroness Marenholtz-Bulow, "Froebel's Educational Views," *Kindergarten and Child Culture Papers,* Barnard's American Journal of Education, 1890, p. 219.

time past the age of seven was too valuable for the "learning of a handicraft. . . . The general disciplines of reading, writing, and arithmetic, etc., and drawing," he believed, must take over after the happy years of kindergarten.[17]

Today it is evident that from the start of the kindergarten there has been more education through the senses and through activity each year and in every part of the school system. Art programs have nearly always shared in the extension of education to more inclusive sensory forms.

KINDERGARTEN AND MODERN ART

What has not been as obvious and as widely noted is the nature of the original kindergarten activities as they relate to present art forms and to contemporary art education. It has been said that Frank Lloyd Wright and Kandinsky were given kindergarten materials as children. How many more of the Western world's present group of senior artists in painting, architecture, music, and other arts were actually enrolled in kindergartens, or used the equipment more freely at home, during the years of its growth, might make a significant subject for research.

There are comparisons of interest which can be made and which merit attention. Susan Blow, quoted earlier in another connection, virtually prepared a preface to a twentieth-century design course when she wrote as follows on the Occupations: "But we must be conscious of ideas before we can express them, and we must gain the mastery of material before we can use it as a means of expression." [18]

We must think of this comment as applying to the use of abstract block forms, thread, paper strips, and sticks as materials for creative constructions by children. Then notice that drawing in the kindergarten was taught as a rigid discipline leading eventually to naturalistic drawing of academic excellence. Free creation was in terms of abstract forms and bits of stuff. Drawing, on the other hand, was a prescribed form of visual grammar.

In 1941, Piet Mondrian, abstract painter, wrote, "In abstract art,

[17] William Tormey Harris, "Kindergarten in the Public School System," *Kindergarten and Child Culture Papers,* Barnard's American Journal of Education, 1890, p. 634.
[18] Blow, *op. cit.,* p. 613.

we see . . . clearly. There the elements of form are no longer veiled by the limited [the naturalistic] forms but appear as the expressive means." [19] Mondrian's reference to naturalistic, pictorial forms is always as "limited" or "limiting"; and while that view of the pictorial vocabulary was not what kindergarten teachers had in mind in their teaching, it may have been the emotional feeling conveyed to the intensely creative children of many school generations.

A large proportion of the dominant performers and thinkers in the arts who are now sixty years of age or older write and speak in some such vein as this: that the eclectic architectural forms, the shapes of historical periods in design, the primarily naturalistic pictorial representation—all of these become tyrannical forms, limiting art expression; and the great need of expression in their work was the recasting of art in fundamental structural shapes.

The apparent direction of visual and tactile kindergarten training in the early years, and of the artists' search for abstract forms during the last seventy-five years, can be related at the least in that both were begun in the same climate of thought.

Since 1900 kindergarten activity has not diminished; but in the United States it has changed. To use a common arts terminology, the child activity has become more individualistic, more romantic in nature, rather than continuing the classical pattern of the strictly Froebelian period. Kindergarten children today use a great variety of materials. There are innumerable forms of commercially prepared play sets for the building of play houses and stores and whole villages. Lengths of wrapping paper, jars of water-soluble paints, crocks of clay, packets of colored papers, boxes of crayons, and other materials as occasion demands are generally available. Many simple tools and adequate table space for working are considered of prime necessity in the kindergarten.

In using these materials the children are given every encouragement to act creatively. The individuality of each child is important, and his choice of activity is respected, in the hope of discovering and developing distinctive personality traits. At the same time there is a healthy interest in the individual's adjustment to the social group, both in using the opportunities which the group makes possible for

[19] Piet Mondrian, *Plastic Art and Pure Plastic Art, 1937, and Other Essays, 1941–43*, Wittenborn, Schultz, 1947, p. 39.

each child and in assuming the responsibilities which each member must have within the class.

What is most conspicuously lacking in the present-day kindergarten as compared to the regime of Froebel is the deliberate effort to teach a series of concepts about geometrical solids, simple tool operations needed in the Occupations, color relationships, and the nature and quality of the materials used. Some of the learning objectives set up for the kindergarten of Froebel made it, in the current use of the term, an art academy for children.

A new academy in adult art education has, since 1918, been extending its generally beneficent influence. It has been inventing and evolving a visual and tactile education of the senses as a foundation for contemporary creation in art. Inevitably, its influence is spreading first to most of the courses in art schools, in colleges and universities, and then downward chronologically to younger students through the work of teachers recently graduated from their professional art-education courses.

The academy here described, the Bauhaus of Germany and its ramified American offshoots, is stressing today, as the kindergarten tried to do in 1852, that education through vision and the sense of touch, and by means of the materials and tools now available, is all-important.

There are three major implications in the primitive work of the Bauhaus. First, there is the interpretation that a liberal education must be changed to include sensory education as the most important aspect of aesthetic comprehension. Second, there is the obvious inference that professional art education must be based, not on coddling abnormal student "sensitivities" or on a craving for a refuge from a coarse world, but on a factual, even scientific grasp of the media of the arts. The student must learn to exploit to the full visual and tactile manipulation, and he must still possess the artist's desire to put his ideas into aesthetic form.

Third, the Bauhaus suggests a different, expanded course of experience for children. The present emphasis upon free expression in paint or clay has seemed desirable in many ways. At the lower age levels, little or no teaching has been done other than offering help merely in the use of materials. The end product for child and teacher has been personally interpreted paintings and three-dimensional objects which represent a satisfying experience in symbolizing experience.

But possibly, creative expression exclusively on a plane of free handling of art forms is limiting to some or all children, and some other kind of expression may be of equal value. Perhaps we will see a revival of more precisely limited and defined experiences with materials, a sort of redefinition of the Gifts and Occupations, which will combine well with the values of the more individualistic experiences in art now common. These experiences would necessarily be formulated to begin the child's familiarity with objects and materials that we know today, pragmatically, scientifically, and aesthetically. The specific objects used might be different from Froebel's. The aims could be very like those proposed by Elizabeth Peabody.

Objection to this comparison of Bauhaus and kindergarten was made by Sibyl Moholy-Nagy [20] after the publication of an article, *Kindergarten and Bauhaus,* in the *College Art Journal,* Fall, 1950. She wrote that the kindergarten became stultified and routine in Germany, that Elizabeth Peabody's interpretation of the creative possibilities did not prevail, and that the Bauhaus was not "academic" because in all its work individuality of result was a goal in the most limited of projects.

These are valuable qualifications. Any system becomes rigid when put in practice by rigid minds and in a social context desiring rigidity. The work of Albers, Itten, Moholy-Nagy, has already suffered that fate in many classrooms. And only a few teachers identify the most creative possibilities in a colleague's work as did Elizabeth Peabody. Finally, the term "academic," used to identify the Bauhaus, is advanced because the Bauhaus did present a carefully organized program leading to specific results. In this sense there ought to be no fear for the consequences if we try to organize experiences which will more successfully help young children to know and use tools and materials on an individualized level of accomplishment. Millions of homes no longer provide such experience as part of the routine of living, and children from those homes become adults almost helpless in manipulative skills.

[20] Sibyl Moholy-Nagy, "Letter to the Editor," *College Art Journal,* Spring, 1951, pp. 270–272.

These avenues of speculation are opened not only by the comparison of the kindergarten and the Bauhaus, but are inherent in many aspects of educational philosophy since 1900, in the several modern art movements, and in the observation of the whole progress of public education. The early work of the kindergarten and its influences upon the arts might be a valuable point of departure for further study.

Bibliography

Barnard, Henry, ed., *Kindergarten and Child Culture Papers*, Barnard's American Journal of Education, 1890 (originally pub., 1881, as *Froebel, Kindergarten and Child Culture Papers*).

Benjamin, S. G. W., *Art in America*, Harper, 1880.

Benson, Eugene, "Museums of Art as a Means of Instruction," *Appleton's Journal*, January 15, 1870.

Bregler, Charles, "Thomas Eakins as a Teacher," *The Arts*, March, October, 1931.

Brooks, Van Wyck, *The Times of Melville and Whitman*, Dutton, 1947.

Butts, Freeman, *A Cultural History of Education*, New York, McGraw-Hill, 1947.

Cortissoz, Royal, *John La Farge: A Memoir and a Study*, Houghton Mifflin, 1911.

Cummings, T. S., *Annals of the National Academy of Design*, Childs, 1865.

Danes, Gibson, "Wm. Morris Hunt and His Newport Circle," *Magazine of Art*, April, 1950.

Eastlake, Charles L., *Hints on Household Taste in Furniture, Upholstery and Other Details*, Osgood, 1878.

Froebel, Friedrich, *Pedagogics of the Kindergarten: or His Ideas Concerning the Play and Playthings of the Child*, tr. by Josephine Jarvis from essays collected by Wichard Lange, Appleton, 1895.

Goodrich, Lloyd, *Thomas Eakins, His Life and Work*, Whitney Museum of American Art, 1933.

Goodrich, Lloyd, *American Watercolor and Winslow Homer*, Walker Art Center, American Artists Group, 1945.

Goodrich, Lloyd, *Winslow Homer*, by Macmillan, 1945.

Heermann, Norbert, *Frank Duveneck*, Mifflin, 1918.

Hegel, Georg Wilhelm Friedrich, *Introduction to Hegel's Philosophy of Fine Art*, tr. by Bernard Bosanquet, K. Paul, Trench & Co., 1886.

Jarves, James Jackson, *Art Hints: Architecture, Sculpture, and Painting,* New York, 1855.

Jarves, James Jackson, *The Art Idea,* Hurd and Houghton, 1864.

Knowlton, Helen M., *The Art Life of William Morris Hunt,* Little, Brown, 1899.

Landgren, Marchal E., *Years of Art: The Story of the Art Students League of New York,* McBride, 1940.

McKinney, Roland, *Thomas Eakins,* Crown, 1942.

Massachusetts Normal Art School, *Catalogues and Circulars; Third Annual,* 1875–1876; *Twenty-Sixth Annual,* 1899–1900.

Moholy-Nagy, Sibyl, "Letter to the Editor," *College Art Journal,* Spring, 1951.

Mondrian, Piet, *Plastic Art and Pure Plastic Art, 1937, and Other Essays, 1941–1943,* Wittenborn, Schultz, 1947.

Mumford, Lewis, *The Brown Decades,* Harcourt, Brace, 1931.

Norton, Charles Eliot, *History of Ancient Art* (prepared by H. F. Brown and Wm. H. Wiggin, Jr., from lectures), Mudge, 1891.

Page, Anne L.; Brooks, Angeline; Putnam, Alice H.; Peabody, Mary H., *Kindergarten and the School,* Milton Bradley, 1886.

Peabody, Elizabeth, *Guide to the Kindergarten and Intermediate Class* (with Mary Mann, *The Moral Culture of Infancy*), rev. ed., E. Steiger, 1877.

Peabody, Elizabeth, *Last Evenings With Allston,* D. Lothrop & Co., 1886.

Peabody, Elizabeth, *Lectures in the Training School for Kindergartners,* Heath, 1886.

Rebay, Hilla, ed., *Kandinsky,* Guggenheim Foundation, 1945.

Roof, Katharine Metcalf, *The Life and Art of William Merritt Chase,* Scribner, 1917.

Shannon, Martha A. S., *The Boston Days of William Morris Hunt,* Marshall Jones, 1923.

Smith, Walter, *Art Education, Scholastic and Industrial,* Osgood, 1872.

Smith, Walter, *Teachers Manual of Free Hand Drawing and Designing and Guide to Self-Instruction,* Boston, 1873.

Smith, Walter, *Examples of Household Taste: The Industrial Art of the International Exhibition,* R. Worthington, 1880.

Smith, Walter, *Industrial Drawing in Public Schools,* Prang, 1875.

Steegmuller, Francis, "James Jackson Jarves: Thumbnail Sketch of a Collector," *Magazine of Art,* April, 1948.

Steegmuller, Francis, *The Two Lives of James Jackson Jarves,* Yale University, 1951.

Watson, Forbes, *Winslow Homer,* Crown, 1942.

Wright, Frank Lloyd, *An Autobiography,* Duell, Sloan and Pearce, 1943.

Figure 5. Drawing in Outline, Light and Dark, in Rendering Type Solids. (From Clark, Hicks, and Perry, "Prang Elementary Course in Art Instruction," Books 1 and 2, 1898.)

IV

The "New Education"

The stages of art education described in the last chapter were concentrated in the years 1870 to 1885. The beginning of the kindergarten in America, the industrial-drawing exercises of Walter Smith, the burgeoning professionalism in American art schools, were widely separated phenomena engaged in by people scarcely known to one another. Yet all three activities have had an influence on present-day art education.

Beginning in the same period and continuing to the years of World War I, educational developments were taking place which finally coalesced into the general pattern of elementary- and secondary-school art work we know today. Though the objectives of art education have broadened, teacher training has improved, and aesthetic understanding is sounder than it was in 1917, essentially little

85

institutional change has occurred since World War I. The history of public-school art from 1870 to 1917 is therefore of particular significance. The social conditions prevailing at the time, the circumstances under which the vast American school system took shape, determined the nature of that art instruction.

We accept, almost without being aware of its meaning, the statement that this period was one of unparalleled growth in the United States. For the public-school personnel it meant fifty years of creating a system of education unlike any known in the world, and of expanding the system at an accelerating rate during the whole time.

Every old city in the East grew vastly in population. Cities in the Middle West which had been founded before the Civil War and were strategically placed for industry and trade grew even more rapidly. The Prairie West, the South, and the Pacific Coast started a little later, but quickly caught up with the Middle West and passed the East in rate of growth. Wherever the soil was fertile, farming populations were increasing and rural school districts were formed all over the country, more often than not meeting the needs of their communities by erecting one-room school buildings.

Urban histories of the period, such as *A Financial and Administrative History of Milwaukee* by Laurence M. Larson, show three major items of public expense: school buildings and teachers' salaries, street and sidewalk paving, and water and sewage plants and pipes. There was never enough of any of the three to keep up with city growth; and budgets were annually fought over by the advocates of education, of health, of transport. Some years the bulk of the funds went for bridges and new paving; other years great stretches of primitive wooden water pipe had to be replaced by more modern installations.

But schools demanded then, as now, a large share of the tax dollar. Buildings particularly were in constant demand. Occasionally the larger municipalities bonded themselves for what were then considered huge sums. Several ward schools might all be erected within a year's time, in which event classes again became manageable because for a little while there were classrooms enough to accommodate all of the children. If, simultaneously, teachers' salaries were raised to put the city in a competitive position to hire a well-trained faculty, then for a short time the school crisis in that city would abate. But in cities the size of Buffalo, Louisville, Cleveland, Indianapolis, Chicago, Denver, and Milwaukee, another decade of immigration started the cycle all over again. In the rural areas, the school district and the one-room school made for an earlier and more flexible solution of the problem. Wherever there were enough children, the political means were established with the district school board, and the financial burden was only what was needed to build a small structure and to hire a teacher for six, seven, or eight months. In the growing parts of the country this effort merely to house all the children who came to school was unending.

From the standpoint of mere economy, school boards might excusably have decided to keep curricular changes at a minimum, and to stay as close as possible to a routine of bookwork, with classes as large as possible. Such a course would permit a minimum of facilities in school structures, and teachers would need no specialized training. Taxes could be kept down. The growth in numbers of children and of necessary housing would then be the only variable in the school organization. Every city and town had its share of voters who urged exactly that.

Other forces, however, required curricular change to match the schools' physical growth. For one thing the increasing school population formed a most heterogeneous group, including both native-born youngsters and the children of immigrant families from almost every nation of Europe. These mixed groups could not be cared for in an orderly manner for a whole school day with little or no activity. Whether or not it was considered desirable, teachers found that they literally could not keep order in large classes on a strictly book, recitation, writing, and ciphering regime.

But more than the simple necessity of activity was involved. Teacher-training schools had been growing in number and in professional competence. European, and particularly German, school experimentation was being studied by many American scholars. The study of the child, his growth, his responses, his observed means of learning, promised to replace much dogmatic assertion with demonstrable fact. Professionalism was growing in the school systems. School superintendents and principals, principals of normal schools,

87

and directors of practice teaching were being paid well enough to attract people of considerable education and abilities, men and women who were energetic in forming societies for the extension of education, in writing books and articles outlining their philosophy, and in a variety of ways securing public support for the improvement of instruction.

THE "TYPE FORM" BLOCKS

This was the environment into which Walter Smith came in 1870 with his course in drawing. The State of Massachusetts asked Smith to start the Massachusetts Normal Art School in 1873 because the legislature had required the teaching of drawing in the schools of that state. As a consequence, specially prepared teachers and supervisors were needed to carry out the provisions of the law.

Smith's drawing lessons and the impulse he gave to the Massachusetts Normal Art School constitute the formal beginning of art in the school curriculum. At least, the art teachers from Smith's time on refer to his practices as a sort of necessary though uninspired starting point. Fortunately, it proved to be little more than that.

The influence of the kindergarten movement, which started in the United States slightly before Smith's arrival, remained a constant aid to teachers who favored any school work of an active, participating nature. Still another influence from the whole curriculum of elementary education, which encouraged teachers of art to expand their work, was the so-called "Oswego Movement." In the 1870's, teachers throughout the country had become aware of the "objective teaching" first introduced in the United States at the Oswego, New York, Normal School. This methodology referred to the use of materials like charts, cards, picture sets, blocks, cocoons, cotton bolls, grain samples, specimens of glass and ceramics, textiles, maps, etc. E. A. Sheldon in 1859 began teaching teachers to make the use of these aids a regular part of their classroom practice.

Even Horace Mann's early enthusiasm for Prussian drawing systems was partly induced by the hope that drawing in the schools would in some way help to foster art interests and abilities. This Oswego approach to teaching, using illustrative objects wherever possible and pictorial matter in the forms of engravings, charts, diagrams, and maps, was bound to encourage some teachers of drawing to go beyond the limits of the rather dreary exercise books to attempt some aesthetic interpretation.

One of the first steps taken toward "pictorial" or "art" drawing as distinct from industrial drawing was the creation of "type form" blocks as models for drawing lessons. These were three-dimensional spheres, cones, cubes, pyramids, and more complex shapes. Obviously the type forms are a kind of "objective" teaching for the drawing class, and resemble the blocks of the kindergarten. The drawing teachers hoped that students who learned to recognize and to represent the "ideal" or "pure" type forms would find it easy to identify cylindrical, pyramidal, cubic, and other shapes in nature and in art forms.

The introduction of the solid geometrical blocks as subject matter for drawing classes does not seem too great a change from Smith's exercise plates. In his exercises pupils drew by locating points on a page and connecting the points. The drawings made from the blocks may seem little enough different, but the fact that personal interpretation could and did show up in drawings made from the same group of blocks became highly significant.

Drawing in the public school began to be considered not only as a possible tool for training manual skill, but as a means of starting art appreciation. For a talented few it was hoped that school drawing could give an early start toward the mastery of representation which all great artists were assumed to possess.

In 1896 the graduating class in normal art at Pratt Institute in New York City listened to John S. Clark talk on the subject, "The Study of Type Forms and Its Value in Education." His remarks give us a clue to the importance placed at one time upon the use of the type forms:

The study of type forms has brought about a great educational advance. Until about fifteen years ago [1880–81] Form Study was practically impossible in the primary and lower grammar schools. There were no suitable materials for such study. Single models served in the higher grades for a whole class to draw from at once, with all the disadvantages of a multiplicity of points of view, making it impossible for the teacher to give any clear explanations applicable to individual pupils. . . . Still later, most of the pictorial work consisted in drawing imaginary solids from copies or from rules of theoretical perspective. The work as a whole was abstract and arbitrary, having little connection with real objects. . . .

The means by which educational reform came about was through the recognition of the Art Idea in the work (that is, the idea of art as the product of the creative human mind), and through the *introduction of type models* into the schools. The introduction of type models into the primary schools was practically the first systematic utilization of the sense of *touch* in primary education.[1]

A summary of Clark's ideas discloses that many of the things we believe are accomplished through art education he thought were accomplished by type-form study. He said that the very simplicity of the models gave opportunity and incentive to exercise the child's imagination; that children use their mental images of the types as keys to understanding all forms. To Clark the sphere is the ideal or "type" of things that possess *unity* and *mobility;* the cube is the "type" of all things that *stand;* the cylinder is the "type" of things that can either *move* or *stand fast.*

Form concepts and the power of idealization were inseparable to Clark, and probably to most of his colleagues in art education. He stated: "By idealization I mean the seeing of an ideal above and beyond an actual visible object or fact, and seeing the possibility of realizing that ideal through the use of the object or fact." [2] They believed that the ability to see geometrical form in all nature was at least of the same quality as the creative impulses which built the Parthenon and inspired the symphonies of Beethoven or Darwin's theory of evolution.

Clark also believed that the child-study movement proposed to abandon children to their own interests and instincts, leaving them without intellectual or social ideals. To illustrate what is meant by intellectual ideals, he writes on the value of form study in mathematics, manual training, science, and art. The subjective idealizing power was the essence of creative ability, and the study of the basic type forms was the means of gaining that power: ". . . let us think of the types and present them for what they actually are,—simple embodiments of man's ideals of pure forms. . . ." [3]

[1] John S. Clark, *The Study of Type Forms and Its Value in Education,* Prang, 1896, p. 3.
[2] *Ibid.,* p. 13.
[3] *Ibid.,* p. 32.

HEGEL'S PHILOSOPHY AND ART EDUCATION

"Pure" form, "ideal" embodiment, "right" seeing, "transformation of material nature in the service of the highest ideals"—these interpretations are characteristic of the American educator of the nineteenth century whose background in philosophy came from Hegel.

Hegelian philosophy and its effect on American intellectuals is an inescapable part of the story of our literature, politics, economic and social history, and assuredly of our educational history. In nineteenth-century art education Hegelian philosophy dominated the thinking of all but a very few of the important teachers in the elementary and secondary schools. The interpretation of Hegel, as applied by the art teachers, assumed that art, "high" art, or "good" art was a revelation of the divine, or at least that the artist's aim was to objectify his own sense of the ideal.

The moving power among men was the power of the spirit, intellect. Spirit was revealed to the soul of man through introspection and also provided man with his highest power, that of "self-activity." This highest power was self-existent, transcendent beyond and separate from man's petty world, but man was under the compulsion of putting himself, through self-activity, in harmony with the majesty of God. In one's work in art it was necessary to determine what kind of training or experience would make possible the doing of an ideal work of art. At once the question arose as to what art of the past had possessed ideal qualities. Before 1900 the art of the Golden Age of Greece and of the culminating painters of the Italian Renaissance was considered to be as nearly an expression of ideal qualities as man could produce.

With these viewpoints in mind, it is easier to grasp what Clark was saying about type forms, and to see why he emphasized their importance in such absolute terms. The educator of the 1890's was hoping that art education would prepare the coming generations to search for ideal forms in art, attaining human insight into the absolute of spirit.

The pragmatic philosophy dominant in the arts today seeks evidence of the qualities of intellect, spirit, of the power of life itself—not in the creation of an ideal form somehow superior to the visual, tangible forms of this earth, but rather, by seeing and touching and literally communing with the shapes of earth and of man—to reveal man and his earthly environment to himself. Sometimes the revelation is of intensive evil, and more often in these days it is a revelation of wonder, of mysticism, of fear, or of abstract structural order. The contemporary artist is trying to visualize the infinite riches and complexities the modern world has found in itself.

Part of the complexity of art today reflects the confusion of values still everywhere in evidence. The philosophy of Hegel is much closer to present-day religious education, while professional and general art education is most influenced by the pragmatism of John Dewey and his colleagues. Consequently, the lay public with its religious convictions, and all the artists and art students who have had a religious family background, are consciously or unconsciously torn between the seeking in art of a definitely unworldly ideal and the pragmatic exploration of earthly forms in the most diverse and personal intepretations.

Examples of individual works illustrating these poles of influence might be found in one of Ryder's seascapes, as representing an unearthly idealism; and, from the same period of time, one of John Sloan's paintings of the New York City slums, as characteristic of art form sought in the most prosaic, even depressing, earthly environment. Pragmatic philosophers and critics point to the "idealism" of mural painters like Blashfield, Cox, and Sargent, who populated our public buildings with inane "Spirits of Agriculture, Justice," and so on, as being the logical art product of Hegelian philosophy. On the other hand, the general public could, if versed in philosophical and aesthetic background, rightly identify some of the self-consciously evil, tenth-rate paintings of the present era as the equally logical outcome of pragmatism.

Either group of examples proves rather that small-bore personalities will produce work of corresponding caliber, whatever their acknowledged or unconsciously borrowed philosophical motivation may be.

William Tormey Harris was for years a leader in American education and among American philosophers. In 1867 he founded the *Journal of Speculative Philosophy* in St. Louis, where he was superintendent of the public schools. In his *Psychologic Foundations of*

Education, published in 1898, the chapter on the "Psychology of Art and Literature" is a good statement of the Hegelian views that had so profound an influence on public-school art work in America.

According to this work, the psychology of the beautiful in art and literature has three aspects. First are the sensuous elements of regularity, symmetry, and harmony—symbolizing the activities of the soul. The second aspect consisted of the several art forms, carefully classified in an ascending scale of values: architecture, sculpture, painting, music, and poetry. Dancing, landscape gardening, engraving, elocution, dramatic art, and rhetoric are classified as accessory to the major forms. All of these major arts serve their purpose as progressively realizing forms of human freedom. The third aspect is the correspondence of any work of art with the work of the three great epochs of civilization, the Oriental, the Classic, and the Modern.

Each of the three aspects is painstakingly arranged in a stepladder scale from low to high. Regularity is of less value as a sensuous element than symmetry, and harmony is the pinnacle of the sensuous elements. Correspondingly, Oriental art is more likely to stress a regular rhythm of forms, Classic art has a high dependence on symmetry, and Modern (by which Harris meant the Renaissance and immediately after) is, at its sublime best, the triumph of harmonic relations or of "subordination of matter to soul."

An interesting interpretation of art history is found in Harris' discussion of his epochs of art. He uses the term "symbolic" to describe Oriental art and means by it that the Oriental artist was least free for personal expression because he had to symbolize the power and the religion and the personal glory of an absolute ruler. Classic art he believes to be the highest form of art "as art," and to represent the greatest of freedom, "in the body." Modern art, the third stage, Christian art—or, using Hegel's term, romantic art—shows the superiority of the soul to the body. Evidently Harris believed that the bodily stiffness and the archaic forms of Byzantine and early Italian Christian art were deliberately employed to demonstrate, as he says, "the renunciation of the body." Present-day scholarship is in partial agreement, but it is unconvincing to project the renunciation of the body into work by Botticelli or Raphael.

Finally, Harris writes of art as a moral force of the highest quality, but not only as it portrays idealism. He grants the artist the right and even the duty of portraying, too, "the conflict of moral ideals" so that humanity may recognize "the successive strata in the evolution of human emotions, ideas, and actions."

Suppose that we hope for a period of integration, of reconciliation of diversity in art education, for the near future. Certainly, for the contemporary art teacher, there is something of a constructive nature in the idealist view of the 1890's. The basis for moral values in the arts is now widely argued, but the need is seldom utterly denied. Harris' unequivocal numbering of the aspects of beauty, of art forms, and of historical epochs in an order of values seems quite naïve today. His obvious lack of background in the history of art, the resources of which we are now able to take for granted, only makes more apparent the increase and improvement of scholarship in that field in the last fifty years. Nevertheless, some of his thinking has significance today.

Our contemporary artist is too apt to place all his values on an intensely personal vision. Harris' idealism had the virtue of putting value on matters of larger concern than the individual's immediate interests or narrow vision. It is a hopeful sign that young artists everywhere are now doing paintings, and work in other media, which attempt to combine a larger sense of the world and their feelings about it with the flexibility of technique and pictorial form which the modern movements of the twentieth century have provided.

DISCUSSION AND THEORY, 1892–1893

The influence of the philosophers upon practical affairs is indeterminate. But whether men like Harris created the atmosphere of art educational thought in the 1880's and 1890's or whether they merely recorded it, the books, the printed addresses, the curriculum outlines of the time—all deal with art as an evidence of human idealism, as a refining influence, as an escape from the harsh realities of ordinary living.

In these contemporary records there are indications of changes of points of view and of classroom practices which forecast some of our present activity. Some things done in the name of producing and appreciating "high" art now look absurd. Other practices and philo-

94

sophical insights expressed are remarkably fresh and close to our own thinking. Too often the insight and professional accomplishment of outstanding leaders are taken as the whole record of a generation. Francis W. Parker and John Dewey did draw together many ideas and attitudes to create a more unified, far-reaching philosophy of education than most of their contemporaries; but before starting on their contribution, a survey of the thinking done by less well-known contemporaries will sharpen the focus on the whole period.

Moholy-Nagy, in his *Vision in Motion* published in 1947, proposes the partially Marxian, wholly German Social-Democratic view that all of the vital channels for art just before World War I were willfully cut off at the roots by keeping the more progressive art education out of the schools. His analysis was possibly correct for Germany prior to 1914. In the United States, contrariwise, art in our schools, the art education in the normal schools, colleges and universities, and professional art schools, assimilated new means and philosophies about as fast as any institutional organization can. Also in contrast to Germany, our schools and school staffs were less solidly established and hence more susceptible to new ideas; then, too, it must be admitted we were less ready in development to grasp some of the most advanced ideas current in Germany at the time.

As American art faculties reach a status in size, vigor of statement, relation to other community interests, where their views are discussed as matters of public policy, art teachers should feel both a greater responsibility and a gratification that the social influence of their work is more accurately recognized. We may hope that Moholy-Nagy's belief in the planned stifling of creative growth will not prove consistently true in our future. Any art teacher or art school has experienced sporadic and more or less tense moments of private and public disapproval of student work; occasional clashes of the sort need not be confused with prolonged programs of restriction and frustration.

Written material and transcripts of addresses made during the nineties indicate a ferment of beliefs and activities in art education. The conflict of philosophical bases is never hidden for long. Inevitably there are some things we can snicker at from the unquestionable superiority of our own sophistication.

An Art Educational Conference was held by the Prang Supply

Company in Boston, April 2, 1892. The gathering considered the topic "Art in the Schoolroom—Pictures and Their Influence." In the course of the day several gentlemen and ladies described their experiences in placing reproductions of art works in school buildings.

Ross Turner had been active in Salem, Massachusetts. In giving his reasons for becoming interested in this problem, he said: "On one occasion I was invited to an entertainment, and on the walls of a rather spacious summer cottage I saw a very handsome reproduction of a photograph of one of Alma-Tadema's pictures. It was so large that, although twenty feet above the eye, it was quite as effective as a fresco painting would have been in monochrome, perhaps in tint." [4]

In 1950, aesthetic judgment has changed and our museums and galleries want nothing of the work of Tadema. His glamorized history is done every bit as vulgarly, and in motion, by Hollywood. Fine color printing makes the monochrome print for the schoolroom an evidence of penny pinching or neglect. It is certainly doubtful that any photo could rival a fresco, and equally questionable that the picture Mr. Turner saw was really twenty feet above the floor. But it must have been at a considerable height, and we may be sure that he found this neck-straining position perfectly customary.

Though we question Mr. Turner's taste in selection of works of art and in his means of displaying them, nevertheless his wish to provide schoolrooms with pictorial art was worth while. Classrooms should have in good quality and quantity any available good pictorial art or reproductions of art. The committee working with Turner depended largely upon contributions of photographic reproductions of paintings and architecture, which was about all that was to be had. Because of its desire to maintain a standard of high quality in what was placed in the schools, the committee experienced difficulties in dealing with unsolicited and unwanted gifts—objects like the Last Supper done in inlaid wood pieces, or portrait studies upholstered with real hair.

A Professor Morse amplified on this theme with the suggestion that children rightly influenced in school will correct the taste of the parent in the home. In his remarks, he emphasized poor design in

[4] Prang Art Education Papers, *Art in the School Room: Pictures and Their Influence*, Prang, 1892, p. 3.

wallpaper and pictures, and the inappropriate use of art, such as the appearance of a Raphael Madonna on a decorative stove medallion. He urged a "chamber of horrors" exhibit occasionally as a corollary to other art exhibitions in the schools.[5] Numbers of American museums have, since that time, used just such material in industrial-design work, textiles, ceramics, and even pictorial work to supplement and contrast with objects of good aesthetic quality.

Finally a Mr. Tetlow proudly described the worth of a complete collection of casts of the Parthenon sculptural frieze which had for twenty years been displayed in the assembly hall of the Girls' High School in Boston.[6] He had made it a practice to give short assembly-period lectures on the history of the sculpture pieces themselves and on the Greek myths and religion illustrated by the casts. These little talks were obviously a favorite hobby with the principal; we can imagine some of the girls in their senior year enduring them in attitudes of impatient despair. His conclusion as to the effect on students was probably a just one, namely, that many girls developed an interest in seeing art in the museums.

A talk given by Myra Martin to the American Social Science Association, also in 1892, was different and her claims more ambitious. Her topic was "Art Education in American Life." She closed her remarks on a climactic note, saying: ". . . as far and as fast as the Art Spirit does become a reality to the people, so far will simplicity and consistency come into our modes of life, and truth and unity and harmony in man's relation to his neighbors become characteristic of that life. . . . To do this, we must have our teachers trained to a right understanding of the Art Idea in human history and in social life; and we must also surround children in the public schools with suitable examples of art work."[7]

The florid prose of the speech, with its earnest insistence upon Art and The Art Idea, might have impressed the Social Science Association as being merely purple passages from the lips of a zealot. The advocates of all forms of special education are frequently accused of assuming that their field of work is the most necessary in the curricu-

---

[5] *Ibid.*, p. 12.
[6] *Ibid.*, p. 16.
[7] *Op. cit.*, "Art Education in American Life," Address by Myra B. Martin to the American Social Science Association, p. 35.

lum for a "balanced life." Only in recent years and particularly in the work of Herbert Read is a more defensible and valid case made for general aesthetic education. Miss Martin's speech was probably accepted as a lovely generality unimportant to act upon. If there is any truth in it as we see things today, we are still no closer to taking action to back it up. The importance of making aesthetic development more common has been frequently acknowledged, but it must come through an aesthetic treatment in the schools of all the liberal-arts subjects, literature, drama, even history, as well as the arts courses, music, visual and plastic arts, manual arts, and home economics.

Chicago held its first and best-remembered World's Fair in 1893. To set off the occasion with memorable events, besides the attractions of the Midway, great "congresses" were held in many professional fields. Incidentally, of course, the congresses attracted new and varied groups to Chicago and to the ticket turnstiles. Among the rest, there was an International Congress of Education, which was subdivided into Departmental Congresses.

Among these was a Department on Art Instruction, another on Industrial and Manual Instruction, one on Rational Psychology, and one on Experimental Psychology in Education. Still other groups were organized on music, business education, secondary, elementary, physical education, and so on. But the first four congresses mentioned dealt with topics especially pertinent to art education. Rather than bearing out the belief that the arts were hampered or ignored in those years of educational development, this record of 1893 suggests that we may have failed in the years since simply in advancing from the best thinking already being done by the time of the World's Fair.

Henry Turner Bailey, a graduate of the Massachusetts Normal Art School, exercised a tremendous influence on public-school art education, and not all for the best. There were many parts of the new education of the day which he could not accept, and his limitations in art interpretation were circulated widely during his editorship of the *School Arts Book*, begun in 1901.

In 1893 he had, however, in common with other reluctant art teachers, agreed to permit children the freedom to draw what interested them, to draw some things as they appeared to the individual child. Bailey called this "illustrative drawing." He believed that illustrative drawing in the classroom was a source of vigor, and that the child should ". . . have sketchbooks and use them constantly, the one aim being expression of life and motion, of thought and feeling." He even went so far as to state: "There is certainly no place here for copies; the technique at this stage is not of the slightest consequence." [8]

If Bailey was convinced of the values of personal expression in drawing, we may be sure they were widely accepted in the schools. The corollary to illustrative drawing, upon which he insisted, was "pictorial" drawing. Here he did not endear himself to our attention by such far-sighted attitudes. He said that truth was the aim of this drawing. Apparently "truth" could only be expressed in a thin line, not a broad, fuzzy one. Color to his academically trained eye was not truth and could be "learned" in no time at all after one had true lines in a drawing making forms where color could be filled in. Light and shade to depict solid form were important, and could be considered an extension of the truth of line.

He remained throughout much of his influential life committed to rationally organized schemes for art training. Children and adult students must master lines first, then the use of lines forming figures, and next proceed to copies of master drawings in which, to be sure, one was to get the spirit, not just servile imitation. Bailey always remained unable or unwilling to believe that a logical art curriculum for children could not be plotted out by adults on adult terms based on nineteenth-century concepts of the art of Renaissance Italy.

Mr. Miller, principal of the School of Industrial Art in Philadelphia, followed Bailey to the platform and stated flatly: "To cultivate creative power is what we are after, whether the process is interesting to the pupil or not. . . ." [9] His subsequent definition of creative power, and the grueling academic exercises recommended to attain this dry-as-dust realism, were even less imaginative, more deadly, than Bailey's "pictorial" drawing. It is no wonder Miller was doubt-

[8] National Education Association, *Proceedings of the International Congress of Education of the World's Columbian Exposition, Chicago, July 25–28, 1893*, the Association, 1894, p. 459.
[9] *Ibid.*, p. 463.

99

ful that students would find his methods interesting for developing drawing power. Bailey and Miller in their ideas about drawing represented a conservatism unwilling fundamentally to go beyond practices familiar in their own student days.

But there were other points of view at the Congress of Art Instruction.

At the second meeting, held on the Fair Grounds in the Art Palace, J. Ward Stimson of the Institute of Artist-Artisans of New York City presented a paper on the "Development of Art Instinct" in which he belabored much of Bailey's approach.[10]

Stimson must have provided a somewhat strange note to the conference when he praised the organic style of Polynesian carving and Pueblo weaving. To most of the art teachers of the time the pseudo-classic Fair buildings were grand and sublime, while the artifacts of the more primitive peoples, which were on exhibit, were of interest merely as oddities. Stimson's awareness of the genuine aesthetic merit of such work definitely placed him in the advance guard of the arts.

Basing his thoughts on the freshness of these art objects, he felt that American art education should protect the student's freshness of inspiration, both by developing personal faculties and by observation of the immediate environment. On the subject of studying the masters by means of copying, Stimson boldly opposed the practice as creating an "incubus of endless precedent."

The students at his Institute had been prepared to follow what he termed "natural principles." They studied the "abstract but essential framework of form," and the optical effects of implied motion, of which he said, "Geometrical ratios are freely generated and played with for pattern (along the marvelous lines discovered by the Japanese and Moors) in order to *quicken* student inventiveness and kindle fertility of imagination."

These student exercises bring to mind the intricate, decorative line studies of Louis Sullivan made for architectural surface treatment in stone, metal, and ceramic; the elaborate motifs created by Claude Bragdon in architecture and for the stage; and the mathematical basis of Jay Hambidge's Dynamic Symmetry. Only a minority of art-

[10] *Ibid.*, p. 466.

ists and craftsmen find their best expression in such work, but Stimson's keen sense of educative values led him to the geometrical-form inventions as a kind of elementary art experience to supplement the traditional cast and life drawing. He must have been convinced that the student expert in life drawing was not necessarily the only potential artist.

Stimson was appreciative also of the kindergarten and hoped that art education could develop similar approaches to art activity. This teacher of art, virtually unknown to us, was anticipating some of our most advanced thought. He obviously understood the art of the Orient and saw in it the framework of aesthetic structure which Arthur Wesley Dow used as the basis for his book, *Composition*, six years later. He saw the relationships of art forms to social customs which our present-day anthropologists have so ably studied. Regrettably, though there must have been a few others who agreed with Stimson, men whose work had no such breadth of view were to dominate art education in the years after 1893.

Ernest F. Fenollosa followed Stimson on the program; what he had to say was not very good, but it is important because Fenollosa was well known as the curator of the great collection of Oriental art at the Boston Museum and because he was a great influence on teachers and artists through his aid to Arthur Wesley Dow.

The curator pronounced the dictum that art training should begin not in nature but in art. He viewed European contemporary painting, by which he meant the impressionists and post-impressionists, as flippant because it cut loose from the old masters. This he believed had resulted in the choice of inartistic and materialistic subjects. In this attitude toward the artist's subject, we note his dependence on the rationalist psychology stemming from Hegel. He could not take seriously a painting by Renoir of a casual riverside picnic. It was only possible for him to see aesthetic qualities in commonplace subjects when they were used by Japanese print makers; then, of course, the subjects were not common to Fenollosa, a European. But he could detect no idealism or universality in a painting of a laundress when done by Degas in Paris.[11]

The meeting on Industrial and Manual Instruction gives another

[11] *Ibid.*, p. 472.

version of the use of tools and materials. Gustaf Larson was principal of the Sloyd Training School in Boston, and, with his Swedish background plus his years of American experience, was able to speak authoritatively on the Sloyd system of manual training as it had been adapted to America. The work was commonly referred to simply as "Sloyd"; Sloyd was a manual training which started with simple carving in wood, using knives designed to be held and manipulated easily by the children. Among the first projects usually done was the carving of a shoehorn, an object then in more constant use than would be likely in the average family today.

Sloyd, as Larson described its important aspects, was manual training especially designed for creative growth and the development of physical skill among elementary-school children. Tools and materials were adapted to the powers of the child; all processes were to be used at once on objects which could be completed by the student, thus giving stimulus to the work and illustrating the need for knowing the processes. Some manual-training courses taught isolated skills, such as whittling out of a squared block as nearly perfect a cylinder as possible. Sloyd, according to Larson, should always offer the incentive of working on useful objects which the child could complete to his own satisfaction. The greatest possible variety of activity and of objects made was necessary; and finally, all the objects to be made should be models of beauty, of simple form combined with utility. It was also a part of the system that children should first be able to draw any of the pieces to be constructed.

"The Swedish system of Sloyd," he said, "was based upon the Froebelian idea of the harmonious development of *all* the powers of the child." A footnote to Larson's speech gives a more liberally minded interpretation of manual crafts than most crafts teachers of today are ready to practice: ". . . the pupil must be led to see and to feel the simple beauty of proportion, of harmony of parts, as well as the grace of outline: elements of beauty which are a direct outgrowth of the useful, as well as the beauty of mere ornament, which is sometimes more or less externally added. For this reason Sloyd attaches much importance to the free hand modelling in wood of solid forms." [12]

[12] *Ibid.*, p. 509–603.

It is not too far-fetched to suppose that these Sloyd practices and educational goals were partly responsible for the free handling of all materials in the basic art-school courses, which was to be started at the Bauhaus after 1919. Nor do we have to be timid about inferring that the present Swedish eminence in design of glassware, ceramics, furniture, and architecture itself was aided by the educational practices started with Sloyd. Unfortunately for us, America welcomed the training in skill, but was not as receptive to the need for developing sensitive uses of materials.

The visitors to the 1893 education congresses and the art teachers who read the volume of proceedings got a good cross section of the state of their profession. Speakers had dwelt upon the need to let children do some drawing following their own fancies; some, but not all, of the same men still wanted to parallel such "illustrative" drawing with a kind of junior academic drawing course too much like the Massachusetts course of 1873. As usual, there were authorities to insist that the study of art must start from the study of masterpieces of the past, and other authorities who wanted students to turn to nature and their own environment, to refresh their inspiration rather than to shackle it to the past. And there was the fine statement on the potentialities of Sloyd manual training, but probably few art teachers heard it or read it. Its significance for the elementary school is still to be properly appreciated.

The other congresses of interest in understanding art education of the time were on Rational Psychology and Experimental Psychology. The first group, in guarded and gentlemanly speeches, established clearly the older and weakening philosophical basis of American public-school education; and the second group, the later modes of scientific psychology which were to dominate twentieth-century education.

The Rationalists were the idealists, the Hegelians, set upon educating children up to a standard of adult values in art, literature, craftsmanship, and citizenship. The Experimental Psychology Congress was embarked on a program of child study as a better basis for improving the schools. One of its speakers summarized its more volatile, less defensive enthusiasm, by comparison with the Rationalists, when he snappishly concluded his remarks with this: "I would say that it would be infinitely better for a man or a woman to have studied three or four psychical phenomena . . . than to have mastered all the rational psychology that we have ever thought we had." [13]

FRANCIS WAYLAND PARKER

Two central themes stand out in the theory and practices of art education before 1900. The first of these was the effort to understand the child and his natural methods of learning. The second was the attempt to understand better the nature of art and thus to improve teaching in art.

Two men were influential in advancing the cause of the first study, not only for work in the arts but for the whole elementary curriculum. These were Francis W. Parker and John Dewey. As they experimented with curricula and incessantly, in speaking and writing, organized their philosophy and its application, they were always conscious of the arts as essential to general education.

Francis Parker was a man who stimulated great plans and attracted lasting loyalty from many of his colleagues. He had taught in rural and city schools in the years before and just after the Civil War, always working toward a more satisfactory method of teaching than the one of "cram and memorize." He went abroad to study philosophy and pedagogy in Germany, and returned to the United States to become superintendent of schools in Quincy, Massachusetts, in 1874.

The accomplishments of his five-year term at Quincy became widely known as the finest example of the "new education." From Quincy he went to a two-year term as a supervisor in the Boston Public Schools, and then he accepted the principalship of the Cook County Normal School in Chicago. The national leadership he so easily assumed put him in great demand as a speaker and as a professor at the popular summer institutes. Parker was not active in writing about his work and his philosophy of education, but his close colleagues and students helped edit and publish his lecture notes. In the years to come, many teachers who had worked with him became frequent contributors to educational journals in their own right.

A great faith in children's potentialities was the basis for all his

[13] *Ibid.*, p. 785.

teaching. He believed in, and practiced as best he could, teaching to develop the fullest capabilities of each individual. He opposed completely all mechanical routines stressing mastery of textbook content without understanding or laborious rote learning of formulae, of rules of grammar unrelated to usage, of poetry essentially uncomprehended by the child, or of geographical catalogues of terms meaningless in the child's own experience.

The gist of Parker's thinking about the arts in the grade schools was that art must be used as one of the "modes of expression" in studying what he called the central subjects. A host of present-day art teachers have been trained to react violently against the correlation of art with the academic subject matter, as implied by Parker's doctrine; other art teachers believe in no other approach. Closer acquaintance with Parker's whole curriculum at least gives the art teacher a favorable argument for a unified elementary-grade program in which art is one means of expression among several.

Francis Parker's famous *Talks on Pedagogics* [14] is logically constructed as a curriculum pattern. Chapter One is on "The Child" and dwells upon the natural spontaneity of children. Parker insisted that learning is not only likely but unavoidable if teaching makes use of the obvious physical, emotional, and intellectual activities and curiosities of young children. The child to be taught is most important to Parker. Curriculum organization is needed, however, and Parker developed a logical plan, based on the most advanced child study; also he was careful that his scheme was capable of change and growth depending upon mutable circumstance.

His fundamental basis for the elementary-school curriculum he labeled the "theory of concentration," by which he meant an arrangement concentrating on his "central subjects of study" in a manner similar to what might now be called a "core" of subject matter. The central subjects were meteorology, geography, geology, and mineralogy for the inorganic sciences; and botany, paleontology, zoology, anthropology, and ethnology (which included history) for the study of organic life. He saw all these as the study of *form* or *law*, and his interpretation of these terms was broad enough to in-

[14] Francis Wayland Parker, *Talks on Pedagogics: An Outline of the Theory of Concentration*, ed. by Elsie A. Wygant and Flora Cooke, Progressive Education Association, 1937.

clude the study of any and all forms man and the natural forces of the universe had created.

To provide the essential tools with which to study the central areas, Parker considered numbers or arithmetic as a mode of "judgment." Then he noted the three modes of "attention" or "study": the first being observation, the second hearing-language, and the third reading. Lastly, but not at all inferior by reason of order, he grouped, as modes of "expression," gesture, voice, speech, music, making, modeling, painting, drawing, and writing.

Parker's whole belief in education was that all teaching must start with the child and the circumstances under which he lives. The "central" subject which must be studied by all children was essentially the immediate and the world environment, which, to Parker, seemed necessary to approach largely from the scientific viewpoint. The means by which the child must be trained to make his schoolwork effective was through the modes of study and the modes of expression. What we call the fine arts were included under the modes of expression. The traditional three R's were the modes of study.

The able teacher was one who was sensitive and alert to the nature and growth of children, who guided them to an understanding of the world in which they lived, and who taught them to get that understanding with a skillful use of the tools of study and the media of expression. Much of the best practice in elementary education today is certainly based on this structure.

For the teacher of art Parker had some positive attitudes, which can be interpreted by some as inimical to art education. His pronounced doubts of the value of the special art teacher evidently waned during his later administrative experiences in Chicago. Nevertheless, he continued to insist on the use of the arts as media for expressing the child's unified school experiences and especially for making the central subjects more vivid through art forms.

But Parker cannot be accused of ignorance of the nature of art activity. He proposed that all the modes of expression should be used freely, and constantly, by all children, and on a child level of technical ability. The most important enlargement of Parker's ideas we might desire would be based on our greater knowledge of man's emotional and aesthetic needs. His outline of subject matter was intellectual, primarily scientific in its direction. Since his time any study of the environment has grown in emphasis on sociology, the study of man and his institutions. The aesthetic modes of expression for both children and adults have gained in popular usage because they make possible the direct expression of the individual's emotional experience. This aspect of the arts is hardly dependent upon whether or not, for example, the child is expressing his concept of rock strata, but it is no less important to the whole school experience.

It is apparent from his writing that Parker would have been among the leaders in using art forms in the service of personality development. Indeed, for all his utilitarian theories, he betrays a considerable acquaintance with the pleasures of working with art materials.

He wrote: "Every child has the artist element born in him; he loves to model objects out of sand and clay. Paint is a perfect delight to children, bright colors charm them. Give the child a paint brush, and though his expression of thought will be exceedingly crude, it will be very satisfactory to him; he will paint any object with the greatest confidence." "Imitation [in art], whatever its kind or quality, is essentially making, minus the best element in making—motive." He thinks genuineness is necessary to a unity of action in expression. "In genuineness . . . no matter how crude the expression may be, there is not a superfluous word, a line too many; there is no waste of breath, ink, clay, or paint; words are used to reveal, not to conceal thought." [15]

In any extension of his thinking, it is likely that he would have held to his ardent belief that elementary education should be unified, with one teacher for each group and each teacher trained to seek a unity of curricular material. The special fields and the special teachers or supervisors must be used to enrich and enlarge the scope of that center of interest. In practice today the great majority of elementary schools follow this procedure. The most damaging criticism to be made, now as always, is that even today far too many grade teachers, and some art-staff members, are still blankly unaware of aesthetic qualities in anything, pictures or pots and pans; neither do they know enough about child art expression to welcome creative

[15] *Ibid.*, p. 183.

107

art work in their classrooms. These teachers fall back on timid copies of adult illustration, or permit their children to waste time on laboriously imitative lettering, charts, and routine model making also cribbed from textbook pictures, apologizing for this aimless busy work as correlation with this or that study and observing in passing that their pupils this year do not seem to have any real talent. No word of suggestion, excuse, or encouragement for this uninspired use of art work can be found in the writing or the lectures of Francis Wayland Parker.

COMPOSITION BY ARTHUR WESLEY DOW

Parker and like-minded educators may well have determined the main direction of elementary education in the United States. But they did not prove as successful in setting a pattern for the special subject fields. This failure has been double-edged in its results. First, there has been the failure to take seriously Parker's dictum that all children need training in the "modes of expression." And there has been the failure to recognize art activities, when they are used, as really expressive media—the tendency to use them instead for exercise purposes, for copying maps, for memorizing other people's poetry instead of having children write some poetry of their own, or for the monotonous droning of stiffly mastered tunes without a particle of spirited interpretation. Vocal and manual classroom drudgery is no substitute for personal and group creation in the arts.

The reverse aspect of the failure to use the arts creatively in elementary education has been the influence of the art specialists who urge the importance of art values independently of all other considerations; who, in Parker's scheme of things, would insist on art becoming the "central" subject. Naturally, a primary interest in art makes it the largest factor in one's life. But with the continued emphasis on unified experiences in the school, teachers of all the arts will have to approach their problem from the angle established before 1900, that of improving the aesthetic quality of the whole range of schoolwork.

For most of the years after 1900, art education was intent on discovering the nature of the plastic arts and on the methods of using that knowledge in teaching. In common with other special fields, art education dwelt upon the separate contribution of art to the individual, and was only vaguely interested in the place of art in the total educational program.

Arthur Wesley Dow was fortunately the dominant influence in the first quarter of the twentieth century—fortunately, because the foundation of his work was good.

Dow was one of those men who develop into a system of education what has been to them an inspiring personal insight. His personality was such that he secured the best academic appointments in the country as centers from which to spread his ideas. His work at Teachers College in New York City from 1904 to his death in 1922, and the earlier years at Pratt Institute, influenced generations of public-school art teachers and supervisors. There is little doubt that the art graduates of Teachers College took over the leadership in art education which had been held since 1875 by the Massachusetts Normal Art School.

The 1899 edition of Dow's book, *Composition*, is prefaced as follows: "The title 'Composition' has been given to this book because the system of art instruction which it represents has come to be commonly known by that name. The term *composition* is, however, too limited, as the system in its full development includes not only so-called composition, but all the stages of the creation of a work of space-art. . . . This is the first publication of any consecutive series based upon the scheme of art education whose elements are here presented." [16]

Dow had been studying art in Paris in 1890 and 1891. He turned to comparative art history and particularly to the study of pictorial structure, or the composition of paintings. There is no evidence in any writing by Dow that he was influenced by the profound structural studies of either Seurat or Cézanne, though his Parisian residence would have made possible acquaintance with the work and ideas of both men. He was indebted, as were the impressionists and many American artists after William Morris Hunt, to the Oriental arts. Ernest Fenollosa of the Boston Museum, whose scholarship in the Eastern arts and whose collection of those arts made for the

[16] Arthur Wesley Dow, *Composition*, Bowles, 1899, p. 5.

Museum, contributed most heavily to Dow's art analyses forming the basis for his system of instruction.

No pronounced originality is to be discerned in Dow's ideas. They were current in many forms in advanced European art circles and among a growing scholarly group in American schools. Dow simply turned from naturalistic representation as the first requisite in the arts to a knowledge of structure, of the organization of the plastic elements of art forms.

Most older American systems of art instruction assumed that only the artist able to draw in a highly naturalistic way was equipped to portray "ultimate truth." The recent agreement to tolerate crude children's drawings as valuable because of the interest the children took in them only put off the day when instruction in "artistic" drawing began. The academic mind did not recognize any value in individual use of design or of color; those qualities were only incidental to a work of art. Opposed to this view, Fenollosa believed that beauty, not realism, was the true aim of art, and Dow's philosophy started with composition as the essence of beauty.

The first edition of *Composition* based instruction on the mastery of the elements of line and "notan." Color was only barely mentioned as a third element. Notan was a term borrowed from Japanese arts to describe value, or dark and light. (See Figure 1, Frontispiece.) Also borrowed from the Japanese was the suggested medium of stick ink and brush. Illustrations used in the book were from Japanese brush drawings. The numbered exercises were just as formally set down as any produced by the Prussian schoolmasters or by Walter Smith. Significantly, Dow's interest was in a new interpretation of art forms and a means of learning the practice of art through that interpretation.

Only much later in life did his writings and teaching turn to educational methods in which student ability and interest determined the kind of work used to develop an idea.

Composition, revised and republished in 1913, contained exercises first in line and in "fine" proportions of spaces created by lines, then in areas of flat forms created by notan. The notan exercises started with black-and-white space division only and then moved on to the use of one or more middle gray values. All the exercises in line and in notan began with lines at right angles within rectangles. Next geometrical forms were used, and finally flower and plant motifs followed by landscapes. In the plant forms and the landscapes, flat decorative forms were used exclusively. Only a few fuzzy charcoal drawings indicate the faintest interest in three-dimensional feeling.

Even in this 1913 edition, color was obviously a minor element, or a difficult one for Dow. He refers to the hue, value, and intensity as properties of color; briefly describes the Munsell system of color notation; and states rather wistfully that ". . . color with its infinity of relations is baffling." [17]

Dow's own work in painting and in the color wood block is uninteresting in color. He worked, of course, as he had his students work, chiefly in landscape, and favored a silhouette of darks forming a network from border to border of the picture space. In effect, he reduced pictorial motifs to flat patterns almost stencillike in the use of masses of light and dark.

The 1913 edition more clearly outlined his Elements and Principles of Composition. The Elements remained as he had first stated them: line, notan, color. The more specifically defined Principles were: opposition, which was defined as the right angle, or the vertical contrasted to the horizontal; transition, illustrated as any line or mass which might be placed at the spot of the formation of a right angle to soften the angle by a diagonal line, a curved line, or some other shape; subordination—of the parts of a form or a design to a single element such as to a central axis or to a dominating mass— was the third principle. Repetition, the fourth principle, was noted as the source of rhythmic feeling; and symmetry, providing a picture or design in exact balance, was the fifth and last principle.

Artists today, unfamiliar with Dow and his influence, are apt to look at his book as nothing more than an archaic trifle. His grasp of the elements of composition seems incomplete. More damaging than the text to present-day esteem are the insipid little student drawings of seascape and landscape in line and value, all pathetically inferior technically and emotionally to the Japanese work used as the major examples. The exercises in little squares of simple and complex line patterns were sneered at by professional art students. The regular

17 Arthur Wesley Dow, *Composition*, Doubleday, 1913, chap. XIV.

art student's chief preparation continued to be life drawing and painting.

Not many years after the Dow composition approach became almost universal in art-teacher training schools, courses using material similar to his space exercises were given in many art schools as design courses supplementing the life drawing. But the fact that for years composition courses were the fundamental work given to teacher trainees, while life class was the backbone of "professional" art preparation, continued to separate needlessly the two groups of students. The normal-school art classes produced graduates weak in drawing and quite inexperienced in almost all painting. The professional art students were realistic draftsmen all too slightly interested in art structure. And both groups were obviously hesitant, ill-equipped technically or through experience to make much use of color.

A fortuitous circumstance created at Teachers College a faculty combination which made the art graduates able to take their national leadership. In 1904 John Dewey left Chicago University and the Laboratory School he had been instrumental in founding to join the Teachers College faculty at Columbia.

Prior to Dow's association with Dewey, it is true that he had shown little interest in the progressive educational philosophy of Parker and the young philosopher, Dewey, who was to broaden and consolidate Parker's work.

John Dewey, while he was on the faculty of the University of Chicago, contributed time and leadership to the elementary Laboratory School. All the art work the children did in that school was closely tied to the general activity of the day or week. Illustrations made by the children were of the social, historical, literary, or geographical material being studied, though the visual interpretation was obviously childlike and individual. Craftwork was also planned to amplify academic study and included work like candlemaking, papermaking, simple weaving, Sloyd work, clay modeling, and sandtable work. The faculty, with the guidance of a special art teacher, welcomed honest child expression, and was more interested in a gradual maturing of art powers than in forced mimicry of adult naturalistic drawing.

It was this preference which was so well met by Dow's approach. Ordinarily, few children readily develop naturalistic drawing ability at an early age. A great many children much more easily acquire a power of organizing line, color, and shapes into a composition or design which possesses a personal distinction.

Teaching art in the elementary school so as to increase the child's ability to compose pictorially has proven closer to natural child-growth patterns than was the older attempt to teach drawing skill.

The booklet, *The Theory and Practice of Teaching Art,* which Dow published in 1908, repeats with variations some of the composition problems already common in many normal-school art courses all over the country, but there are glimpses of change in point of view about the application of the system to children's work. He had come to observe that younger children might wish to paint directly, and that picture making of a direct and naïve sort might have to precede for some years the beginning of any more intellectual exercises.

In the Introduction he wrote: "The purpose of art instruction is the development of [creative] power . . . the education of the whole people for appreciation." [18]

The happy accident of collaboration between a philosopher who believed in child expression in the arts and an artist-teacher who formulated a system of aesthetic education which aided the child's creative power gradually changed the objectives of general art education in this country.

Dow was not to contribute much more to the literature of art education after 1913. He did, in 1917, write one of the few magazine articles by any American art teacher welcoming the work of painters like Gauguin, Van Gogh, and Cézanne.[19] He agreed with the almost unanimous opinion of the day, that the artists were technically crude, but he suspected that it was a crudeness of strength, of new directions, not of ignorance. His thoughtful position, taken in the midst of the art critics' bewilderment about French modernism, was the logical outcome of his study of the vigorous though imma-

[18] Arthur Wesley Dow, *The Theory and Practice of Teaching Art,* Teachers College, Columbia University, 1908, Introduction.
[19] Arthur Wesley Dow, "Modernism in Art," *American Magazine of Art,* January, 1917, p. 113.

ture work of children. Dow, the great educator of teachers of art for children, was in advance of the teachers of the professional art schools, and of the large majority of professional artists, when he comprehended these paintings, so utterly unlike anything he, as artist, ever could or would try to do.

John Dewey, of course, continued his interest in the arts, which culminated in the world-wide influence of his book, *Art as Experience,* in 1934 (pages 202–206).

The students of the collaborators Arthur Wesley Dow and John Dewey were many in number, and they have been tremendously valuable and productive in their teaching positions. Inevitably, the outstanding persons among them were to provide the leadership in elementary and secondary art education up to the present time.

Bibliography

Brooks, Van Wyck, *New England: Indian Summer 1865–1915,* Dutton, 1940.

Butler, Nicholas Murray, ed., *Monographs on Education in the United States,* Lyon, 1900.

Chicago Art Institute, School of, *Circulars of Instruction,* 1901–1902, 1913–1914.

Clark, John S., *The Study of Type Forms and Its Value in Education,* Prang, 1896.

Clark, John S., *Teachers Manual, Prang Course, Parts 1–6,* Prang, 1898–1900.

Clark, John S., and Parker, Francis W., *Some Vital Principles in Education: A Discussion on the Place of Art in Education,* Prang, 1895.

Clarke, I. E., *Art and Industrial Education* (Vol. II of *Education in the United States,* ed. by Nicholas Murray Butler), Albany, J. B. Lyon Co., 1900.

Dow, Arthur Wesley, *Composition,* Bowles, 1899; Doubleday, 1913.

Dow, Arthur Wesley, *The Theory and Practice of Teaching Art,* Teachers College, Columbia University, 1908.

Dow, Arthur Wesley, "Printing From Wood Blocks," *International Studio,* July, 1916.

Dow, Arthur Wesley, "Modernism in Art," *American Magazine of Art,* January, 1917.

Dow, Arthur Wesley, *Illustrated Catalogue of Oil Paintings and Draw-*

ings, *Ipswich Prints from Wood Blocks—and (Japanese) Collection,* American Art Association, 1923.

Fenollosa, E. E., *"Mural Painting in the Boston Public Library,"* Curtis, 1896.

Fenollosa, E. E., "Modern Spanish Art to the Fore in the Salon of 1908: Decadence of French Influence," *Craftsman Magazine,* September, 1908.

Harris, William Tormey, *Psychologic Foundations of Education,* International Education Series, Appleton, 1898.

Hollis, A. P., *The Contribution of the Oswego Normal School to Educational Progress in the United States,* Heath, 1898.

Larson, Laurence Marcellus, *A Financial and Administrative History of Milwaukee,* University of Wisconsin, 1908.

Mayhew, Mrs. Katherine (Camp), *The Dewey School: The Laboratory School of the University of Chicago, 1896–1903,* Appleton-Century, 1936.

Morris, William, *Hopes and Fears for Art,* 1882.

National Education Association, *Proceedings of the International Congress of Education, World's Columbian Exposition, Chicago, July 25–28, 1893,* the Association, 1894.

National Education Association, "Report of the Committee of Ten on Elementary Art Education," in *NEA Proceedings for 1902,* the Association.

Parker, Francis W., *Notes of Talks on Teaching Given by Francis W. Parker,* ed. by Lelia E. Partridge, E. L. Kellogg & Co., 1885.

Parker, Francis W., *Talks on Pedagogics: An Outline of the Theory of Concentration,* ed. by Elsie A. Wygant and Flora J. Cooke, Progressive Education Association, 1937.

Partridge, Lelia E., *The Quincy Methods,* Kellogg, 1886.

Prang Company, *Lectures at the Prang Art Educational Conference,* Prang, 1892.

Western Drawing Teachers Association, *Annual Reports,* from 1894.

Figure 6b. "Interesting poses [which] can be attempted in high schools." (From James Hall, ed., "The Applied Arts Book," March, 1902.)

Figure 6a. Drawing of Boer War by Seven-Year-Old English Boy—the Picture to be Studied as an "expression of the child's life." (From Earl Barnes, ed., "Studies in Education," 1902.)

V

Art, Education, and Modernism

Some historians judge that the United States left adolescence about 1900 and began its struggle for maturity. After the Spanish-American War our national affairs were no longer merely local in importance, although to this day many American citizens wish they could be managed without regard to the rest of the world.

Art and art education also encountered a different kind of influence from abroad than had been experienced in earlier centuries. Previously American artists and teachers had studied in European countries and had returned to spread the word of new developments in their work. We had imported teachers like Walter Smith and the first kindergarten teachers to begin schoolwork which certain alert leaders believed we wanted, or ought to have.

What steps were taken in art education prior to 1900 all seem to have been attempted in the most sanguine spirit. The best of European art education and of general education, as exemplified in the kindergarten, was dedicated to liberal democratic objectives and seemed altogether available for transplanting into our schools.

After 1900 this process continued, but the country was no longer disposed to look to Europe as an unchallenged fountainhead of all wisdom in the arts, nor to accept European innovations as readily and unquestioningly as in the past. For we were possessed of a large group of established and recognized artists, schools and art curricula, and a large corps of teachers with a vested interest in the school system; so that new influences from any source were meeting with the reluctance of a fully organized society to change its ways too speedily.

Then, too, the new century in America brought the beginning of doubt and of reconstruction in all phases of society. This was evident in the arts, just as much, if not more prominently, than in political life, in economic matters, and in social customs. In the twenty years before 1917, the Congress was confronted with problems like the Spanish-American War, and the unruly conscience with which some Americans rebelled at supporting a government of imperialistic intentions. The laws to attempt the curbing of monopolistic trusts, to protect natural resources from unrestrained exploitation, to equalize economic opportunity through the federal reserve banks and the income tax, and finally the decision to enter a war with the stated aim of preserving democracy beyond our boundaries were certainly efforts to stabilize and to adjust a form of society.

The arts and art education during this time met problems which could not be solved simply by encouraging more activity. The new influences to be assimilated were decisive in nature, hard to understand, and are not even yet quiescent as leavening elements. The very basis of aesthetic quality was being called into question, and fundamental differences of educational method and objectives were bitterly debated. A discouraging stalemate ensued, but it was probably inevitable. No progress of value could be imagined without serious questioning of a great deal of the early teaching of drawing and the arts.

CHILD STUDY IN ART FORMS

The Chicago World's Fair Congresses on Rational Psychology and Experimental Psychology represented opposing forces on a fundamental issue. The experimentalists won out, and the subject of child study became the dominant form of psychological inquiry in university departments of education and in the leading normal schools.

Studies aimed at discovering what children are replaced treatises guessing at their ideal potentialities. One of the most useful implements for these purposes of discovery was the product of the art and drawing classes.

English and German scholars early in the 1880's published studies on child nature as revealed through drawings. American studies of similar nature appeared not long after. In the published work on the subject up to the year (1908) of James Parton Haney's *Art Education in the Public Schools of the United States,* there are two directions of significance. One group concentrated on the study of the child, his reactions, his intellectual and emotional growth, and the insight into the progress of that growth offered by the "absurdities" of children's drawings. The other group of teachers was more involved in the arts. Their observations and conclusions, while directed at and formed upon the work of the child, were always to be rationalized with adult concepts of aesthetics. This latter two-way preoccupation ultimately delayed some of the now obviously needed renovations in art teaching. Nevertheless, child study was to prove more rewarding in later decades than the rest of the confused and often misdirected elementary art education of the first two decades of the century.

A cross section by child-study experts of their observations of child art shows how objectively they studied this work at a time when most artists and art teachers were blind to the positive values of child art. The drawings of young children were seen to have individualized character. Educational values greater than just the encouragement to go on to more disciplined drawing were recognized when boys and girls of the lower grades drew freely. Particularly it was noted that imagination was stimulated and child experience was organized in the processes of the drawing.

These aspects of child work were acknowledged long before the forceful qualities of color and of individual pictorial forms, common to many children, were noticed. At the 1894 meeting of the National Education Association Art Department, the president of the department, Christine Sullivan, said: "Of course, these illustrations by little children are, from an artistic standpoint, simply ridiculous; still, educationally they are priceless." [1] It is difficult to tell whether she is apologizing because she really liked the children's work or because she distrusted the encouragement of this activity and had to present some rationalization for permitting it.

Another contributor to the same program left no doubt as to his position. J. L. Todd, Director of the Public Industrial Art School of Philadelphia, asked: "Why should not children draw elephants or chickens or fish if they can, in the first grade? Why should they be chained to cubes and hemispheres—abstract forms or some other traditional system? Why should they not think for themselves? Why should definite results according to a system be expected from individual minds, each one created on a different plan for some special purpose?" [2] The questions he raised contain more than suggestions of change from a graded system of instruction in drawing specific forms to one permitting children to draw pictorially at an early age. Todd was insistent on such a change because it seemed to him a better way to aid the development of the individual.

M. V. O'Shea, then of the State Normal School at Mankato, Minnesota, and later of the University of Wisconsin, presented a paper dealing with careful observations of children's drawings. He was one of a small group of university professors of psychology and pedagogy who had been interested since the 1880's in making such studies, and his conclusions are probably representative of the day.

He claimed as of first importance that nearly all children between the ages of four and nine enjoyed representing objects, people, and animals, and that they drew easily and with few misgivings. Next, he recorded that they evolved personal and favorite diagrammatic

[1] National Education Association, *Journal of Proceedings and Addresses, Session of the Year 1894*, the Association, 1895, p. 896.
[2] *Ibid.*, p. 903.

schemes of showing such things as "house," "man," "woman," "dog," and that they used these diagrams without change, regardless of the change in the appearance or the position of any model from which they drew. This led to O'Shea's final point, that there were no logical relations of proportion in the drawing or in the visual perception of young children.[3]

O'Shea's first two generalizations would be accepted today. His last statement has been modified in view of the fact that children's logic in drawings is usually more severe than the conventional practices of professional artists. But children's visual logic is based on their own experience and vision. Sometimes the simple clarity with which children interpret their views of the world results in dumfounding, even terrifying pictures, but these works are seldom illogical in reference to the child experience and understanding from which they emerge.

Earl Barnes published two volumes of *Studies in Education,* the first covering the years 1890 to 1897 when he was on the faculty of the new Leland Stanford University. The second volume was issued in 1902, and was based on material produced partly in England and partly in America. Both volumes dealt with child study, but the second book included ten studies on aspects of children's drawings.

Barnes made his commentaries from actual sketches made by children, and accompanied each article with a reproduction of the drawing. He continued this interest in the field, and in 1908 contributed to Haney's symposium the article on "Child Study in Relation to Elementary Art Education." In that chapter Barnes summarized the publications from Germany and England, together with those of his American colleagues and his own work.

Art education in 1908 apparently accepted the worth of child study and approved heartily of the studies in art. Certainly the common practices in drawing classes were not changed very quickly by the insights available from the psychological studies. It took many more years of gradual assimilation before classroom teaching in art was done with a real understanding of the child's capabilities. These studies in the art forms of children suggest that before 1914 the psychologists and professors of education were closer in spirit to the

[3] *Ibid.,* p. 1015.

advance guard in modern-art experiments than they were to their art-teaching colleagues, or to the majority of practicing artists.

There is a fascination in following their trend of thinking. It is as if we were on a hillside watching a group of people search for a path clearly visible to us but full of dead ends to the people coming through the thickets. This group made much progress; its followers lagged behind for a while, but eventually caught up. We can wonder, perhaps with some profit, what paths, which we are following with every confidence, are to prove blind alleys.

Not any part of the most sympathetic professor's background could prepare him really to enjoy child art at that period of time, though some of the writers came close to doing so when they described the personality attributes of the children doing the work. For instance, they realized that children could produce such convincing effects with small pictorial resources because they would venture to try anything that came to mind. One characteristic drawing on which Barnes commented was a scene of action in the Boer War (Figure 6a, page 116). The boy's line drawing of fighting in progress is as vigorous and inclusive of imagined detail as anything we might expect today from schools providing an ambitious art program. Strong emotional power was discerned in the drawings, too. And in every analysis, the child's need for showing action and movement was commented upon. Only the final step for the professors remained, that of perceiving that the quality of the work itself possessed strong emotional character, often a marked feeling of movement and action, and zestful interpretation of whatever story or subject matter was being used. This step was beyond the aesthetic limitations of the scholars. But they did grasp fully the possible good influences on the child of the opportunity to produce such personal expressions.

Of course, young children did and do enjoy drawing. Further, they make constant use of their own experiences as a primary, and indeed only, source of subject matter. The child-study group observed that children's power of organizing and giving voice to their experience could be improved noticeably through drawing. More than once it was noted that each individual expressed ideas better through one medium than another. With no more pretense at meeting the problem than most art teachers now display, it was acknowledged that the beginning of adolescence, and a marked feeling of insecurity as to what one might draw, go together.

An important part of child study in drawing and arts activity was the analysis of drawings in large enough numbers to insure sound generalizations. Again this kind of study was inaugurated in Germany. It was soon taken up by the English, and shortly after by the Americans.

Studies of the sort brought out conclusions in three large areas. First was a better understanding of child ability to learn some of the mechanics of drawing. Second, there began to be established an observable pattern by which children come to a maturity of visual perception and picture making. And third, there were the hazy and often contradictory attempts to reconcile excellent views on the nature of children and their art with the prevailing doctrines on art and beauty and philosophical idealism.

It was at once apparent that drawings done independently of dictated lessons showed no interest in abstract or geometrical forms. An art program based on the painstaking drawing of squares in the first grade ran counter to any normal child interest. Furthermore, few young children showed any great interest in ornamentation of the surface of crafts objects, or in drawings of ornamental borders or all-over patterns on paper. Perspective as a formally taught discipline was also listed as impossible to the lower grades, and even in the upper grades there was a difference of thought. Some believed that the study of perspective and proportion should be deferred until the upper grades; and other opinion voted realistically that even in the upper grades, proportion and perspective were learned, "here a little and there a little." In this connection, too, undefined opinions are often found that some sort of "grammar" of drawing is needed for the upper grades. What the grammar would be, what classroom activities would be used to teach it, is not made clear.

The child study of this period created an impression of not being much concerned with adolescents. In art, as well as in other fields, this field of research has been most helpful for its illuminating work among boys and girls of the nursery school, kindergarten, and primary grades.

122

One other phase often dwelt upon was that of media used in drawing, and here there was some confusion. Generally, writers were still sure that pencils and line drawings were most acceptable to children and most useful in portraying their ideas. Occasionally, though, there were teachers who began to urge the use of larger drawings, of paint and a wider use of color. Doubtless these ideas started the overemphasis, still current in some places, on painting on large papers as almost the only adequate means of art expression for the younger child. But in the years when studies of child art were new, this urge to enlarge the number of media to be used was an improvement for the art classes.

The subject matter in children's drawings and the stages of growth recorded, from the use of crude and personal symbols to a more adult and realistic use of form, were popular areas of study.

Statistical tables were made on subject-matter preferences by grade and sex. These varied a little from place to place, but did arrive at some similar results. Boys were preoccupied with subjects of speed and action, including all the figures of American folk mythology: the Indian, the cowboy, the locomotive engineer, and the speed-demon automobile driver. The girls drew children, family activities, and pictures of girls doing things. A few girls, "tomboys" of course, preferred boyish subjects.

The relationship between personality status and growth on an individualized basis, and the effects which these have on art subjects, were not studied at any length.

Personal symbols created by children for all representational forms were watched both for the process of change as the child's observation became more acute and for detecting individual differences in the way the symbols were developed. Sometimes the researchers were upset because the pupils being observed used much the same shapes to draw a man, regardless of whether the man was to be an old duffer in an overcoat or a circus acrobat on a wire. Among many children in the early school years, there was obviously no effort to depict a particular kind of person or to indicate any unique aspect of body or clothing.

But it was always evident that these symbols did change with age and experience. Naturally it was easiest to chart the changes in the drawing of the human figure, in the progression from the irregular, bulb-shaped object, with sticks protruding from it as arms and legs and ears, to the stiff but reasonably all-inclusive figure possible to the children of the upper grades.

The changes in some children's work from placing all figures in full frontal position to the profile view; the gradual realization of the body trunk and of the attachment of arms and legs thereto in approximately the usual location; the growing interest in the details of the face, the hands, and simple clothing; and finally the use of many figures in complex narrative pictures—all these were noted carefully and with enthusiasm. As the studies are fully comprehended, one becomes aware of the utter removal they portend from Walter Smith's practices of art education and the use of items like the type-form blocks.

The university people and their graduate students who were making the studies were, however, chiefly interested in psychology. The significance of their work in art teaching was still to be realized by the majority of art teachers. And part of the reason for this slow absorption of research into practice was that the psychologists themselves were uncertain when their material was matched against popular and professional art standards.

Whenever child drawings were discussed as art, it was an almost uniform procedure to agree that the "standard" children set for themselves was too low. To that admission there was often added the lament that the requirements of "high" art, or the idealistic best of art, were so distant and virtually unattainable that it was questionable whether children should even be burdened with the thought that their work was art. It was realized that enthusiasm and vigor of expression came first for children, and that any mastery of the skills of art must be acquired later.

The whole scheme of evaluation was based on the notion that the uncompromisingly "perfect" figure drawings of the academic art schools were the only valid criteria of artistic heights. Any knowledge of the broadening of aesthetic values—as seen in the work of artists like Van Gogh, Cézanne, Toulouse-Lautrec, or Arthur B. Davies and John Sloan in this country—is not in evidence.

In philosophizing on the arts and the work of children, some valuable insights were expressed. A relationship in form was seen between child art and the arts of adults in primitive societies. Since then that comparison has been more closely examined. The positive forms and the nonphotographic picture organization are seen to be common to the work of children and the primitive adults, while the expression of the primitive societies is adult and based on maturity of experience, making their art forms essentially unlike any child's illustration or craft product.

Contradictions remained for later decades to solve. How could the awkward, even brutal drawings done by many children as forceful expressions of experience become, in course of time, transformed into expressions of the "beautiful" and, hence, artistic? One study pointed out that children identified things and views that they liked as "pretty," regardless of the fact that the adults conducting the study had much more limited definitions for what they accepted as pretty.

Somewhere along the line, usually deferred for the indefinite upper grades, all the vigor and energy of the young child's expression in drawing and painting would have to become channeled into the expression of beauty. This was essential for the achievement of the universal culture.

Thus, while the studies in psychology were giving direction for the healthy development of arts experiences for young children, a blind spot prevented carrying the work into the years of adolescence. The "grammar" of drawing could be deferred, but it must not be evaded; sooner or later all true growth in the arts was still sought in the dry draftsmanship of the academies.

THE MODERNISTS IN ART REACH AMERICA

This grammar of beauty, the ritualistic ideal human forms called for by Hegelian art concepts, was being attacked by other persons and groups, and far more consciously than by the students of child development.

The people who started educating the United States to see the modern art of the late nineteenth century and early twentieth century, and to accept other values in art than those of ideal beauty, were artists turned educators, or they might be accurately described as art missionaries. There was an atmosphere of dedication in the efforts they made to educate the American public in the arts. Since 1914 we have been busy assimilating the significance of art forms, contemporary, historical, and primitive, which were unknown or largely ignored before that time, and which certain artist groups succeeded in forcing upon the attention of this country.

Delacroix, Corot, Daumier, and Courbet—the first as early as 1825 —had exercised great influence on their younger colleagues, painting pictures unlike anything American students encountered in West's studio. The impressionists, from the early days of the 1860's, and the post-impressionists of the 1880's, based part of their practices and their art philosophy on the growth of all French nineteenth-century art. These men and the movements in which they participated were before 1900 but little known even among the artists of this country. As for public-school art education, there was no glimmer of awareness of these great changes in the arts.

Eventually some individuals and small groups sensed the importance of this gap in our national background in the arts. Every recent history of American art or survey of contemporary art tells the story of the work and influence of Alfred Stieglitz, of the one and only exhibition of the artists who called themselves the "Eight," and, of course, of the huge 1913 Armory Show of paintings and sculpture first shown in New York and then in Chicago and Boston.

All three of these jarring impacts on the serenity of the public eye were initiated by men whose knowledge and understanding of art put them well beyond the conventional art attitudes common to other art professionals.

It followed that they were denounced by a majority of American people interested in the arts; and also that extremists uninterested in a free flow of ideas, and fundamentally without a feeling for democratic processes, loudly urged that modern art be banned completely from public exhibit halls. The artists responsible for introducing the new movements, starting from a high pitch of enthusiasm for the variety of new expression, often fell victim to seizures of gloom and great distrust of the public when they discovered how slowly any intelligent responses were being made.

However, in a world relatively free and flexible, interchange of ideas in every field, art included, had to come. Alfred Stieglitz, gifted with more than ordinary discernment, with a great zeal for public education, and with the advantage of a reliable independent income, was a unique figure in aiding this intercontinental exchange in the arts.

He had been one of the young Americans to study in Germany during the eighties and nineties, and during that time began his own great creative work in photography. In 1897 he became active in the Society of American Photographers and began his editorship of the magazine *Camera Notes* (in 1903 renamed *Camera Work*). Stieglitz kept it going as a personal venture until 1917. In 1905 he started his eventful career as exhibitor of advanced experimental work in photography, and of the most radical of contemporary European and American art in painting, drawings, and sculpture.

In the course of years, the Little Gallery at 291 showed work of Picasso, Van Gogh, Picabia, Rodin (the drawings), Matisse, Toulouse-Lautrec, Cézanne, and Renoir. Younger American painters whose work was welcome at the 291 gallery were John Marin, Marsden Hartley, Arthur G. Dove, Abram Walkowitz, Alfred Maurer, and Max Weber. In Stieglitz' magazine, articles appeared on the work of each of these artists. The articles that appeared on photography were uncompromising in a devotion to experiment, to seeking the true development of the medium, to exposing the phony, the imitation painting or etching achieved falsely through altering the print from the film.

The gallery attracted unbelievably large numbers of people and is unrivaled in the currents it set in motion from so tiny a spot and with so slight an endowment. Stieglitz' intensity, his unfailing judgment, great courage, and complete generosity in using the funds he had, created an institution unequaled in the past and unapproached at present.

Other gallery owners and directors then and now have wished to show "the latest thing," but the art Stieglitz sponsored broke all too clearly from the art forms customarily admired at the time. His exhibitions were almost always from the work of artists who insisted on experiment, both in the media they used and in the organization of their pictorial subject matter. Matisse's flowing, unstudied-looking drawings and his violent use of color, Picasso's structural analyses of

127

forms in varied planes, were both negations of the supposed classical pictorial values best shown in the fetching ladies in Greek robes adorning American public buildings of the period.

At its simplest, the visual aspect of modern art claimed for the painter nothing more than the right to use any visualization he found forceful. This might be derived from the magnified distortions of African sculpture, from the unconscious symbolism and vagary observed in children's work, from the pictorial organization practiced in the Orient, or by making use of the arbitrary and brilliant color usage of the Persian ceramist.

Literally hundreds of explanations and dissertations try to account for the change in pictorial art in the nineteenth and twentieth centuries. Much scholarly work explores the subject on trivial and profound levels, and still more publication and public discussion are aimed at the education of the general public. Two fairly evident assumptions may be based on a generous sampling of this material. One is that pictorial art in painting, in photography, in motion picture and animated cartoon, even in television, will continue to reflect the mass of experimentation that the "new vision" of the twentieth century has produced. That vision will persist because it is a combined product of diverse elements which cannot and will not be canceled out, forgotten, or ignored. These include the science of optics and of color, the broader view of the world and of world arts furnished by archaeology and anthropology, the independence of the artist from the narrow demands of a court or church patron, and, in this century particularly, the use and influence of the mechanics of camera, projector, and electronics in picture production and dissemination.

The second assumption, which few are likely to question, is that the general public will continue to be confused and baffled and at the same time conditioned by manifestations of what we call, too vaguely, modern art. The perplexing associations and dissociations of much modern painting will continue to infuriate millions of people when they see reproductions in the mass press, particularly so when the publication using such pictures does so with editorial comment likely to stir up resentment for the unfamiliar. In the same publication a large proportion of the biggest advertising pages will make use of pictorial devices for catching attention which were unknown in 1900.

The exhibit of the "Eight" was held in 1908 and was deeply disturbing to the art world. The novelty it offered has long since been accepted because the painters changed only the content of their pictures, not the form of picture making. To raise a ruckus among art lovers, all these painters did was to submit, as examples of serious art, pictures of men and boys caring for pigeons on the rooftops of the slums, or shopgirls going in to a dance hall, or the portrait of an old bum with his hat pulled down over his eyes. In 1908, subjects like these were distasteful as "fine" art because the activities and people portrayed were common, not "elevating," even though the manner of painting employed by the artists was not difficult to comprehend.

When the group of artists was attacked as having set old values at nought, it proved exhilarating to some of them, especially to a man like Arthur B. Davies who was alert to the art of Europe. He was aware of the fact that some of the recent painting of Paris deviated infinitely more from the work of the past than did any of the pieces in the exhibit of the "Eight."

The story of the Armory Show is a perennial favorite among artists and writers, probably because it is one of the few times that a carefully planned event lived up to its advance billing and to the hopes of its sponsors. This 1913 art event introduced to the New York City art world post-impressionism, Fauvism, futurism, and cubism. Works in these categories were the spectacular items which caught the eyes of newsmen, caricaturists, guardians of the public morals, and all the artists, young and old, the most conservative ones, and those most eager to welcome change. More quietly, the exhibit showed much work, European and American, of the nineteenth century which unfortunately had been missing in the public or private American galleries.

In 1893 the art exhibitions at the Chicago World's Fair had been devoted almost exclusively to salon painters, both French and English, covering yards of canvas with full-length peasant girls blushing vividly at handsome noblemen mounted on shiny horses. The great men of the beginning of the century, David and Delacroix, all the impressionists, the young leaders of the decade before 1893, Seurat, Lautrec, and Van Gogh—all were missing at Chicago; the latter were, of course, not much better known in Paris itself at the time.

But in the Armory Show all this panorama of growth was on the walls—and more, too, in the first revival of interest in the three American painters, Eakins, Homer, and Ryder. Their paintings, in the aurora borealis setting of the exhibit, displayed more quiet strength and durability than the work of their better-known contemporaries.

Reams of paper were used up and quantities of ink spilled in criticism and comment on the show. If it had been the absurd indignity that some believed, its chief works would now be remembered with such freaks of nature as Tom Thumb. On the contrary, the total exhibition has been regarded with increasing respect in the years that have passed.

As had been the case in the arts of canvas and sculptured stone and metal, so it was in architecture. Louis Sullivan in 1910 was a somewhat forgotten, sharp-tongued eccentric, tremendously able in architecture but unwilling to adapt himself to the "direction and needs of American business." Wright was Sullivan's young disciple, architect of a hundred unusual and distinguished homes of rather bizarre exterior appearance; he was seldom approached to work on major industrial or office structures for fear he might not be amenable to compromise.

Both men, however, were leaders in the thinking which was to create the architecture of the future. Frank Lloyd Wright had had examples of his work widely circulated in national magazines. An excellent volume of text and over a hundred pictures and plans of his buildings to the year 1908 had been published by the Wasmuth firm in Germany, where they were given wide recognition by progressive architects and designers.[4] Wright's ideas, based on Sullivan's and developed in the course of fifteen years of independent work, were reaching a larger public every year.

Louis Sullivan, during the last twenty years of his life, had less reason to feel that his teachings in architecture and aesthetics were or would be successful. He wrote the series "Kindergarten Chats" for the magazine *Interstate Architect and Builder,* which published

[4] C. R. Ashbee, *Frank Lloyd Wright,* Wasmuth, 1909.

it during 1901–1902. But at the time only a few reactions to his ideas reached him. He wanted desperately to teach young architects to see the sham of eclectic architecture, of the style shopping which constituted most of the architectural work on large American business and public buildings. Sullivan was intensely the idealist, the thorough artist, who desired that architecture should be an organic art form, reflecting, and at the same time shaping, a fundamentally democratic life.

It has become a commonplace to say that Sullivan was ignored and neglected for twenty years before his death. A listing of his buildings and the bibliography of his occasional writings suggest, rather, that he had enough work to keep him busy, and that he had some status as a philosopher in the field. He was assuredly not, in the days that he lived, the dominating figure he has since become.

When he died in 1924, his sense of accomplishment must have been small, because architecture in America was still almost entirely all that he derided. He was yet to be the great teacher of hundreds of young men not then out of the elementary-school years.

The photographer, gallery director, art missionary Stieglitz, the American painters who began their work under the influence of the 291 Gallery, the painters who formed the "Eight" and later led in organizing the Armory Show, and the architects and designers whose work shared the creative direction best known in the work of Sullivan and Wright—these artists were and are great art educators. Not one among them failed, through writing, actual teaching, or in personal activities, to teach compellingly. The fervor of their wish to reach the public may have been an indication that all of them were philosophically ardent democrats and defenders of individualism, and wished to transmit a democratic aesthetic to their society.

Education and the schools were constantly in their thoughts. Some would say that they were always on the offensive against the schools. A more productive view of their contribution to education would recognize that men like Sullivan in "Kindergarten Chats," and Robert Henri as he was quoted by his students in *The Art Spirit*,[5] were taking for granted the existence and power of the huge American school system. It was because they were aware of the extent and

[5] Robert Henri, *The Art Spirit*, Lippincott, 1923.

power of the schools—not always exercised on high levels—that they were so ambitious to make an impression on the minds of young artists, teachers, and designers.

Criticism and evaluation of art forms are implicit parts of any art education. The artists and the exhibits we have been reviewing, the work of these artists, considered in their total impact on education, demonstrated convincingly that the arts of our time must face forward; must evolve their own forms based on our social organization.

They taught the leaders in their generations, and we are now fairly united in accepting the doctrine that, while the principles of art and life in the Greece of Plato's time may be valid today, nevertheless the contemporary interpretation, the pictures painted, the books written, buildings erected, cannot reflect principles except in art forms likely to be as strange to Plato as the automobile or the airplane.

Too much of the art of the nineteenth century was predominantly a continuation of the outward forms of the past. Many artists and art teachers whose instincts for the good life were offended and often directly thwarted by the disorganization, the dirt and clutter, of twentieth-century urban life looked toward art—the art of the past— as a mode of spiritual release from the torments of the present. This doctrine was not acceptable to the modernists. Art, they believed, must be of its day, expressive of the life being lived, and, one might hope, partly improving the conditions of life. Whatever contribution art might make to society must be as an interpretation of the society of the present, or as an architecture shaping a more tolerable existence.

In April of 1912, at Stieglitz' gallery, paintings done by children were exhibited.[6] Part of the children's subject matter was that of the streets and the city. It might be protested that the city was not beautiful, was not the ideal spot for children to live and play and study; but it could not be denied that the city was for them, most of the time, the boundary of existence, and their art was based on experience. It was no longer a uniformly accepted article of faith that art must depict idealism or whimsy. Children were using the arts as in-

[6] Sadakichi Hartmann, "The Exhibition of Children's Drawings," *Camera Work*, No. 39, Spring, 1912, p. 45.

terpretation and as imaginative creation, too, but the impulse to expression must come from themselves and from their world.

"SCHOOL" ARTS

The world of the big cities, the factories, and the railway lines was ugly in all its forms, was wholly cut off from the arts, in the opinion of Henry Turner Bailey. Bailey was a graduate of the Massachusetts Normal Art School. He had been State Agent for the Promotion of Industrial Drawing in Massachusetts, and he became the first editor of the *School Arts Magazine*. In that capacity he was influential in art education, especially in the work of the elementary grades.

A pamphlet by him, *City of Refuge,* issued in 1901, is an eloquent statement of the point of view so vigorously fought by the modernists. For Bailey, art was above all a refuge, a haven for the spirit above the grime of daily existence. Teachers of art were, in Bailey's words, "blessed" because they could pass on to children the "keys to the celestial city, that dream city more real than all our New Yorks and Chicagos, to which in all ages the human spirit has looked for satisfaction." [7]

Louis Sullivan was no more fond of Chicago or New York than was Bailey; for lyrical invective on the evils of urbanism, he was a master compared to the *School Arts* editor. But Sullivan did look upon art as an instrument capable of creating great cities in the present. The apparent conviction that only medieval Florence was, or could ever be, a magnificent dwelling for the human spirit was utterly stupid in Sullivan's eyes. Art could serve democracy even better than it could the Medici's wool-growing and money-lending plutocracy. Bailey wrote:

. . . and when the child becomes a man, though shut in a factory by day, and lodged in a city of bricks by night, he will know that

> Yon ridge of purple landscape,
> Yon sky between the walls,
> Holds all the hidden wonders
> In scanty intervals.

What a privilege is ours! To free the spirit of a single child is to do a divine thing. [8]

[7] Henry Turner Bailey, *The City of Refuge,* Davis, 1901, p. 5.
[8] *Ibid.,* p. 18.

Sullivan could not believe in an art which was to exist only as a dream of beauty forbidden to waking reality. Neither could the painter John Sloan. In 1906 he painted the picture *Dust Storm,* a whirl of dust circling the base of the new Flatiron Building while people on the sidewalk bent their heads and clutched their hats and clothes. Down the street came one or two automobiles. Such paintings were condemned by the idealists as travesties on beauty. Now we see Sloan's painting nostalgically as a charming record of an earlier time in the history of the great city.

The artists could not see how the most characteristic aspects of their day could be ignored in the creation of contemporary arts. Huge cities, vast rail lines and yards, the factories, the laboratories, the complexities of science, the urban slums, and the huge office buildings were the dominant visual aspects of American life.

But for the first twenty years of the century, art in the schools was narrowly presented as an expression of the beautiful, beauty that was to be found only in beautifully formed people, in pastoral landscapes, or in the "cities of refuge" of one's dreams of a golden past that is no more.

The Applied Arts Book first appeared in September, 1901. It was described in the Foreword as the Voice of the Applied Arts Guild, and it was "Prepared under the eye of Fred H. Daniels, Guild Master, in Consultation with Henry Turner Bailey, State Agent for the Promotion of Industrial Drawing, Massachusetts, and James Hall, Supervisor of Drawing, Springfield, Massachusetts; Guild Craftsmen." [9] The sublime crowded the prosaic in the description of membership in the Guild. "Membership in the Guild involves the promise of perpetual interest in the coming of Beauty into life and the annual subscription of one dollar for the Applied Arts Book."

The first page of text in the first number forecast the never-failing success of the publication. The teacher subscribers, or Guild members, found there "An Approved Outline for September Work in All Grades." It was this specific outline of what to do and how to do it which secured and held a large professional following.

Two years later, in September, 1903, Bailey was made editor and the title was changed to the *School Arts Book*. He continued as editor until 1919, when the post was taken over by Pedro J. Lemos.

[9] Applied Arts Guild, *The Applied Arts Book,* September, 1901, p. 5.

Probably no other publication has been used as faithfully by as many teachers in the elementary schools as has *School Arts*. The essential quality of its attitude toward the arts has changed somewhat in the intervening years. In its first decade the emphasis was dictated by Bailey's opinions on what constituted the mission of the arts.

Drawing from nature was a constant ingredient for all grades. Subjects were plant fronds; branches from trees, preferably with nuts and seed pods visible among the leaves; clumps of long grasses; selected garden flowers; and fruits and vegetables mounted singly on a display board or arranged in a basket. The composing of these natural forms in compact pictorial areas was freely borrowed from Dow—and properly acknowledged. Lettering was stressed for the middle and upper grades, as was design for craft objects in metal, leather, and wood.

Both in design and lettering, the dominating aesthetic influence was that of William Morris, with a discreet touch of *art nouveau*. The most approved designs were a kind of stiffening up of plant motifs in the manner of the exercises in Dow's *Composition,* with now and then a more willowy, vinelike form permitted. The continuous border across the ends of textiles, along the edges of woodwork, around the lips of ceramic pots, was a favored scheme for decoration. This was varied by the division of space into elongated vertical panels, with conventionalized ground and root forms at the base and flower and leaf forms at the top. The lines defining the sides were, of course, the stems, trunks, or vines of the plant form on which the design was based. Much was made of the need for adapting ornament to the shape available and to the material used in the object; flatness of decorative forms was also insisted upon. In all this the work and the writing of Morris and his disciples are clearly seen.

The *School Arts Book* for its first ten years created a world all its own. Perhaps the isolation from the cold logic of cubism and the hot color of Fauvism was not too great a loss at the time. Maybe the concentration upon one man's nature-centered concept of beauty and art was vigorous enough to be a stimulation in the schools, a source of satisfying activity for the children his magazine influenced. The time did come when the continuation of that influence became stultifying.

The most frequent contributor of pictorial matter to the magazine was the editor himself, Henry Turner Bailey. That frequency of editorial contribution was questionable as an aid to creative schoolwork.

In each issue Bailey reproduced a "blackboard" calendar, which was redesigned monthly for a different arrangement of pictorial panels to surround the numerals. Invariably the panels were filled with drawings in white chalk of plants, trees, and animals to symbolize the passing of the seasons. Accompanying each calendar picture were directions for securing the oak sprays, or for observing the tree forms at first hand and for creating a personal version of the pictorial suggestion which the editor submitted for the month. Directions were given, too, for the precise use of the chalk, broadside, stippling, staccato lines, and many more methods for making possible the various effects. The love of nature's seasons was obvious and also the desire to communicate that emotion as an aesthetic experience; indeed, as *the* aesthetic experience. The hope expressed that the teachers and some of their gifted pupils would make a creative variation on the magazine drawing was probably seldom realized. More likely, in hundreds of schoolrooms the drawing was reproduced as exactly like that of the editor's as could be managed.

And such emulation was at the time not too disturbing to the editor or to his subscribers. In the 1906 volume he contributed a supplement, "The First American Thanksgiving." [10] It was reproduced in the author's own handwriting and with his drawings of the Pilgrims' common house, of Squanto, of one of the Pilgrims bringing home a turkey, and of a circular still-life vignette composed of a sword, a pewter plate, and an iron cooking pot. In later issues, student work is frequently reproduced in which these line drawings were lifted directly for use as booklet covers, as mural decorations for history, or as topical art work for the month of November. Editorial comment shows no concern over the undesirable effects of this borrowing of art forms.

"Pictorial" drawing, that is, the disciplined learning to represent objects in Occidental perspective, was all-important. The lessons in this category, from first grade through the ninth, were planned to teach all children a conventional, impersonal group of realistic forms

---

[10] Henry Turner Bailey, "The First American Thanksgiving," *School Arts Book,* November, 1906, p. 108.

as the "correct" ones for people, animals, trees, wagons, buildings, and still-life objects. Again there is little evidence that the editor and his art-teacher writers had encountered the idea of individual interpretation of visual forms. The insight of the child-study psychologists into the pattern of individual growth and expression had not reached the *School Arts Book*.

Other attitudes toward the arts and art education than those held by the editor were recognized and given generous space.

During the summer of 1908, a great Third International Drawing Congress was held in London, from which reports appeared in *School Arts* of September to June 1909. Three reports were of considerable significance. The first was a survey of the luncheons, teas, banquets, lawn receptions, and exhibitions held at various castles and sponsored by the English nobility.[11] Bailey wrote this article. At one of the banquets he had spoken for the American delegation. It was to him a source of wonder, of pleasure, and of pride that important personages treated the Congress as an important event; his hope was that America might one day put art education on such a level of importance.

At another time a Prussian schoolmaster's comment was published. He lamented the laxness and freedom of expression in the Prussian lower schools as contrasted with the drive and discipline our best work showed for lower-school grades. The writer obviously disliked the emphasis on creative art work stemming from Froebelian practices, and he found the discipline and accuracy of representation in American school exhibits more satisfactory.

The third of these important articles was an enthusiastic review of the children's work done under Professor Franz Cizek in Vienna. One of the most interesting exhibits at the London meetings had come from him. Miss Lucy Silke reported on Cizek for *School Arts* readers:

The free paper tearing and cutting from memory without drawing, the exercises in original construction and in colored poster work are not of course new with us, but they were here made the vehicle for creative expression to an extent seen nowhere else in the exhibition. The subjects had been sympathetically chosen, simple materials had been developed to

11 Henry Turner Bailey, "Editorial, The London Congress," *School Arts Book*, September, 1908, p. 455,

their full possibility, and the tendency to small, cramped drawing which is the result of too early restriction to the pencil point, had been to a large degree overcome. Moreover, by means of appeals to an imaginative equipment in this case above the average, the interest had been sustained so that the work had not become formal but remained spontaneous and child like. The technique reminded one of that acquired in play, in which the child's desire to realize his mastery over his own small world is expressed in his tireless repetition of processes and his keen interest in the growth of his own skill . . . it augurs well for the future of art education that a practice school of this character should be incorporated among the regular departments of a leading art school like that of Vienna.[12]

In the same article, Ebenezer Cooke of England was described as a leader of art education whose ideas were unorthodox but acceptable and likely to be influential in art education in his own country and elsewhere.

Miss Silke's eager interest in men like Cooke and Cizek could not have been hers alone. Cizek's work with children later became one of the most valued forces in expanding child art experience. It is a little surprising to come upon such enthusiasm for Cizek in so early a number of the *School Arts*. But Bailey did not prove to be as impressed as was his correspondent, at least not to the extent of following up the article with additional material or illustrations on Cizek's classes.

One additional feature of the *School Arts Book* of that time, which is significant today, was that of a Workshop section, conducted by William Hammel. His monthly projects were actually constructional and scientific experiments rather than what would then have been considered art work. No effort was made to relate this experimental work in materials and processes to art, though the ingenuity, the encouragement to design and build for particular purposes, was more like our present aesthetic approach in furniture and the crafts than most of the so-called design problems in the rest of the magazine. An example from the Workshop offerings was a suggested construction of an attic woodworking corner, to be built in the home and to make use of the open spaces between the two-by-four studs. The plan for the bench, for the shelving between the studs, for tool racks, and for drawer space was all most cunningly devised, and in such fashion

---

[12] Lucy Silke, "The Work of Normal Schools," *School Arts Book,* May, 1909, p. 879.

that any older boy whose home included a space like the one mentioned would be able to begin his own scheme. There were many other projects, such as those with bottles and candles to explain the need for oxygen in keeping a flame burning.

Such activity has gradually been absorbed into the manual-arts shops and the science curricula for the elementary grades. Now we face the problem of relating and integrating Hammel's workshop ideas with the rest of what is more readily recognized as art. It is desirable that much of the material Hammel taught as interesting tricks should now be used as a basis for understanding science concepts, and it is also valuable to have well-equipped woodworking shops in the schools. What is regrettable is that as these activities have been made more effective, it has too often been assumed that the educational qualities they possess are not valuable in the arts.

Yet, more than ever before, art concepts of our time require good craftsmanship, Yankee ingenuity, an understanding of the properties of materials, as the basic resources of the creative designer. School art in 1908 was not ready to relate the workshop projects clearly to the heights of fine art.

The London Congress brought forth as the most important American record of contemporary art education the volume previously referred to, *Art Education in the Public Schools of the United States*, edited by James Parton Haney. The editor's own article summarized historically "The Development of Art Education in the Public Schools." Earl Barnes prepared the equally valuable summary on child study and art education. Other contributors surveyed art education in the elementary grades, the high schools, evening classes, the normal schools, colleges, and art museums.

Illustrations throughout the book, which do not in any case attempt to illustrate the sections in which they are placed, undoubtedly reflect as accurate and favorable a view of student work as do the articles. The reproductions of young children's drawings were chosen to show, far more emphatically than would the *School Arts Book*, freely done work of strong individual nature. But there are not many examples of such drawings. The bulk of plates show upper-grade and high-school craft and lettering. Ceramics, leather work, booklets and hand-bound books, jewelry, small furniture pieces, and textile weaving and printing are included. The ornament is in the usual twining vines and chopped-up plant stencil forms of the *art nouveau* persuasion, with Morris-style structure.

Secondary students were fewer in number than now, and those who did take art were expected to attain a greater technical proficiency than is generally found among present-day secondary students. In one particular the work pictured is uniformly of higher quality than much shopwork we see today, and that is in the use of materials. Metal and clay surfaces are handled distinctively, not similarly. Metals show the mark of the hammer if shaped by the hammer, not otherwise. Wood surfaces are finished to bring out the best of the appearance and texture of the wood. The shift over the years of some of these activities from the art class to the manual-arts shop has been technically understandable. The all-too-common disinterest of shop teachers in any aesthetic consideration for materials and structural design is not understandable or defensible.

The Morris style referred to above is only superficially well known as a mode in furniture and interior decoration. The whole work of William Morris did affect American arts and art education, though most imperfectly; and it is worth while to know what was welcome from his teaching and what was rejected by our countrymen.

William Morris died in 1896. His crusade to establish the superiority of handcraftsmanship over what he felt was the evil system and product of the mechanized factory was a strong force in America until the postwar years of the twenties.

It is dubious whether Morris' most ardent American followers would have been a pleasure to him. For Morris was an artist-craftsman who took a deeply felt and active part in socialist societies. His philosophy was all of one piece; he believed the English society of which he was a part had degenerated aesthetically because of the Industrial Revolution. Consequently he admired the honesty, the clarity of design, and the use of materials in the handicrafts of the English workmen before the coming of the steam engine. The artist, as he saw the situation, could not produce objects of beauty based on an environment of ugliness and dirt. Working for what he believed was the only hope, he advocated socialism politically for the control of industry to the point where most of man's work would

140

again be made by hand. In his own craft design and workmanship he returned to the heavy stability of the medieval period, finding but little charm in the graceful elaborations of Chippendale, Adam, and Sheraton. In the use of all material—cloth, wood, paper, the printed page, metal—he held that an artist guilty of imitating one material with another was literally a moral delinquent.

Morris was consistent and thorough in observing the consequences of his belief. Any workman should be expected to start and finish all of a certain object. In no other way could the craftsman feel the responsibility for the quality of his work; he could have the satisfaction of knowing that his work was well done in no other way; and only thus was he likely to have a decent regard for the materials he used and the tools of his trade. A day's work, in Morris' thinking, should be man's most rewarding experience.

Mass-production industry seemed to make that idea impossible. If mass industry was to persist, Morris took the humanitarian view that work hours must be reduced, since there was no likely way to bring pleasure and a sense of accomplishment into subdivided work processes.

How much of this well-knit if hopeless philosophy made real headway in American art education? Primarily a superficial and slightly precious version of Morris' discrimination between individual and mass production.

Any handmade object was assumed to be without question superior to all factory-made pieces. Art was a rare and beautiful activity. Works of art also were beautiful and few in number. Since handicraft and the products of the craftsman were becoming rare, it followed that all handicraft was closer to art and beauty than could be true of any machine-built object. It was this truncated interpretation of Morris' work which dominated our art education. Morris saw art unseparated from all of English life or from the economics of the nineteenth century. His broad conclusions were far from the sympathy or even from the comprehension of most Americans; but art education avoided the problems he raised, rather than disagreeing with them, by the neat process of admiring him as the apostle of handwork, and ignoring the total meaning of his work. The emphasis for art teachers was always on extending the province of the arts;

how or where, and to what ends, were questions better left unasked. If there was public apathy for this high endeavor, it was with ease and practice attributed to lack of education in "sensibility."

Only the artists and architects, again, were touched by Morris and his vigorous followers, either to agree or disagree. For instance, Frank Lloyd Wright's best-known early public expression was on *The Art and Craft of the Machine*,[13] the Hull House lecture of 1901.

Here he stated his eagerness to come to terms with the machine, to use it as a tool of greater capacities but no less aesthetic potentialities than the hand tools of the individual craftsman. Wright was like most of his contemporaries when he spoke in opposition to Morris' ideals, but he was like him, as the educators were not, in being able to see and willing to take a stand on the relation of the arts to the people and community.

ART-EDUCATION ASSOCIATIONS

Associations in education grew in numbers and in membership as the enormous expansion of the school system gathered momentum. In this branch of activity American schoolteachers proved as eager to write constitutions and to elect officers as any group of their fellow citizens.

The associations, perhaps unfortunately, multiplied in two ways: one, by the process of forming organizations for the enlargement and improvement of individual subject-matter fields; and second, by forming national, then regional, and finally state associations of the same type. Nowhere near as often were associations formed on the basis of differing approaches and philosophies for education in general.

Frederic Lynden Burnham, writing for Haney's symposium, listed some of the early art-education associations and the dates of their founding.[14] An Art Education Department of the National Education Association was begun in 1884. In 1888, the Connecticut Valley Art and Industrial Teachers Association was formed. At the World's Fair in 1893, the Western Drawing Teachers Association organized. By

[13] Frederick Gutheim, ed., *Frank Lloyd Wright on Architecture*, Duell, Sloan & Pearce, 1941, p. 23.
[14] In James Parton Haney, ed., *Art Education in the United States*, American Art Annual, 1908, p. 353.

1899, the Eastern Art Teachers Association created a larger unit into which the earlier-formed Connecticut Valley group was absorbed. A large and growing number of local associations, both state and city, were listed in Burnham's paper, all with quite similar objectives.

The membership of practically all the associations included teachers of drawing, of manual arts, and of industrial or mechanical drawing. There was assumed to be a community of interest among the teachers of these areas. In fact, in many school systems, there were supervisors appointed to organize and administer joint programs of drawing and industrial arts. A healthy relationship seemed to be taken for granted and to be capable of continued growth; every influence of the past several decades was helpful in unifying the arts and the crafts.

Not alone William Morris, but a large group of European architects and designers like van de Velde, Peter Behrens, William Voysey, Rennie Mackintosh, and Victor Horta, as well as the Americans Henry Richardson, Sullivan, and Wright, all favored shopwork, drawing, and art experiences taught in a closely related manner.

Regrettably, the unity of aim and of continued mutual development did not prosper. No sooner did the educational associations begin to organize annual meetings than the separate interests and points of view became apparent. Divergence was common; efforts to seek out common goals were infrequent and more often verbal than real when they were attempted.

The art groups were still preoccupied with their overprofound descriptions of the "fineness" of the arts. The shop teachers were increasingly eager to prove their value in training boys directly for local industry. Manual-arts faculty members finally formed a wholly separate organization, the National Society for the Promotion of Industrial Education, for the specified intent of securing federal funds for the support of vocational education. The aim was realized by the passage of the Smith-Hughes Act, providing federal aid to vocational and agricultural education beginning with the school year 1917–1918. By the time the United States declared war on Germany in 1917, even the associations which had been jointly organized had become almost entirely devoted to the teaching of shop techniques.

In 1910, the Art Education Department of the National Education Association renamed itself the Department of Manual Training and Art. In 1914, it became the Department of Vocational Education and the Practical Arts, and by 1919 even this was shortened to the Department of the Vocational Arts. Not until the thirties was an effort made to re-create a department of art education. By then all thought of coördinating shop and art education was assumed to be mere wishful thinking on the part of a few diehard art teachers. Shop teachers felt that the arts had little to contribute to their work.

Unlike the NEA department, the Western Drawing and Manual Training Association changed its name in 1919 to the Western Arts Association, and as such it has continued to represent the interests of art, home economics, and related arts and manual-arts teachers. To be sure, more success has been achieved correlating home economics and related arts and art curricula objectives than has been possible with the manual arts.

The problem of relationship in these fields is one that is forced on our attention today, and it will require thought and action constantly in the years to come. Art teachers are forced by many recent developments in their field to seek and use more shop equipment. Shop teachers, on the other hand, in many small schools are being encouraged to teach crafts that have generally been done by art-staff members. This has happened as school boards begin to want craft classes for their creative and recreative values in addition to the strictly vocational courses. Each group of teachers, the arts and the manual arts, is in need of some of the preparation enjoyed by the other.

EDUCATION IN THE MUSEUM OF ART

One more contributor to the encyclopedic 1908 symposium was Florence Levy of the *American Art Annual.* She prepared a paper on *The Educational Work of the Art Museums.* While she surveyed quite completely the best work of American museums in publications, newly formed museum guide services, exhibition organization, library services, and the like, she did not refer to the valuable concept of the museum in art education, which was then in operation. Her article did not refer to the Newark Public Library and the work of its director, John Cotton Dana.

Dana was librarian of the Newark Free Library from 1902 until his death in 1929. The products and the practice of the arts interested him all his life. As librarian in Denver, starting in 1889, he began to amass a circulating picture file for general and school use; and he began, too, quoting his own words: ". . . to settle, out of hand, many of the questions that I see from the reports of your [art teachers'] meetings you are still puzzling over." [15]

A young art teacher, Mr. Collins, helped John Cotton Dana "settle" the problems of art education in Denver. To judge from the results in the form of exhibits later initiated by Dana, their settlement of problems was fresh and unhampered by precedent. Dana created rather than followed precedent in public education in the arts.

From 1902 to 1909, he carried on art activities on the third and fourth floors and in the art room of the Newark Public Library, which had fortunately been built with much extra space for future expansion. During that time a picture collection for circulation was growing immensely. Also, any organizations with some concern for the arts which needed space for meetings were welcomed to the library rooms. Dana managed to use increasing sums from the library budget to begin a collection of fine art prints and original works of art.

His thinking in art was formed on the theme that art was a part of every person's daily experience. He was more helpful to teachers and especially to art teachers than any librarian or museum director in the country; when he criticized their work, it was a privilege he earned by his close knowledge of their classroom practices. He observed that teachers might teach their students successfully to model, to paint, to weave, to bend iron, and to make boxes, and yet fail to plant the seeds of aesthetic understanding, to "breed, by exposure, suggestion and practice, the habit of having feelings about all that they see." [16]

The Newark Museum was founded as a separate entity in 1909 and continued to operate in the Library building under Dana's direction until it moved to a building of its own in 1925. The first decade of Museum affairs included several momentous exhibits which, taken

[15] John Cotton Dana, "Relation of Art to American Life," *School Arts Book*, September, 1906, p. 3.
[16] *Ibid.*, p. 4.

together, established an example for a broad museum-of-art education program.

In painting, the works of Arthur B. Davies, Ernest Lawson, and John Marin were shown, along with paintings from many other artists whose work was better known at the time and more pleasing to the public. Max Weber was given his first important one-man show in 1913, complete with printed catalogue presenting an introduction of the artist by Dana and of the work itself by the artist. Dana anticipated a lack of favorable public response to Weber because the artist's work was not altogether intelligible even to Dana. But he believed that contemporary artists should be the first concern of the interested public, and further that those artists whose integrity he could respect, but whose work was more difficult of approach than the majority, were most in need of public showing. Then, too, the public must find the culture of its day, in art as in books, in the works of men who necessarily cast a different light than that shed by their predecessors. As with Fenollosa and A. W. Dow, Dana's enthusiasm for the arts of the Orient made it more natural for him to welcome the art of the twentieth-century modernists.

Exhibits of photography, of simple objects excellently designed which could be bought for sums less than fifty cents, of the products of the New Jersey clay and ceramics industry, were some of the unusual events held in the Newark institution.

Sometimes Dana's mottoes accompanying exhibit material were considered in poor taste, and not really adequate for raising the level of public interest in art. One of these was, "Beauty has no relation to price, rarity, or age." If one believed this blunt statement, it cast a shadow over the latest European masterpiece acquired with large sums of American money. The viewers might conclude, and entirely logically, that whether or not they found a "masterpiece" or a floor tile beautiful depended on qualities inherent in the object and in their personal understanding, rather than in a knowledge of the price paid.

Dana did not balk at some of the obvious interpretations of his attitude. He wanted children to look more carefully at their newspaper comics, at neighborhood billboard posters, at new stores and factories. If they found something attractive and interesting in their ordinary experience, that was all gain. If they became aware of much that was dull or even drab, then they at once contributed to the impulse to re-create, to improve their local environment. The museum could help to accomplish either or both of these outcomes for the children and adults who were its visitors.

Nothing was more fantastically stupid to Dana than the fixed policy of American art institutions to ignore contemporary art and particularly American contemporary art. He was not chauvinistic in this regard. He simply felt that we must begin in art, as in farming or business—or in making a library or an art museum—with the land or the natural resources, or the writers and the artists that we possess. Of course, we can secure for ourselves some of the products, as we can some of the lessons from the experience of the past, and make use of both in understanding the present. But the art museums did not see their collecting and exhibiting function as primarily of importance to a living art and to living artists. Rather, they were building up huge repositories of the past purely for their interest in the past.

The Newark Museum's purchases were not large, but they were made from the work of living artists. Newark's Library and Museum under Dana added to the educational museum program of this country elements of unique value at the time and now widely copied.

Miss Levy's article indicated a flourishing growth all over the nation for public education in the museums. Already, in 1908, Chicago Art Institute's Ryerson Library was becoming one of the best and most usable art collections available to scholars and artists. Toledo Museum had started to achieve its present eminence in schoolchildren's use of the museum. The New York Metropolitan, the Boston Museum of Fine Arts, and others were welcoming larger numbers of visitors, were providing lecture and museum guide staffs, and were issuing publications, including postcards of works of art as well as scholarly monographs.

But it was the Newark Museum which circulated art prints as the library did books. In this case it was Dana's application of library methods to art-gallery resources that proved so beneficial. Newark was first to engage an artist, Max Weber, to redesign and work out color schemes for its gallery rooms. Newark was foremost in showing

147

contemporary work under the patronage of a large public institution. And Newark looked for art, and called attention to its finds, in the products of the factory or from shelves of inexpensive goods in the local retail stores. Nevertheless, Dana was not, as some artists and museum professionals protested, either a sensationalist or a vulgarizer.

He merely insisted stubbornly that art was always the product of today and of the place where we live. The past works of man in other parts of the earth and in our own land can be most valuable to our development. But finally we must find and nurture our own artists. Dana's museum practice was directed at uncovering whatever art forms were being created, as the first step toward a richer and more varied future production.

WAR AND POSTWAR

The war years 1914 to 1918 slowly whittled away much of the energy and zest that would otherwise have brought a consolidation of many valuable elements in art education. Of course, any number of hasty and ambitious projects were outlined, some started, and a few completed to prove that art in the school had some talents which could aid the nation to wage war. Fundamentally, though, the arts are constructive, and war in its most favorable light can only claim to be defensive of human values, not creative. The arts, possibly more than any other part of human life, lose energies and intelligent direction during and just after war years.

By 1920, many once-valued intellectual and aesthetic movements seemed to have been forgotten. Much of the prewar work needed to be freshly seen in the light of a different and rather strange world. As an example: what child study revealed of the processes and products of child art was by no means lost, but it faced the necessity of new evaluation in the light of Freud, of the behaviorists, and of Gestalt psychology.

The modernism of Stieglitz and his painters, of Davies as the godfather of the Armory Show, of the architects Wright and Sullivan— these men and movements were temporarily in eclipse in 1920, submerged as far as the sophisticated younger art generations were concerned by new European art movements: purism and dadaism and the internationalists in architecture.

Art teaching in the elementary and secondary schools, while it continued to be impressed by the formulas of men like Bailey, did, after the First World War, begin to synthesize, as best its young teachers could, the mass of ideas bequeathed to it by the psychologists and artists, photographers, teachers, architects, and museum directors.

Bibliography

Allison, S. B., "A Study in Theories of Art," *Elementary School Teacher,* March, 1905, pp. 385–395.

Applied Arts Guild, *The Applied Arts Book,* September, 1901.

Arts and Crafts Club, *Art and Industry in Education,* Teachers College, Columbia University, 1912.

Ashbee, C. R., *Should We Stop Teaching Art?* Batsford, 1911.

Bailey, Henry Turner, *The City of Refuge,* Davis, 1901.

Bailey, Henry Turner, *The Flush of Dawn, Notes on Art Education,* Atkinson, Mentzner, and Grover, 1910.

Bailey, Henry Turner, *Art Education,* Riverside Press, 1914.

Barnes, Earl, *Studies in Education,* the Author, 1896–1897, 1902.

Burk, Frederick, "The Genetic vs. the Logical Order in Drawing," *Pedagogical Seminary,* September, 1902.

Cahill, Holger, "John Cotton Dana and the Newark Museum," *Magazine of Art,* November, 1944, p. 268.

Caswall, Muriel, "The Children's Art Center," *American Magazine of Art,* August, 1918.

Chicago Art Institute, School of, *The Sketch Book,* February, 1902.

Curti, Merle, *Social Ideas of American Educators,* Scribner, 1935.

Dana, John Cotton, *American Art: How It Can be Made to Flourish,* Elm Tree Press, 1914.

Dewey, Evelyn, *New Schools for Old: The Regeneration of the Porter School,* Dutton, 1919.

Dewey, John, *Democracy and Education,* Macmillan, 1916.

Dewey, John, "The Psychology of Drawing," "Imagination and Expression," "Culture and Industry in Education," *Teachers College Bulletin,* March, 1919.

Eddy, Arthur Jerome, *Cubists and Post-Impressionists,* McClurg, 1914.

Eshleman, Lloyd Wendell, *A Victorian Rebel: The Life of William Morris,* Scribner, 1940.

Fenollosa, Ernest F., "The Fine Arts," *Elementary School Teacher* September, 1904, pp. 15–28.

Fiedler, Conrad, *On Judging Works of Visual Art,* tr. by Henry Schaeffer-Simmern and Fulmer Mood, University of California, 1949.

Fry, Roger, *Vision and Design,* Brentano, 1920.

Hall, G. Stanley, *Adolescence,* Appleton, 1904.

Hambidge, Jay, *Dynamic Symmetry in Composition as Used by Artists,* Brentano, 1923.

Haney, James Parton, *Classroom Practice in Design,* Manual Arts Press, 1907.

Haney, James Parton, ed., *Art Education in the United States,* American Art Annual, 1908.

Hartmann, Sadakichi, "The Exhibition of Children's Drawings," *Camera Notes,* No. 39, Spring, 1912, p. 45.

Henri, Robert, *The Art Spirit,* Lippincott, 1923.

Kandinsky, Wassily, *Concerning the Spiritual in Art,* Wittenborn, 1947.

Kuhn, Walt, *The Story of the Armory Show,* Kuhn, 1938.

Larkin, Oliver, "Alfred Stieglitz and '291,'" *Magazine of Art,* May, 1947, p. 179.

Lukens, Herman T., "A Study of Children's Drawings in the Early Years," *Pedagogical Seminary,* October, 1896.

Maitland, Louise, "What Children Draw to Please Themselves," *Inland Educator,* September, 1895.

Mellquist, Jerome, *The Emergence of an American Art,* Scribner, 1942.

Mellquist, Jerome, "The Armory Show: Thirty Years Later," *Magazine of Art,* December, 1943, p. 298.

Morris, William, *Architecture, Industry, and Wealth, Collected Papers,* Longmans, Green, 1902.

Munsell, A. H., *A Color Notation,* Ellis, 1913.

National Education Association, *Journal of Proceedings and Addresses, Session of the Year 1894,* the Association, 1895.

Pach, Walter, *Queer Thing, Painting: Forty Years in the World of Art,* Harper, 1938.

Santayana, George, *The Sense of Beauty; Being the Outlines of Aesthetic Theory,* Scribner, 1896.

Sargent, Walter, *Modelling in Public Schools,* Hammett, 1909.

Sargent, Walter, *Instruction in Art in the United States,* Department of Interior, Bureau of Education, No. 43, 1918.

Sargent, Walter, and Miller, Elizabeth E., *Fine and Industrial Arts in Elementary Schools,* Ginn, 1912.

Sargent, Walter, and Miller, Elizabeth E., *How Children Learn to Draw,* Ginn, 1916.

Smith, Margaret Santelle, "Children, Art Museums, and Stories," *American Magazine of Art,* June, 1918.

Stieglitz, Alfred, ed., *Camera Notes,* 1897–1903; published 1903–1917 as *Camera Work.*

Stimson, J. Ward, *The Gate Beautiful*, A. Brandt, 1903.

Sullivan, Louis, *Kindergarten Chats and Other Writings*, Wittenborn Schultz, 1947.

Wright, Frank Lloyd, *On Architecture: Selected Writings 1894–1940*, ed. by Frederick Gutheim, Duell, Sloan and Pearce, 1941.

Wright, Willard Huntington, "Impressionism to Synchronism," *Forum*, December, 1913, p. 757.

Wright, Willard Huntington, *Modern Painting: Its Tendency and Meaning*, Lane, 1915.

Figure 7. The Later Bauhaus Seal, Designed by Oskar Schlemmer, 1922. (From Bayer, Gropius, and Gropius, "Bauhaus 1919–1928"; Branford, 1952.)

VI

Progressive Education

The progressive-education movement has exerted a more widespread influence in American education than anything that came before it. There are people who condemn and distrust what they call progressive education; there are others who resent the slightest criticism of any aspect of "progressive" dogma. The very use of the words "progressive education" has reached a point where it sets off automatic emotional reactions pro and con among those persons who take fixed positions as liberals or conservatives.

Avoiding, as far as possible, the heated misinterpretations of the progressive movement which are current today, and which reflect

152

more upon our times than upon the original apostles of progressivism, let us see how valuable the movement was to the development of art education. There can be little doubt that the art curriculum was expanded in the elementary and high schools and that an extension of some art work into additional thousands of schools was accomplished during the most vigorous decade of the progressive program, the 1920's.

It is currently in order to comment upon the inadequacies and even the downright foolishness of some aspects of progressivism. When such an evaluation is made in an effort to understand the past and to make forward progress, it is justified. But to infer that the whole progressive movement was crazy at best or subversive at worst is to attempt to defeat educational advance. A major portion of this discussion concerns the extent to which art education has developed beyond the position it claimed in 1929. The present healthful and promising outlook for art education is, in my opinion, based on the scholarly inquiry and exploitation of resources in the arts which were so greatly advanced in that postwar decade.

MONTESSORI AND CIZEK

In the closing years of the First World War, two European influences in education were of particular interest to the American art teacher. The first and least permanent was the importation of Montessori-trained teachers in a few places in the United States.

The system developed by Madame Montessori in Rome was enthusiastically praised by English and American visitors. Briefly stated, its characteristics were these: school was held in homes or homelike quarters as pleasantly located and furnished as possible; children were trained to come in and go out as they might in visiting a friendly family, greeting the teacher as a hostess. Activity programs in Montessori classes resembled those of the early kindergarten. They employed ready-made paraphernalia of string, pegs, cardboards, yarns, balls, and so forth. The criticism was made of this curriculum, as it was of the kindergarten, that routine requirements were set up in each activity game and that individualized use of the materials was frowned upon or absolutely refused. Certainly, Madame Montessori left no doubt as to her complete disapproval of the unrestrained, inexpert use of such media as paint and brushes. The physical messiness was as distasteful to her as the aesthetic value of the children's work was unrecognized.

The emphasis upon quiet kindliness, upon dignity and polite restraint of action, was particularly attractive to observers and international visitors. The American schools following the Montessori approach, again like the earlier kindergartens, tended to liberalize their interpretation of the European original.

The second influence was of a more positive and lasting sort in art education, for it consisted of the work of the children's classes of Franz Cizek. Following the London conference of 1908, Cizek had been attracting the attention of many art teachers. During and just after the war, some American and English articles appeared on his work, and shortly afterward groups of the work of his children were sent out on exhibition to both countries. The work itself, brilliant in color, large in scale, together with the occasional articles of appreciation and teachers' convocation talks that had been made since 1908, were bound to shape the teaching of some of the younger and more experimentally minded teachers. Many acknowledged their debt to Cizek during the twenties.

"THE CHILD" ARRIVES

With the end of the war late in 1918, many ideas for improving education, shelved for the duration of the conflict, emerged.

By the middle of the next decade (1925), the ideals and practices of progressive education were firmly established, as were the personnel and some institutional framework to give the ideals wide circulation.

There is every indication in the philosophy of William James, the early practice and philosophy of Dewey, the child-study movement, of a time when the relatively uninhibited activity and the unfixed interests of the child would come to dominate temporarily the approach to teaching. For a century of public education, textbooks and a fixed quantity of factual subject matter had been of prime importance. Then, as the psychologists became better acquainted with children and the philosophers left the realm of the ideal society for a more pragmatic interpretation of human acts and motives, it was

154

to be expected that education should be approached from the point of view of those to be educated rather than from the angle of what constituted an adequate store of knowledge.

It was believed by the educational leaders and experimenters after 1920 that creative activity and the development of children's natural interests could be relied upon to produce a curriculum better than the older ones. Most of the nineteenth-century curricula, it was assumed, were established by adults with little understanding of children, or of the learning processes.

The forms of art expression were inevitably pushed as the most creative of all possible child activity. Margaret Mathias, a Teachers College, Columbia University, graduate, taught as supervisor of art in the Cleveland Heights public schools in the early twenties. Demonstrating the results of that work, in 1924 she published the book, *The Beginnings of Art in the Public Schools.* It is still a classic, though now more often overlooked than read.

Patty Smith Hill's Introduction states, on the philosophical level, the approach of the art teacher in a progressive-education curriculum. She wrote: "Art ceases to be art in Miss Mathias's scheme of education, if any form or technique, no matter how good, is imposed from without. In other words, if it fails to grow out of the child's own expression and feeling of need as they lead on to higher levels of appreciation and control." [1]

This philosophy was interpreted throughout the rest of the book by its author. Her concern for influences like the work of Cizek is evident. His wide variety of art media, his encouragement of the children to use the studio as an artist might, were taken over by Miss Mathias. Her work did not parallel the approaches of the Montessori group except as they both used tangible materials for child activity.

Art in the Cleveland Heights school was based on child growth in the use of the materials and, more than that, on child expression of ideas. The need children have to give expression to their developing concepts of the life they know was dwelt upon at length. An outline of "Steps in the Artistic Process" was given. Manipulation was the first step and referred to the almost universal desire to feel, to try

[1] Margaret Mathias, *The Beginnings of Art in the Public Schools,* Scribner, 1924, p. ix.

out, to experiment with materials, to see what happens to them. The stage of symbolism was used by Mathias to cover roughly all the work a child does which is only vaguely representative or naturalistic, but which he describes positively as a cow, a tree, or whatever else it "symbolizes" for the moment. The third stage was that of realism.

Under educational principles, she states one axiom which, if taken alone, could indicate the kind of drifting attitude toward education which critics of the progressive movement are so emphatic about: "Training is harmful when it precedes the development of the power to be trained. Training should, therefore, be given as the need for it arises and is felt by the children." [2]

It is dubious, however, that the art work in Cleveland Heights was on any catch-as-catch-can basis. Problems were to be provided that would "lead to growth and development." Children must develop the "ability to use individual liberty and so respect the rights of others," and the "ability to give and take constructive criticism."

In the chapter *"Materials Suited to Child Experiences,"* [3] the author is factual and altogether helpful. She concedes that some material is not useful at certain ages; that other media will serve as well. Much of the rest of the volume deals at length with standard materials and their potentialities: clay, wood, cloth, paint, and by-products.

Extremes in child freedom of expression were to be found in the twenties and early thirties, but more often the plea for creative activity was modified sensibly, as in Mathias' outline of the materials and their usefulness at various age levels.

The need for creative experience with materials to be physically handled and shaped was eagerly accepted by all progressive educators. Since 1924, we have taken that need as a point of departure. The great contribution of progressive education has been continued as we have investigated the nature of the art expression and the psychological bases for the individual's means of communication.

WHAT DEVELOPS "ART APPRECIATION"?

One other aspect of the arts claimed by the progressive group to be of paramount importance was that of art appreciation. It was as-

[2] *Ibid.,* p. 10.
[3] *Ibid.,* p. 12.

sumed to be an outcome of art expression. Miss Mathias stated the problem in this way: "If we are to hope for a society with art appreciation and some ability to meet art problems, an adequate art course must provide for developing ability for self-expression and for understanding the expression of others." [4]

Simple and straightforward, this dual objective of expression and appreciation for education in the arts appeared in all the aims and purposes of several valuable publications of the time.

The Francis W. Parker School in 1925 brought out a study on *Creative Effort* as one of its Studies in Education. Teachers contributed from the fields of writing, melody, rhythm, design, drawing and painting, clay work, and shop. Characteristic expressions of the new faith were made by the faculty contributors.

We presuppose that in varying degrees and with wide individual divergencies and tendencies, all normal children possess impulses to create . . . All normal children have the right to live in a rich environment, to exercise to the full all their powers of expression, and to have every avenue to their souls open and in use. . . . "Given freedom, children will create. This we say over and over.[5]

The Progressive Education Association, in the most ambitious project it had ever attempted for its new magazine, *Progressive Education,* produced an entire number on "The Creative Experience." It was dated April-May-June 1926. Without doubt its contributors reached the pinnacle of optimistic certitude on the topic of the child and the arts. (See Figure 8, page 158, for an illustration of a child's creative work.) Hughes Mearns expressed the hope and faith of the day: what past ages had not achieved might yet be possible—and through the agency of the school helping the child to attain his full stature.

In the lead article, "The Creative Spirit and Its Significance for Education," Mearns wrote: ". . . but adults are in the main wingless; convention, tribal taboos, mechanistic living, long years of schooling, something has stilled the spirit within or walled it securely. It is to children we must go to see the creative spirit at its

[4] *Ibid.,* p. 1.
[5] Francis W. Parker School, Studies in Education, *Creative Effort,* the School, Vol. 3, 1925.

Figure 8. Linoleum Block Print by Twelve-Year-Old Child, Carson College, Flourtown, Pennsylvania. (From Hartman and Shumaker, "Creative Expression," John Day, 1939, and "Progressive Education," Vol. III, No. 2, 1926.)

Figure 9. Grade VII. Line and Dark and Light, Designs for Glazed Bowls. (From Belle Boas, "Art in the School," Doubleday, 1924; now pub. by Odyssey Press.)

best; and only to those children who are in some measure unco-
erced." [6]

Mearns, like Mathias, was aware of limitations, of adaptations and
refinements due to come as the years interpreted their work. "Education is at last learning to use the natural creative impulses. At
present it is experimenting and the results are good; it has no assured techniques as yet, but the beginnings are in sight." [7]

Appreciation of art as a primary motif runs through the magazine,
but nowhere as extensively nor as roundly as by Frederick G. Bonser
in "My Art Creed":

> I believe:
> That life itself is the finest of all arts and that its richest realization is
> art's supreme excuse for being. . . .
> That the mission of art is to teach a love of beautiful clothes, beautiful
> households, beautiful utensils, beautiful surroundings, and all to the end
> that life itself may be rich and full of beauty in its harmony, its purposes,
> its ideals. . . .
> That all progress in art lies in the expression of the experiences, the
> hopes, the ideals, and the aspirations of our own times, and of our own
> lives.

Bonser followed those three statements, somewhat optimistic as
they are, with a reaching for the infinite which harks back to Hegel
by way of the rational psychology of Harris:

> [I believe] That the appreciation of beauty in the thousand common
> things of daily life will result in the final appreciation of beauty as a dis-
> sociated ideal. [8]

In a book *Art in the School,* Belle Boas tried to assure forward-
looking art teachers that the coming of good taste and aesthetic
judgment into the lives of the young was just as sure as their eagerness to develop creative expression. (An example from the book will
be found in Figure 9, page 158.) She wrote: "Probably no one who
has been drilled in design will be content with chaos and discord. If
he can be made profoundly miserable when in contact with them he
will have gone a long way toward eliminating them. . . . All a

[6] Hughes Mearns, "The Creative Spirit and Its Significance for Education: The
Creative Experience," *Progressive Education,* June, 1926, p. 97.
[7] *Ibid.,* p. 101.
[8] Frederick G. Bonser, "My Art Creed," *Progressive Education,* June, 1926, p. 104.

teacher can do is to produce dissatisfaction with evil; he cannot compel the attainment of good." [9] This negative note underlines the dubious hopes entertained for any large-scale change in public appreciation of the arts.

Art expression on an individualized basis and the analysis of fine art as to its qualities of line, mass, structure, dark and light values, and color—these were to be the keys to art appreciation. While we no longer feel that they will accomplish the job, we are not positive about either a substitute or a means of amplification. It is time, however, that we try to make a distinction between the "art appreciation" of 1926 and alertness to the much greater span of values implied by Dewey in his classic, *Art as Experience*.

A step in the right direction would be that of junking the term "art appreciation." It suggests an activity almost impossible to experience for millions of American citizens. A work of art, a masterpiece, is an object of rarity. Most works of art are believed to be in museums; and a few, in the shape of buildings, are in faraway cities, frequently in Europe. Hence, to urge the importance of art appreciation is, in most students' minds, a request to become vicariously excited over a remote object existing for them only in a small reproduction.

There is too great a limitation in the connotation that has grown up around the word appreciation; we think of polite tea-table chatter when we really hope for strongly held creative convictions upon which people will take action.

We have continued to develop in the creative work of the art classroom since the twenties. The drive to give an organized expression to experience, and the frustrations which hamper expression, have been made more familiar to us by the psychologists. We are better equipped to encourage individual creation because we know child development in the arts and something about the most marked differences in personality types and their influence on art production. Herbert Read and Viktor Lowenfeld have supplied us with more material than we have learned to handle.

But in the development of mature aesthetic judgments, a comparable progress has not been made. For the majority of the American

[9] Belle Boas, *Art in the School*, Doubleday, 1924, p. 3.

people art is still held captive to the tradition of the framed painting in oils. Art is a product of dead men, or of other countries than our own, or it is a property to be owned by wealthy people or museums, an object famous enough to be written about in book or magazine. The tendency among artists and teachers to rely upon the relative handful of famous works and famous artists to explain elements of quality in art simply reinforces this attitude.

Any college student taking a survey course in art is much more likely to be informed about the aesthetic quality, the structure, the glass, the sculpture, and the sociological and economic background of Chartres Cathedral than about any structure in his home town or state. When we come back to this side of the Atlantic in our search for quality, we find ourselves still in a rut, with most texts published showing, as representing the best in historical or regional development, the same buildings and the same old paintings for which photos are easily obtainable. It is no wonder that children and adults grow up to feel that art is not in their community; has nothing to do with their lives.

The building arts which American schoolchildren grow up with include the mass-produced Cape Cod cottages, the new drive-in shopping areas, and the Victorian mansions. These are what the teacher of art needs to deal with. His knowledge, his firsthand observations of masterworks wherever he has traveled, are needed to find and to make known to his students the individual qualities of their immediate environment.

Pictorial arts have been approached in the same way as have the design and architectural arts. The teacher's professional background has been such that he has emphasized works foreign to his students. For them, movies, advertising, magazines, comics, television, are a major part of their experience. And they too often find that what the instructor counts as important art does not help them to form qualitative habits of seeing. Picasso's *Guernica,* powerful as it is, may be a poor piece to dwell upon for many students, and the work of Baziotes is beyond the sympathies of most beginners in thinking about pictures. As in the development of their own painting, art understanding can be built only upon the basis of the individual's experience.

Kouwenhoven, Giedion, Pearson, and others are helping us to see what the relationships are between Bill Mauldin and Daumier, Piet Mondrian and Radio City, the Marx Brothers and Aristophanes. The problem for the art teacher dealing with children from the sixth grade and upward is that of finding and making opportunities paralleling class activities, of calling attention to the aesthetic content of the world the children know. The great contribution that Giedion and others have made is that of helping us to see how the excellent, the really bad, and the oversupply of the mediocre, taken altogether for any period of time, constitute the soil from which the finest art forms spring. The child who lives engrossed in the comics is satisfying his aesthetic hunger with cheap and vulgar fare, to use Dewey's terminology. But the tragicomic masterpiece, Charlie Chaplin's *Gold Rush*, will be found to appeal to the same hunger. As the child approaches and enters high school, he is capable of making some of the analyses necessary to understand the contrast between ephemeral and lasting works.

It will always remain the teacher's task to grow in his own vision and judgment and to guide his students' growth with all the materials that can be found. When the teacher begins this job, he must demonstrate the personal courage and ability to apply his broader background to a stimulating use of the resources of the child's environment. He must use clippings, slides, motion pictures, TV programs, as he thinks they can be assimilated. But no amount of these materials frees him from the responsibility of finding qualitative distinctions for the child to grasp among the buildings in his home town, the automobiles on the street, the movies shown in the local theater and on the network TV screen, as well as among the objects that may be shown in the local art museum.

Appreciation of the arts, which was to have grown casually as a by-product of individual art expression, has to give way to deliberate education in aesthetic awareness. Because a boy paints with an intense emotional projection, particularly strong in color relationships, we no longer count on an automatic emergence of his aesthetic judgment. But when the intellect is ready (that may be any age from eight to twelve), his interest in everything—paintings and automobiles, technicolor and public-park gardens—can be enlarged by

162

becoming conscious of comparative values. For such a boy, his dominant expressive use of color might well determine and be the chief enrichment of his individual vision of all these things.

As Mearns put it, ". . . we have no assured techniques in sight," but we realize that "appreciation" should be improved upon by an aesthetic awareness as fixed a part of the personality as the sense of balance.

THE PATRONS OF PROGRESSIVE EDUCATION

Progressive education at the pioneering height of its influence, and when it was most concerned with the power of expression in the arts, was distinctly a manifestation of its own time. In the 1920's many artists, writers, and musicians took up more or less permanent residence in Europe because they found their American contemporaries, to use Hughes Mearns' words, "wingless . . . stifled in tribal taboos."

Schools which eagerly welcomed progressive ideas were for the most part public schools in wealthy suburbs or private schools in still wealthier areas. It was as if the people whose frustrations Sinclair Lewis so aptly described in *Main Street* and *Babbitt* were hoping to secure to their children a more fruitful and sensitive experience in life. The outspoken criticism of editors like H. L. Mencken and George Jean Nathan regarding the aesthetic illiteracy of the American middle class must have impressed many of its victims. To some of these the liberating influence of an education which dealt first with the children and their unbounded potentialities promised a next generation free from the deserved rebuke of the critics.

The same people who had interested themselves in the Armory Show were aware of the exhibit of Cizek's classwork. After the Armistice the Provincetown Playhouse group stimulated a tremendous growth of American traditions in playwriting, and in the new designing of the theater stage. Every step taken in the theater, every artist exploring the directions suggestion by the Armory Show, were familiar to the people active in the new movement in education. As one example of many, it may be noted that Mrs. Avery Coonley, for whom one of the greatest of the pre-1914 Frank Lloyd Wright houses was built, was the patron who made possible the use of the many expensive art color plates in *Progressive Education* magazine.

Maturing art interests in the theater, architecture, literature, painting, music, became a force in the schools, increasing and improving art education in particular.

Another impulse toward improving education was that of the negative social aspects of the twenties; recognition of current social evils became a goad to discover a more adequate education, one which might claim that its aim was to create values in life and in action rather than in "mere" book learning. The bootlegging era of prohibition, with its widespread law violation and the rise of frighteningly efficient gangs; the vast apparent increase in general prosperity, artificial though it might be; the radical change in relationships between men and women—these movements were a great menace to the stability of young people. Progressive education offered the hope that children active from an early age in educational pursuits aimed at self-reliance and the development of the individual would take such social turbulence easily. A child creatively educated might have a power of judgment and selection that would guide him past the dead ends of dissipation, of unrestrained sensuality, of too exclusive a reliance on economic success.

It has been suggested, too, that the reason education turned in this liberal direction for salvation from general laxity in society was a superficial but generally accepted interpretation of the Freudian theories. Such an interpretation accepted the notion that many personality defects were, without qualification, the product of needlessly strict inhibitions imposed on most of us during childhood. After 1918 there was considerable belief in the idea that almost all inhibitions were stifling and dangerous. To a parent holding this doctrine, the more-flexible educational plans appeared as a great improvement over the strict regime through which he had suffered.

PROFESSIONAL STABILIZATION: THE 1920's

Had the progressive pattern of art education come into existence in only a few schools through the enthusiasm of a few gifted teachers like Mathias, Mearns, and Boas, it might not have spread its influence as we find it today. The groundwork of the past had been solid enough, however, to support a good company of teachers who welcomed the expansion of outlook and furthered the acceptance of public art education in the 1920's.

One group of teachers concerned themselves with the place of the arts in the complex structure of the American public-school system. C. Valentine Kirby in Pennsylvania, William G. Whitford of Chicago University, Leon L. Winslow in Baltimore, and Sallie Tannahill in New York taught and wrote extensively. As school organization financially and sociopolitically was of paramount interest in the twenties and early thirties, it was inevitable that the status of the arts and art education should be examined in those terms.

Kirby's little volume on *The Business of Teaching and Supervising the Arts* was printed in 1927, Winslow's *Organization and Teaching of Art* in 1928, Whitford's *An Introduction to Art Education* in 1929, Tannahill's *Fine Arts for Public School Administrators* in 1932, and Klar, Winslow, and Kirby's *Art Education in Principle and Practice* in 1933.

In each of these volumes a statement on the aims of art education underscores the authors' belief in creative experience. These leading educators reflected the cumulative growth of a "child-centered" philosophy of art expression. All of them, too, expressed their hopes for improved social and civic life as one of the outcomes of education in the arts. Their major preoccupations dealt with the art teacher's relationships to every aspect of the school and surrounding community. Suggestions were made to help the art teacher-supervisor meet elementary teachers, pupils, principals, and parents, each on his own level of interest. Outlines were worked out for courses of study, subject-matter areas, the ordering of supplies, and the keeping of inventories, all in the most businesslike manner possible.

Most of the volumes go into the problem of art appreciation, and in doing so reveal a still-considerable gap between their art interests and the work of the artists of the time.

Whitford is the most exhaustive of the group. His survey of art needs, courses of study, theory and methods of art instruction, tests, and measurements is detailed and outlined in charts (Figure 11). The Klar, Winslow, and Kirby book follows somewhat the same pat-

Figure 10. Space and Line Elements in "Purposeful Design." (From Teachers College Arts and Crafts Club, "Art and Industry in Education," 1912.)

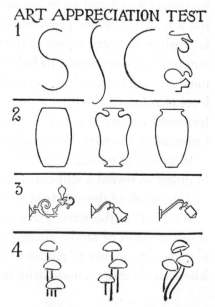

ART APPRECIATION TEST

Figure 11. (From William G. Whitford, "An Introduction to Art Education," Appleton, 1929.)

tern, with perhaps more emphasis on the museum as an art resource and upon the integration of art activities with other subject matters.

Tannahill's book, frankly addressed as propaganda for the administrator, puts a greater value on the nature of the creative experience than do the others. It is a persuasive tract, putting the argument for art education in concise form for principals and superintendents.

An evaluation of the place and the worth of this kind of art-education leadership is necessary. Unlike the thinking and record of work coming from the unusual classroom teacher, it tends to be a little prosaic in content and phraseology. But what might have been the outcome for the arts in public education in this period and in other eras if the insights of Parker, Dow, Mathias, etc., were not given the support of men and women whose contribution is that of organization? Sometimes the organizational framework is too cumbersome for its avowed purpose; sometimes it is so impressive it frightens the teacher away from using the material except in small parts. Occasionally the basis of interest in the arts appears only barely discernible in the heaping up of charts, diagrams, and lists.

But texts of this nature provided a framework for art curricula. They have been used through the country in teacher-training schools and colleges, where their value has been in the building up of confidence that art classes may be sensibly, carefully established, and that the objectives of art education have an important place in the schools.

Organization applied to school and social forces was not the only effort to organize in the art education of the twenties. In the field of design and composition there were influential teachers able to provide leadership. George J. Cox's *Art for Amateur and Student* (1926) was the best of several works which used Dow's earlier text on composition as its basis. Cox, following Dow's principles and elements with certain variations and improvements, wrote a book accompanied by well-selected plates which added greatly to the student's ability to see art forms through the media of the author's definitions. Cox's use of superior and poor work comparatively on the same plate was excellent. His shortcoming was still to treat three-dimensional forms as two-dimensional façades and to see their design as a combination of views like an architect's drawing.

167

Charles de Garmo as early as 1913 discussed the aesthetic qualities evident in the automobile.[10] The *Essentials of Design*, produced with Leon Winslow in 1924, showed an awareness of the industrial-design problem. The Goldstein sisters' well-known volume, *Art in Everyday Life* (1925), anticipated the more-explicit design approaches to materials and techniques which were to be shown in the machine-art exhibits of the thirties.

Design, as these teachers saw it, had already ceased to be a decorative motif cribbed from nature and pasted in some form on a surface. By way of the William Morris tradition, they were looking for design in the structure, for an understanding and feel for material in the craftsmanship of each object. Like Arthur Wesley Dow in his last magazine article, they were as alert to the changing and growing values in aesthetics as any artist-designer in the country; this on the part of persons primarily active in teaching was a good omen for the future.

DEPRESSION DECADE

The economic depression, beginning in 1929 and reaching its most distressing depth in the election year of 1932, set apart in complete relief the decade of the twenties and that of the thirties. Art education matured in the thirties. Professional art schools moved forward more rapidly than ever before, and in every phase of art education an integration of philosophy, of new practices arrived at in Europe, of psychology, of more exact studies of the nature of the arts, was at least begun before the bombing of Pearl Harbor in December, 1941.

Part of the forward movement of the thirties was due to the depression itself and to the public agencies inaugurated to cope with deflation and economic disaster. But significantly, a large share of the growth and improvement in art education can be traced to the continued good health of American institutions and foundations, and to the alertness of the people who set them up and the professional personnel carrying on the work. A recapitulation of the state of art education in 1929 is essential for understanding later accomplishments.

[10] Charles de Garmo, *Aesthetic Education*, Bardeen, 1913.

ART EDUCATION IN 1929: THE ELEMENTARY SCHOOL

The most advanced position in education in the visual and plastic arts in 1929 seems to have been that of the best teaching done in the elementary schools. Children were using as media the ordinary water colors, the powdered dry colors, crayons, and chalks. Small-size drawing papers were still much in use, but large-size papers were more and more common. If anything, there was an overemphasis upon the need for encouraging young children to draw, and particularly to paint in large and bold fashion. Paintings done by children in the grades up to and including the sixth were, at their best, freely conceived, painted in personal and brilliant color, and individual in the drawing of form. Already the relationship of the best of children's work to the work of the German expressionists and the French Fauves was being understood, not that children were maturing at an excessively early age, nor that some contemporary professional artists were attempting deliberately and witlessly to retrogress. Rather, the professionals sought the emphatic statements possible when color and forms on the canvas were used arbitrarily and independently of naturalistic appearance. At the same time, the thoughtful teachers of children were aware that a child using reds, oranges, and blues strongly to create a spring landscape was doing so to suggest the verve, the wonderful excitement of his response to living in a manner which he would lose altogether if required to make his whole painting in cautious repetitions of green pigment. The advanced painters and some young children were achieving an emotional expression foreign to academic drawing, to school "studies" of still life.

HIGH-SCHOOL ART AND ART SCHOOLS

In the schools only the progressive elementary curricula showed much concern with changing art concepts. The high school continued to teach a watered-down version of art-school drawing, and to adorn craft objects in clay, leather, or wood with slightly stiffened versions of *art nouveau* decoration. Here and there in the crafts, slight manifestations of cubism had appeared.

In the high schools, as well as in the professional art schools, the encroachment of courses in painting and finally in composition was almost complete. It is more than a little difficult for us now to consider composition courses as a radical innovation, but it took almost fifty years to establish them firmly as part of a desirable art background. By 1920 a professional art student could expect to be in a drawing class for his full four years, but he would also expect to begin some approach to creative pictorial composition, especially during his last two years. Even there, draftsmanship was still dominantly naturalistic or representative; though advanced teachers were overly insistent that the subject matter was of no interest, and that the form, the design, was the only truly significant aspect of any good painting. Clive Bell's dictum was in general circulation; a thirteenth-century altarpiece or a landscape by Seurat were equally masterpieces because they possessed "significant form." [11] For the moment, the place of these respective works in social contexts, the intent of the artist, were matters of little or no concern. The Chicago critic, Bulliett, wrote a book, *Apples and Madonnas,* the theme of which was established by the statement that an apple by Cézanne was of equal significance with a madonna by Raphael.[12]

As a consequence, the chief characteristic of study in an art school was a painful, introverted effort to achieve "significant form," when all the while most students were still struggling with conventional form representation problems of the usual subject matters, still life, landscape, and figures.

Technical study of media was slight, and not very good, being for the most part little personal recipes and tricks achieved by the teacher in the course of his own painting. There was widespread advocacy of devices like dynamic symmetry in pictorial organization, or like "scientifically" set color arrangements for the palette. Drawing, painting, and, in the larger schools, sculpture were the only serious occupations of the professional student.

Craft media, lettering, commercial arts, design, all were considered lesser activities taken by students majoring in education or commercial art; the determined fine-arts student took such courses before leaving school only as a kind of last resort to help him eke out an income.

[11] Clive Bell, *Art,* Stokes, 1913.
[12] C. J. Bulliett, *Apples and Madonnas,* Covici Friede, 1930.

In the years since 1929, courses and course content in art schools have changed immensely. Colleges and universities have entered the field of professional studio courses in art, as they had only timidly begun to do then. But to record only the change in courses would be relatively meaningless. For the whole concept of the arts and art education has been clarified and broadened since that time. To the considerable distress of many artists and teachers, drawing and painting from the nude are not likely again to dominate the art experience of the professional art student of the next half century. In important aspects of his work he will be closer psychologically to the successful child painter. At the same time the professional art student will take for granted an acquisition of technical skills in many media which his counterpart of the 1920's would not have believed possible.

A great body of philosophy, scholarly studies of the past, research projects, governmental sponsorship of the arts, museum education, and art historical scholarships dealing with the arts in Europe, Asia, among primitive peoples, and in contemporary as well as historical periods—all came to something of a climax in professional art education before the entry of the United States into war with Japan and Germany.

INDUSTRIAL DESIGN AND THE BAUHAUS

Industrial design in this country is sometimes designated by its best early performers as a product of the depression. One reads that the effort of leading railroads to recapture passenger traffic drifting to the motor buses and to the private automobile led to the designing of the first streamlined, air-conditioned, refurnished coach and sleeper trains on runs between important cities. Of course, the effort to relate art to the environment, to make the designing of everything from communities to kitchen pots a concern of the artist, did not spring into existence only with the coming of the depression. Some artists and art teachers have always been interested in that legitimate activity for the designer, as witness the discerning words of Horatio Greenough in 1848–1851 discussed in Chapter II.

But we can be reasonably accurate in assuming that the practice of designing for the huge mass production of American industry in the twentieth century, by artists competent to deal with the machin-

171

ery, began with the attempt to find markets during the depression years. And with the development of industrial design came a new orientation in the practice of art and in art education.

As always, there were roots in the past. Artists have seen what is needed and what must come long before it actually arrives. The Italian futurists had publicly announced their desire to live in and by the mechanisms of the twentieth century. Their "manifesto" of 1909 is now seen to have overtones of the fascism of the Black Shirts, but their disgust with trying to be artists in the twentieth century, in a country where the chief industry is the adoration of the arts of dead men, has continued to strike a responsive chord in most artists of this century. Such a sensitive and appreciative visitor to Italy as Henry James expressed virtually the same plea for arts, for building, for thoughts appropriate to our time, for minimizing the nostalgia for the past.[13]

Dadaists in Paris after the First World War were even more violent on this score than the futurists. They proposed to junk all aesthetic values belonging to the past. The present and its inevitably mechanistic future they would glorify, and, to show what they meant, it was believed entirely appropriate to use sections of toilet and bathroom plumbing as collage material in a dadaist exhibit.

At the time the dadaists were making their serious postwar jokes, another group of men were painting canvases using only severe forms based on rectangles, cylinders, and geometric forms and lines, and doing some three-dimensional pieces in complexly interrelated solid geometrical forms. These "purists," so-called, included men who later did more work in architecture than in painting, as well as in typographical design and design for industry. Those who continued to paint continued also to relate their work with what they believed to be the inevitable, the right direction, for all the arts of our time. Le Corbusier, Leger, Oud, Mondrian, were all of this period and of this conviction.

This direction was uncompromising revelation in all things of the structural pattern and the materials used. A house depending on steel and concrete and glass for its support and its sheathing from the weather would show those materials freely, as well as the proba-

[13] F. O. Matthiessen, *The James Family*, Knopf, 1948, pp. 289–290.

ble arrangement of space within, to all who might glance at it or examine it closely. There was to be no concealment of iron posts by concrete molds of Corinthian pillar, no thin casing of marble precariously pinned on a concrete wall, no elaborately carved sills and moldings to mitigate the shape of a window rectangle in a flat concrete wall.

When an able group of artists starts to think in terms quite rigorously clearing away and rejecting the ingrained habits of the immediate past, it is only a short time before someone will begin to plan a school curriculum to develop the new thinking in a group of students.

The German Bauhaus, first of Weimar and then of Dessau, came into existence as the first great school to establish a twentieth-century art curriculum.

Walter Gropius, assuredly one of the most valuable artist-teachers who ever lived, agreed during the years of the First World War to take over the direction of a combined institution at Weimar, which included the old crafts-and-design school and the fine-arts academy. The agreement he reached with the Duke of Weimar, when he began work in 1919, gave him as great a freedom to recruit staff and to establish a pattern of studies as might be desired.

What was accomplished by the Bauhaus, as the new institution resulting from the merger was named, was unique in art education, and has had to be understood and used to an extent by every worthwhile art school of our day.

Gropius, together with the talented men who joined him on the faculty, believed that a school in which many art forms were being taught and each art activity influenced the other was unquestionably the best possible improvement over the classical academy.

The effort to deal with more than hours and days and years of routine life drawing and painting was a clearly revolutionary concept. Painting, sculpture, architecture, typography, ceramics, metal work, photography, and motion pictures were all counted as important art media. A new kind of elementary course had to be created. The plan was to devise a first-year experience which would acquaint the young student with the common and unique qualities of all the usual materials: wood, metal, paper, glass, stone, plastics, textiles,

173

rubber, etc. Use of the material was to be approached so as to exploit and handle freely the inherent qualities: flexibility, brittleness, reaction to heat and cold, tools possible to use, forms which could be created, combinations of materials, and many other possible analyses. All students planning for work in any of the specialized fields worked in this first studio course. Josef Albers, Johannes Itten, and Moholy-Nagy developed the work and, since its start, contributed most to spreading its influence in Europe and America.

This is the activity from the Bauhaus best known to America. Josef Albers brought his interpretation of it to Black Mountain College in North Carolina in 1933. Later Moholy-Nagy, inaugurating the Institute of Design in Chicago, as a matter of course designed a first year of work based on the old Bauhaus principles. The abstract paper-sculpture forms, the carved sculptural "handies," the wire-mesh three-dimensional forms, the photograms, the collages of all kinds of material and textures, and the painstakingly done representational drawings of small objects and surfaces are easily recognized problems emanating from the practices of the first year of the Bauhaus training.

To ignore this aspect of training in the arts today is well-nigh impossible. Unfortunately, as is frequently the case, far too many teachers and schools of narrow vision have only seized specific problems from the Bauhaus to replace their old regime of six weeks on a charcoal study of the values to be seen on a plaster cast. The basis for such work in a constantly fresh approach to each material, and in the potentialities of tools and processes, may too easily be lost to view.

As Bauhaus students went on in their work, they became more specialized. And another distinctive approach of that faculty to education in the arts was exhibited in the specialized work. First of all, every student upon graduation was expected to qualify for a journeyman's license in his craft as far as technical skill was concerned. Second, each teacher in a major field was expected to be a first-rate artist in that work. For several years this necessitated two people in some crafts—an artist-designer and a craftsman. Later it was possible to complete the faculty with men and women who combined design competence with the craft technical background. Here, too, the influence upon American art-school practice is becoming apparent as we see more splendid artist-craftsman teaching in many of our high schools and in professional departments and colleges.

Some kind of coöperation between the senior student designers of the Bauhaus and German industry was hoped for, but, though a beginning had been made, some products actually being placed on the market, the internal trouble of Germany first seriously interfered with the school; Gropius resigned in 1928; and then, after Hitler took over, closed it for good in 1933.

The most vigorous period of the school was from 1919–1928. But its influence in America was slight until the post-depression years. Partly, I believe, the stimulus of our growing field of industrial design turned American art schools toward the Bauhaus program. Partly, the general interest of art professionals and particularly of museum curators in the art of the machine directed educational thought to that school which had done so much to comprehend and instruct its students to work for machine production.

In 1933, the New York Museum of Modern Art held an exhibition on "Machine Art," for which Philip Johnston wrote an excellent and influential catalogue. The show was circulated in many museums on an extensive tour. "Machine Art," as elegantly set forth in the museum, was a relatively new term for this country; but it was inevitable that design for industry, the attention paid to the products of industry by the more active museums, and the spreading knowledge of the curricular innovations of the Bauhaus should come to have an influence in American schools.

The largest full-scale recognition and public display of the Bauhaus work in the United States came at the Museum of Modern Art in 1939. By that time magazine articles were being published on the subject, and it was only a question of time before the more intelligent schools began making direct use of the principles of Bauhaus education. In 1944 Gyorgy Kepes published his *Language of Vision*, and in 1947 Moholy-Nagy's *Vision in Motion* was published posthumously. Both books have enjoyed a large circulation and have been used as texts of the new design.

Moholy-Nagy and most of the other Bauhaus teachers and former students would emphasize, as the first Bauhaus contribution to education, recognition of the need for developing the individual, drawing forth in each personality those unique creative potentialities which each individual and particularly the art student may be expected to possess. In the Bauhaus publications and in the works published in America since 1933 by those who took part in this rare scholastic enterprise, it is the first objective mentioned.

"The most important task is the liberation from dead convention in favor of individual experiences and revelations." Thus Sibyl Moholy-Nagy quotes from the early Bauhaus program of the foundation course.[14]

Yet, it is a question whether that emphasis is the greatest contribution the Bauhaus made to schools in America. First, an art education which hoped to develop the strength and growth of the individual was in full swing here at the same time the Bauhaus was starting its work. Teachers like Robert Henri and Kimon Nikolaides were striving toward that goal during and after the First World War. The influence of Dow and Dewey in teacher education was to aid in the effort. American schools using only slight variations in content from the academic regimes of the nineteenth century were, nevertheless, aiming at the kind of a school experience and independent thinking necessary to produce strongly individual artists and artist teachers.

What the Bauhaus provided was a broader range of experiences in materials to accomplish the purposes of individual development. It could be and has been argued that only the experimental attitude toward materials and processes which the Bauhaus faculty originated could offer a range of experience ample for countless individual expressions; that any art-school experience based only on a small number of media in life drawing, painting, and composition was so constrained that individual development would necessarily be limited too. There is a degree of truth in thus defining the handicap of limitation in materials. There is even more justice in supposing that conventional practices can breed conventional minds.

However, a minimum of materials, employed by teachers who are seeking and showing by example a maximum of individualized in-

[14] Sibyl Moholy-Nagy, "Letter to the Editor," *College Art Journal*, Spring, 1951, p. 271.

terpretation, can develop students capable of future growth when material limitations may have changed.

So it can be argued that the Bauhaus showed this country's best art teachers how better to implement a creative teaching which they had been working at ever since the first efforts of men like Eakins, Stieglitz, and later the Eight.

Whether or not one may with scholarly certainty state that the Bauhaus' inventions for students, deriving from an urge to provide forms for individual growth, were of greater ultimate importance than the philosophy, it is obviously true that the Bauhaus' instructional devices used in a context of prescribed routine can be just as stultifying as the academic procedures they displace. Both an experimental approach to materials and a planned freedom for student development are essential to the valuable coördination of Bauhaus discoveries and all subsequent art education.

THE MUSEUM OF MODERN ART

Not the first but one of the best points of contact between what the Bauhaus had been, and had hoped to become, and our American art development was the catalogue written by the Gropiuses and Herbert Bayer and issued by the Museum of Modern Art in New York for the 1939 Bauhaus exhibit.[15]

Museums all over the United States had been working slowly in the direction mapped out by John Cotton Dana and Newark. The Museum of Modern Art was incorporated in 1929 and began its work in a converted mansion on the site of the present building, which was erected in 1938–1939. The Modern has led all other museums in certain functions; in others, it has carried on superlatively well practices established before its inception. Not just in sponsorship of the Bauhaus exhibit, but in several other fields, the Modern seemed to find for itself museum duties which others had not assumed and which now seem peculiarly appropriate to it.

Its series of exhibits in the 1930's—starting with the comparative exhibit of Art Nouveau and Design of 1933, followed by Machine Art, then presenting the Objects of Everyday Use, the work of the

[15] H. Bayer and W. and Ise Gropius, *Bauhaus, 1919–1933*, Museum of Modern Art, 1900.

Aalto group in Finland, the competitions in organic furniture design, the Bauhaus showing—focused attention on furniture, textiles, household objects, and the precise beauty of machine-made tools as no amount of writing could do. For each of the shows, handsomely illustrated and well-edited catalogues were printed. In exhibiting such material, the museum was not an originator. We can recall the forerunners, the thinkers who made such museum exhibitions virtually a necessity, from our reading of the work of contemporary art historians, including Nicholas Pevsner, Herbert Read, Lewis Mumford, Siegfried Giedion, W. R. Lethaby, Charles De Garmo, and others.

Preservation of the monuments of the art of motion picture became one of the Modern's unique historical and educational functions. This task, begun in 1935 as the Film Library, has achieved enormous proportions in the size of collections and, quite as important, in the widespread circulation and showing of its films. Few small or large museums in the United States have failed to run some of the series of films from the Film Library files.

MUSEUM EDUCATION IN THE DEPRESSION

A curious twist in human affairs caused the decade of the thirties to be particularly fruitful in the arts. As employment and payrolls dropped during 1929–1930 and 1931, little time or energy went into new enterprises in anything. But eventually the whole population began to accommodate itself to an economically stringent regime. As it did so, all over the country museums, libraries, the programs of free summer concerts, the adult evening classes in vocational schools, all reported a steadily expanding and an intensely serious patronage from all age groups and from a cross section of intellectual and educational backgrounds.

Catering to this large and eager clientele, the American museums of art which possessed collections and endowments permitting some creative activity entered a period of educational exhibits never before equaled. Certain types of ventures stand out in retrospect. First in public attendance and probably in general interest were the historical-survey exhibitions held in conjunction with the three great fairs, at Chicago in 1933 and 1934 and New York and San Francisco in 1939. Then there were exhibits of the work of primitive cultures, the Pacific islands, the pre-Columbian culture of Mexico and South America, the art of the American Indian, the sculpture, especially of the African tribes. Large and small exhibitions of this sort were carefully organized and presented. The relationship of the arts to the study of anthropology was more than ever important and influenced professional scholars in both fields while it broadened and deepened the public awareness. Arts were seen to be inclusive of the symbolism of African ebony carving, the clean lines of a boat propeller, the twenty minutes of clowning in a Keystone film comedy, and the concrete walls of Frank Lloyd Wright's 1904 Unity Temple.

Museums and their exhibits, the exhibits and their special publications, reached a high point in public education in the years following the Wall Street crash. Something of the magnitude of their work in the last two decades can be appreciated by assembling in any reasonably large library of contemporary art all those volumes which were produced in connection with a major museum exhibition.

The Boston Museum of Fine Arts, the Metropolitan Museum, the Whitney Museum of American Art, the Museum of Modern Art, the Brooklyn Museum, the National Gallery in Washington, the Philadelphia Museum, the Carnegie Institute, the Cleveland Museum, the Chicago Art Institute, the Detroit Institute of Arts, the St. Louis City Art Museum—all have resources to create important exhibits, to present them adequately, and to publish catalogues.

Different in the nature of their contribution and important in another way have been the activities of the increasing number of art and general museums not included in the list of major institutions.

The smaller museums of the country perform a quite different service. Their permanent collections are usually far less significant and more apt to be excellent in some small area of art and no other. Often they use their collections only occasionally as interim exhibit material for the reason that they lack exhibit space for showing temporary exhibits together with a permanent collection.

The smaller galleries are performing their greatest service in annual exhibitions of local art of importance. Such showings include the public-school art work; the prints of the local photographic

179

groups; painting, sculpture, crafts from special art clubs, such as businessmen, physicians, night-class groups; the work of any museum classes for children and adults; the work of faculty and students in local art schools and colleges; and, somewhat less regularly, significant design in local industry or in local advertising and merchandising.

To make the service of these museums more than simply provincial, however valuable that activity is, the American Federation of Arts, the Museum of Modern Art, and the Metropolitan Museum conduct regular programs of circulating exhibitions, which are made available at reasonable rental and transportation rates. A survey of exhibition listings through the year in the United States would indicate that when most small galleries wish to attempt an educational collection on some worth-while theme, they go to the current circulation units from one of these sources. The reason is obvious. The circulating units are better in individual pieces included and in editing than the resources, in personnel and in finance for shipping and insurance, of the small institution can make possible.

The AFA and the MOMA catalogues of circulating exhibits list fine groups. On one important score, however, the tendency to rely on these bookings is to be deplored. It is comparable to the tendency of the small-town newspaper to rely on syndicate material for editorial comment, as well as for news, comics, fashions, health articles, etc. Fine as is the staff of the AFA and the Modern Museum, the whole art field is benefited when some of the smaller museums plunge into creating their own exhibitions. In the last decade, leadership of this sort has been taken by a few college and university galleries, where academic personnel can do some of the work of planning; and most conspicuously of all by the Walker Art Center in Minneapolis. This gallery has achieved extraordinary influence and distinction for its work in its "Everyday Art" gallery and for its small quarterly publication of the same title. The Walker has not ignored painting and sculpture either, for in those media it produces outstanding regional exhibits of contemporary work.

Despite the excellence of work already accomplished and the wide coverage of museums now in an active state, the educational values of art museums are too largely available only to the urban resident.

True, the museums do set and advance art values which extend far beyond their walls, and the small-town and rural resident is influenced by the museum whether or not he ever enters a museum door. But he lacks the consciousness even of his own indisputable acts of aesthetic purpose and intent, partly because we have not found as yet the way to bring to all the parts and people of the nation the kind of cultural understanding the museum provides.

Education in museums has not been limited to the influence of the exhibit, the publications, or the gallery tours conducted by the staff. It has become a widely accepted part of the museum job to offer classwork in a variety of art activities. Of course, some of the largest and oldest museums are the parent institutions for our best-known professional art schools, but in recent decades even the largest museums have not made any effort to enter that field. Instead, they inaugurated that kind of instruction suited to the aesthetic education of the general citizens, child and adult, who have some art interests. As a result, schoolchildren with special aptitudes have been able to do more art work than would be possible in their schools alone, and not only more art work but frequently work of freer possibilities, with more complex materials, than those offered by the regular school situation. In the larger cities, these classes are oftentimes staffed by young artists; they bring to their museum teaching a somewhat more stimulating and interesting flavor than is likely in a public-school, five-day-a-week situation.

In smaller communities where museum classes are held, the instructor is more apt to be one of the regular school art staff. Even so, there is still the element of environment, and the encouragement of a class group having more than ordinary interests, which makes art activities in the gallery a most welcome addition to the community cultural resources.

To some extent the museum class can serve as an experiment station for new materials and for untried class group organization. For the reason that it is free from the requirements of an interlocked curriculum, the museum can venture more easily than the school. It should not wish to emulate the more organized, slow-changing patterns inevitable where many interests are to be reconciled.

NATIONAL GOVERNMENT IN ART

Probably there is now a far greater spread of able artists and artist-teachers in all parts of the country than might have been thought possible in 1929. This situation, if it prevails to the extent artists and art magazines think likely, is partly due to the work of the various federal art projects and sponsorships of the 1930's. The detailed story of all the cultural projects is yet to be written. Some books treat of parts of the program, and a large body of periodical material remains as yet the best record of the subject.

When, in 1934, a relief program for artists was made part of the whole Works Progress Administration, rather than provide mere relief payments in the form of cash or food and rent, the aim of WPA was to provide gainful employment in work which the recipient of the relief check could do. Where possible, this could be achieved by setting up projects using particular skills and talents; such was the Art Project.

Accomplishments accredited to the Art Project, up to the time of its dissolution in 1939, were varied in quality and effectiveness. Some of the accomplishments have never been adequately recognized, while others have been unduly criticized.

The actual work the artists produced was amazing in quantity and quality: paintings in all possible media; stone, metal, concrete, and wood sculpture, much of it for specified architectural settings; prints in all possible techniques, including a production in silk-screen printing which led virtually to a new industry both in the fine arts and in commercial practice. Then there was the now far-famed Index of American Design, the collection of thousands of painstakingly done plates illustrating copiously the folk arts of the whole nation for the past three hundred or more years. The personnel of this unit was composed largely of older men recruited from the workers in lithography, engraving, and printing.

Besides the works of art produced—all available for the cost of the materials to public institutions requesting them—the people on the Art Project participated in hundreds of teaching and museum projects for children and adults in special-interest groups. The artists taught, lectured, and demonstrated from New York City to North

Dakota and points in between and beyond. At first the bulk of the artists on the Art Project rolls were fairly experienced men and women; in its later years, large numbers of recent art-school graduates sought employment until teaching or part-time work gave them a more favorable income.

One of the valuable results of the Project was that of keeping a considerable group of younger artists in their home communities. As they left their respective schools, New York, Philadelphia, or Chicago could hardly be said to be a golden lure. Artists were sleeping in subways along with laborers. So scores of talented artists, realizing that the Project gave them the opportunity to continue and mature their work beyond its student level, took advantage of whatever activity their local Project office provided. Gradually, most of the younger Project artists worked their way into art and art-related jobs in their home towns or state. A roll call of one-time Project artists is revealing in showing the numbers of them who are not and often never have been working any length of time in the New York City area.

Project artists found that they could work with schools and school administrators, with hospital directors, with architects, with museum staff members, and with any number of other people in the community. What is more impressive, the communities where art projects were active found that the artists were not too difficult to endure; and that often, in the most unlikely of community undertakings, Fourth of July parades or Christmas festivals, they willingly and successfully provided designs, posters, floats, all manner of decorations, stage settings, and any other related necessities.

To some extent in many places, they led the way in general art activity that we see at its best today in the community participation in schools, colleges, and museums. Many staff members in those institutions were Project members in earlier years.

The later-inaugurated Procurement Division in the Treasury Department evolved a form of artist contribution which served to encourage private support of art projects. This division worked out a jury system of awarding mural and sculpture contracts as part of the construction program of federal buildings. The artists submitted studies of specified size and proportion to the jury. From the jury selection one artist was commissioned to do a job on a specific building; the largest number of these jobs went into small post offices the length and breadth of the country. Here again the artists commissioned had to work with others and under definitely prescribed conditions. Of late years it has been commonly said that the total body of work was too narrowly, superficially historical in subject matter. That may be so, and it is possible that only a few works above the average will be sought out as the years go by. But the competence acquired by the artists, their greater professional preparation, their wider spread geographically in the nation, will continue to be felt as a more important influence over the years than the actual work finished and distributed during the existence of the project.

The influence of the museums and of the government art projects was felt keenly by the public-school art faculty and by the college, university, and art-school teachers. A healthy sort of competition bloomed between the artists and the art teachers, for many project artists conducted late afternoon, evening, and Saturday classes for children and adults. More than once, a young and intensely devoted artist forced a change in the "regular" art teaching of his community because of the verve and sense of accomplishment he brought to the classes under Project sponsorship.

Lacking so direct and possibly unflattering a stimulus, hundreds of cities and towns benefited and felt a jump in art interest by reason of the Project. They were presented with a mural in their new post office, or they appropriated the comparatively slight funds needed to buy some project art works for their schools and hospitals. Project artists were invited by local museum directors, by high-school art teachers, by the local librarians, to give lectures with slides or with a demonstration in some art field. In earlier Project years, the advent into some smaller communities of artists attempting to propagandize a rather abstruse point of view created minor storms. As the years went by, however, those artists better qualified to judge the audience level of response were used as the public-relations experts. A whole collection of folk stories are exchanged by the artists concerning demonstration lectures, involving struggles with materials, unusual lighting arrangements, and the inevitability of strange and frightening chairmen of the gatherings.

184

This sort of thing was all on the positive side. The arts and the artists were in circulation, were mixing with the public, making their way as best they might. Negatively, the acknowledged impermanence, the small income of the Project workers, made long-range planning an impossibility.

It is fortunate that American museums, schools, colleges, and some private agencies tried to carry part of the Project gains over into the war years. The war itself has made it all but impossible to determine how much success there has been in that.

The Federal Art Project served an obviously temporary purpose. Time will prove that in those years major permanent gains were made for our whole culture.

THE OWATONNA PROJECT

A recurring tragedy of human life is the stagnation or disintegration of cultural progress which war causes.

The First World War interrupted and delayed a vigorous art growth in America. However, the activities of the nineteen-twenties and thirties accomplished more than a rebuilding of the structure of 1914. Much more mature points of view in the arts were developed; and before the world was involved in the next chapter of the twentieth-century wars, this maturity in the arts was expressed specifically in two important educational projects.

Both were begun in public-school systems in September of 1933. One was an intensive project on a local scale, the Owatonna Art Project; and the other was a nation-wide study of the secondary curriculum, now known as the Eight Year Study. Each has a considerable importance for education in the arts and for the greater understanding of the need for arts in general education.

While few school people would say that war years have ruined the one-time value of either of these noteworthy studies, it is true that their impact has been slowed up and made less decisive than might have been the case if their major publications had been printed in a peaceful period of time. Introductory monographs on the Owatonna Project were issued in 1935, 1936, and 1938, but the books describing the years during which the project was in opera tion were printed in 1944.[16] The concluding volumes on the Eight Year Study were copyrighted in 1942.[17] Simple delay in making use of these excellent jobs in educational planning and experiment is not necessarily a great loss, and the reinterpretation which delay has produced could be an actual enhancement of their values. What ought not to happen is for school people to forget them, to repeat the same work without benefit of the labors of their predecessors.

Particularly in art education, we have too often rediscovered, with cries of delight, approaches to our work which have already been thoroughly exploited and documented for all who can read. The objectives and the work of the Owatonna Project for art education need to be kept fresh in our professional background.

The story of the Project is well told in the fourth volume of *Art for Daily Living.* Dean Melvin E. Haggerty of the School of Education, University of Minnesota, was the responsible agent in getting the Project started. A speech of his given at a Western Arts Association meeting had dwelt with vigor upon the meager aesthetic quality of ordinary life on the Midwestern plains, which the dean had experienced as a boy and which he assumed was not too much improved in his intervening years. Subsequently the Carnegie Foundation suggested an educational project based on the theme of the convention talk, "Art a Way of Life."

The plan proposed was to create an art activity in a representative small city which would be based on the natural aesthetic interests of the population. The city picked, Owatonna, was one of reasonably diversified industry, close enough to the University of Minnesota for administrative and observational purposes, and sufficiently deprived of art activities in the immediate past as to make easily noticeable in community life whatever the Project did. As in many cities of its size, the depression had cut out art classes in the public schools.

Three persons formed the resident staff for the Project in 1933. One of them, Edwin Ziegfeld, was designated to restore art instruction in the schools; his time schedule was identical to that which is a commonplace in scores of American towns and cities. In the morn-

[16] Owatonna Art Project, *Projects in Art Education,* University of Minnesota, 1944.
[17] Progressive Education Association, *Adventure in American Education,* the Association, 1942.

ing he supervised the art periods taught by the elementary-grade teachers in their own rooms, and in the afternoon he taught one junior-high-school class and one senior-high-school class.

The other two members of the Project spent their time for the first year in all kinds of "service" projects and in unobtrusively becoming familiar with and documenting photographically the physical environment of Owatonna. The service projects consisted of advice and assistance in planning for interior and exterior paint jobs, landscaping, interior decoration, and window displays in private homes, business places, factories, institutions, and even in the city parks.

Over the whole five years of the life of the Project, the activity of staff and community separated into two major areas: the community adults and their art interests, and the school program for the children.

In the community at large, the Project provided an infinitely more concentrated art experience than could have been available to Owatonna unaided by university and foundation money. This is not to say that the Project is thus heavily discounted in an evaluation of its work. Rather, it is necessary to note what valuable activities were made possible, and to assess the ways and means available for such a community to maintain some of those values on its own initiative and financial resources.

Service projects already referred to bulked large in staff activity through all five years. During the first years, evening classes for adults were held, and in the Owatonna experience as much or more desire for classes in understanding and appreciating art works was shown as for the more commonly scheduled night classes in crafts.

During the first two summers, art classes were also carried on for three different groups. Children's classes continued the kind of work begun in the school year with such variation as summer and longer time periods made possible. Adult classes stressed activity in art media, alternated with lectures and discussion, as an approach to contemporary arts. And for two summers a class of art teachers was formed, carrying a program of work for university credit and based in part on observation and discussion of the whole scope of the project.

Besides taking care of classwork in the winter evenings and for the six-week summer term, the project staff was always available to city clubs and study groups for lectures on as many aspects of the arts as their professional background permitted. To supplement this service, foundation funds made possible several lectures each year by widely known designers, artists, art directors, and university staff members.

Last, but not less useful, among the community-wide influences which the Project had was its aid to the public library and, conversely, the aid given the Project by sympathetic librarians. To begin with, the librarian made all possible efforts, as soon as the Project staff members arrived, to add to the art-book collection and to aid the work in other ways. Clipping collections were enlarged, prints purchased, and a room in the library was eventually redecorated to serve as an exhibition space.

So successful was the library in making use of art facilities and materials that the Carnegie Corporation felt justified in granting it two of its art-equipment sets ordinarily given only to larger institutions. The first of the sets included two hundred volumes and several hundred photographic prints on the arts. The second and later set was a music collection of six hundred records and a phonograph and loud-speaker.

A hasty reading of the Owatonna story might give the impression that in the later years of the Project the art staff withdrew somewhat from its all-community activity, putting most of its effort primarily into school activity. To a degree that seems to have been true, but the move can be interpreted as a withdrawal of the staff from quite so much active professional designing and planning in order to give still greater encouragement to students and the community to begin working out their own solutions.

During the last three years of work, much of what the staff had done to begin with as art service now began to be worked upon by school groups and even by individual students. From the school flowed dozens of projects, single home-interior redecorations, garden plans, planting schemes for park and school, color schemes for high school and grade schools, redecoration of the high-school auditorium —all of these as well as continued work, this time by students on such projects as window displays, large-scale illustrated albums, ticket booths, drapery designs, and so on.

In short, the serving of the community as aesthetic adviser simply was transferred, as was appropriate on the part of a good teaching staff, from the faculty to the students, the faculty contribution taking the form of guidance and evaluation. The first couple of years had served a purpose in that faculty design on such projects had become an example to be followed up by students who had become confident of their own abilities.

Still another reservation one might have in regard to the whole picture of the Project art activities in the school is that of wondering about the place of individual creative activities like painting and sculptural work. True enough, there are careful and well-worked-out units of work in these media for the various age levels, but they are somewhat slight in proportion to all the activity described.

In comparison to the kind of art work which much current practice stresses, the Owatonna schools probably did minimize such art experience. Everywhere nowadays a decided accent upon art as an individually creative experience is evident, and in many places the need for art as mental and emotional therapy is definitely overstated; overstated not because art is not legitimately helpful therapeutically, but because the emphasis on art's therapeutic values is likely to reduce its quality as a creative experience, and, at the same time, effectively reduce its value as a mental or emotional corrective.

More important than any of these considerations, however, in thinking about the Owatonna work is the fact that the art teachers in the last part of the five-year period had gone far beyond the limits of *the* art period. The art period was still being spent on creative, individual work, though the tendency to base the work on the home, school, and community environment always predominated.

Of unique significance is the fact that much of the staff activity was no longer teaching art in the art period, but expanding the aesthetic emphasis of the general educational pattern of the whole school in all subjects. It was not until the Project was completed that Herbert Read issued his *Education Through Art,* in which he postulates that man can only be educated through art, hence the absolute necessity for improving the quality of the arts, and more than that for becoming aware that all "subjects," from history to agriculture, are of absolute necessity taught or transmitted through the generations by the art forms of language, literature, pictures in the form of maps, diagrams, charts, and other pictorial media. The basic effectiveness of all education rests upon a more qualitative use of the aesthetic tools of our culture.

That is exactly what the Owatonna staff was working at in its gradual but certain expansion of art thinking into every class and subdivision of the curriculum.

How do we judge the Owatonna scheme's significance to the average community unsubsidized and unselected by foundation directors?

In cities the size of Owatonna, young art teachers are likely to be employed in two- to five-year periods of service. They cannot do a tenth what the Project staff did; at least, that is a first reaction to the problem. But it may not be justified. The Owatonna Project did explore many activities possible to any art teacher, however modestly equipped and supported.

In many communities, the public library already has become or will become, upon invitation, an invaluable aid to art education. Books are added all the time to any collection. Art books can be more legitimately ordered if the local art teacher provides his professional assistance. Print collections are not impossible and again are more likely to be attempted if there is artist advice in selection and purchase to be had.

Already the vocational school has started to expand its cultural activities for adults, including orchestral and choral groups, drama, crafts, art survey, and other classes. Since the close of the Owatonna Project, the number of art graduates from professional schools and colleges has increased greatly, and few good-sized towns and cities do not possess one or more young married women who have had a quite professional background in art and who can be induced to add to the professional coverage of the full-time art teacher by agreeing to teach a single class or a part-time schedule.

In the realm of instruction and guidance in landscape gardening and interior decoration, public education, by means of magazines, has advanced in quality and circulation in the last decade. Concerted efforts by interested laymen can now accomplish, with the aid of far greater reference materials, much that the Project staff got started in Owatonna.

There is not, and cannot be, any substitution for at least one good professional art teacher in a school system the size of Owatonna. On this point, a detailed consideration of the range of activities under the Owatonna staff, together with a review of the art implications of the Progressive Education Association's Eight Year Study, suggests one of two conclusions. Either the art staff member in Owatonna would need to be joined by an associate or else there would need to be a quite different use made of the art teacher's time. The Eight Year Study in certain respects provides surprisingly similar conclusions for art education to those reached at Owatonna.

THE EIGHT YEAR STUDY

Both these studies came into existence because someone followed up ideas expressed at educational meetings, a reassuring fact when one thinks of the disparaging comments so well merited by most convention speakers. Perhaps, with the economic effects of the depression bearing down on everyone, there was a feeling that sound ideas worth expressing might just as well be implemented to get some activity set in motion. So few parts of the social network were operating at capacity that there was an oversupply of people and a great dearth of things for them to do. Money was scarce, but there were times when it seemed wise to try to get an enterprise started, with or without cash in sight.

A meeting at Washington, D.C., in April, 1930, on the subject of secondary education turned inevitably to the heavy hand that college requirements placed on efforts to improve or make more flexible the high-school curriculum. A commission on the relation of school and college was set up under the sponsorship of the Progressive Education Association. The commission then met for a year's time and issued a report on the areas of inadequacy and needed improvement in the American high school. Under the heading of school and college relations, in addition to citing the various difficulties as they appeared to both institutions, a plan of experimental activity was proposed.

191

A select number of high schools was to be designated. For a period of years (later set at eight) the graduates of these schools would be admitted to most important colleges in the country without submitting a list of required units and subjects. All graduates were not to be admitted without regard to qualitative status in their high-school work, but the content and quantity of that work were left to the judgment of the high-school faculties.

What it meant to the high schools involved was that they were to be free of specific subject and credit requirements imposed by college entrance regulations. Among other things, the study was to prove that college entrance requirements were not the only, nor event the worst, restrictive influence on the secondary curriculum.

Finally, in 1942, five volumes of records were issued, including a chronological narrative of the study, a survey of the curriculum studies and experiments, a record of student achievement, a survey of the college records of graduates, and a brief summary of the record of each of the thirty schools participating.[18]

Eventually it will be seen that the record of the study furnishes an absorbing picture of secondary education during the 1930's, including as it does the description of curricula before the experiment started, the bases upon which faculty members planned new work and new approaches to the standard course contents, and the story of student reaction and development during the life of the study. The economic and physical limitations of the depression were always a part of the background. As evidence of a state of mind generally prevalent because of the depression, we see that the high-school faculties of wealthy suburban schools, as well as those of large industrial city systems, felt obligated to teach the importance of improving and broadening economic and social opportunity as the way of bringing true democracy closer. On the other hand, there is a difference in attitude toward the need of vocational education in high school. The large-city schools were definitely more eager to enlarge specialized facilities in shop, science, art, music, and business education. The suburban schools and the country day or boarding schools were more prone to accept core curricula with a pronounced emphasis on liberal education.

[18] Progressive Education Association, *Adventure in American Education: Thirty Schools Tell Their Story,* the Association, 1943.

A most significant discovery for all education was that almost every school faculty involved made more or less progress in the study depending upon the degree to which the whole staff was active in planning and carrying out innovations. Where brilliant schemes were handed down from administrators or from isolated small faculty committees, success was much less likely. Schools careful to plan with the whole faculty, and with at least the consent and nominal advice of representative parent and community groups, completed the years of the study with the greatest real gains.

Nowadays many American citizens under the age of fifty are familiar with the organization of the traditional high-school course. At least three academic subjects and a gym class twice a week, with a fourth academic class or some variation of electives in fields like shop, music, commercial courses, art, and the like, complete the students' schedule of classes.

As the schools participating in the study found out, the difficulties of changing this scheme are considerable. When one teacher is responsible for a group of students all day long, as in the elementary school, flexibility is easily achieved. Use of new equipment, trips, supervision in special fields, shift of curricular emphasis, all may easily be brought in for the classroom teachers' use.

But the high school has traditionally been devoted to the values of specially trained faculty members, specially trained in subject-matter areas, not in the teaching of the adolescent citizen.

Every possible variation or improvement on the secondary curriculum has to be done by men and women prepared to teach limited subjects, English, mathematics, history, or art.

Two major directions emerged in the attempted reorganizations of courses. One was that of creating a core curriculum based on one of two themes: either the culture epoch or the unit based on contemporary life.

Some schools worked with the culture epoch, studying a single quite-complete cultural complex. As with the Experimental College at the University of Wisconsin under Alexander Meiklejohn, the most frequently used period was that of classic Greece. The study of a single period was conducted, as best the faculty could manage, in such a way as to create a related body of knowledge and attitudes on the part of the students. As the year progressed, the skills formerly isolated in mathematics, English, or social-studies periods were to be incorporated in various ways in the study of the culture.

More of the schools used as a core center the study of the students' environment, beginning with the immediate community and expanding to the state, the nation, and the world. Still others created a core center in the direct adolescent interests of the student group, studying the individual, the school itself, the family, in the setting of the larger community. Obviously, the thought animating any variation of the core curriculum was that a central unit of study would not only be valuable for itself, for the facts and the attitudes that could be taught by focusing on an easily understood subject close to the students' experience, but that the use of language, mathematics, history, and the acquisition of skills in music, art, business practice, shop, and home economics would be more easily mastered when used in connection with such work. Elementary schools and college curricular planners, too, have kept on stretching themselves to grasp some such focal point as an improvement over an ill-assorted, rather unrelated group of "subjects."

The second large grouping under curricular change was that of trying several integrations of the standard subject-matter fields. In this category, the most common and most successful schemes were the integration of the social studies with English and an integrated course grouping in the sciences, sometimes including mathematics, though this latter was eventually disowned by most of the mathematics teachers.

All curricular experiment resulted in certain values, regardless of the particular types attempted. One of these was the enforced faculty meetings to determine what common grounds could be agreed upon. This outcome of the study underlined the fact that such meetings ought to be a regularly scheduled part of a teacher's activity. Many schools are now holding regular professional meetings, not as an extra burden after full days of teaching and an extracurricular program, but as an activity worthy of its place in the semester's work.

Regardless of the curricular schemes proposed in separate schools,

194

the teachers' acquaintance with one another's professional fields must have proved invaluable.

For determining the impact of the whole study upon art education, the best source of information may be found in the volume *Thirty Schools Tell Their Story.* Here it is apparent that the arts in general improved their status, were found of greater value to the whole program of secondary education, than had been true in most of the schools before the study began. Fortunately, this increased art emphasis was not achieved by art-education pressure groups, but by the general awareness of faculty groups and committees that the arts were not prominent enough in their schools. A great majority of schools, in their statements of objectives, set a better and more general art education as one of their goals.

They proposed to reach that goal in varied patterns characteristic of the personality of the individual school. Required semester or year courses of art which had been common in the junior-high-school years were adopted in some senior high schools. The plans for required art courses usually urged work of general interest to all students. The especially interested student in most senior high schools had ample opportunity to continue with his art work beyond the limits of the introductory requirement.

Variations of the required course consisted of a requirement for having each student do work in at least one fine-arts field, with the fields broadly defined to include shop, music, visual and plastic arts, drama, creative writing, and dance. Schools establishing this type of requirement usually had outlined an arts area as one of the necessary elements of secondary education.

Less often, but frequently enough to be noteworthy, schools offered required courses in appreciation of the arts, or, as some of the more journalistically slanted course titles put it, "consumer arts." When these appreciation courses are described, there seems to have been a heavy emphasis on literature, architecture, and painting, particularly in the historical context of European history from the medieval period to the present. Art teachers who have labored to do a course in appreciation of the arts, sometimes with enlarged sections of students numbering fifty or more, have raised bitter questions as to the value of requiring such work of all students or indeed of any students, except under very favorable circumstances with adequate equipment and classes small enough for extended discussion. The revised art-appreciation class would seem to be the least desirable method of enlarging the scope of art in high schools. It is a talking about art at a time in the life of the individual when he prefers, as much as possible, direct action, real grappling with the tricks of a trade, skill, or vocation. It is easier for a high-school student to think about activity and its implications if he is simultaneously working at it.

Integration of art with other subject fields, particularly with English, history, foreign language, and less frequently with the sciences, was done in several schools. The success of this kind of integration depended entirely on whether or not art faculty members were assigned some class time for coöperation with scheduled art teachers on a roving basis for a part or whole schedule. They were thus available to be called upon by the French teacher to show slides and to conduct a discussion on the characteristics of the Gothic cathedral, or by the chemistry teacher to explain the aesthetic aim and qualities of the scientifically interesting technique of fresco painting on a wet plaster wall.

All of these schemes—the required credit of all students in studio work, or more broadly in some one art field; the art-appreciation course which tended to stigmatize art as a polite accomplishment for the well-rounded citizen; and the widespread practice of calling on the art teacher to contribute to academic fields by interpreting aesthetic history more completely—these three kinds of expansion in the arts have continued to influence present-day secondary schools.

Students in most of the schools of the chosen thirty enrolled in greater numbers in all arts and shopwork. The sound feeling that the manual-arts and home-economics shops were closely allied to the work in visual arts and to music, dance, and drama was more and more common, not by arbitrary faculty arrangements alone, but because students saw them as having similarities. The greatest increase in arts enrollments occurred in a few schools where a studio course was required of all students, but where that course was conscientiously planned on a "come-on" basis. Experiment with materials and different crafts was fostered in such semesters or even half-semesters of work. Naturally, the elective classes of additional work were well filled, a proof of the effectiveness of the introductory unit.

If arts and shop and music and drama classes became more popular in the thirty schools, some other fields must have suffered. They did. Foreign languages and Latin experienced the greatest dropping off of enrollment. Freedom from some fairly strict college entrance requirements of language credits showed this result immediately. For the art teacher to take this result as natural and even highly desirable would be short-sighted; it would suggest a narrow partisan interest in "my" subject as a competing unit among others all out for the greatest possible attendance.

To rest on this response would be to ignore the greatest lesson of the whole study, which was that beyond all other achievements it aided—even forced—the high-school faculties participating to think in terms of the whole curriculum and, to employ a cliché of the educational trade, the "whole" student.

A better evaluative point of view to take toward the increased art activity would be to note that activity of any sort in the years of adolescence is more than ever important; that aesthetic understanding is important in every phase of experience and makes its appearance in the planning of all good teachers. Furthermore, any secondary curriculum is outmoded if it does not encourage and strive to make possible interfaculty contributions to one another's special fields.

One further generalization would appear valid and of more than casual interest to art education. The tendency in all but a few schools of the group obviously was toward an increase in the effectiveness of general or liberal education and a somewhat lesser concern for the strictly vocational courses.

This would seem to most art educators both natural and desirable. Vocations employing a little or considerable of the skills, the design ability, the general philosophy of the arts, should be well known to the secondary-school art teacher; but specific preparation for those vocations certainly ought to be the responsibility of the industry itself in apprenticeship programs, of post-high-school courses in the vocational school, or of longer and more professional courses in the art school or in the college and university art departments.

Meanwhile, high-school curriculum plans are still slow to change. When change does come, and as it comes, the art teacher needs to be prepared to show the value of a greater art participation for general education. The *Eight Year Study* needs to be better known and its implications better understood.

Bibliography

Bailey, Carolyn Sherwin, *Montessori Children*, Holt, 1915.

Barnes, Albert C., *The Art in Painting*, Harcourt, Brace, 1928.

Batchelder, Ernest A., *Design in Theory and Practice*, Macmillan, 1921.

Bayer, Herbert, and Gropius, Walter and Ise, *Bauhaus 1919–1933*, Museum of Modern Art, 1938.

Beck, Minnie, *Better Citizenship Through Art Training*, McClurg, 1921.

Berry, Ana M., *Art for Children*, Studio, 1934.

Best-Maugard, Adolphe, *A Method for Creative Design*, Knopf, 1926–1927.

Boas, Belle, *Art in the School*, Doubleday, 1924.

Bonser, Frederick G., and Mossman, Lois C., *Industrial Arts for Elementary Schools*, Macmillan, 1923.

Cheney, Sheldon and Martha, *Art and the Machine*, Whittlesey, 1932.

Cizek, Franz, *Das Freie Zeichmen*, plates from the work of students in the Vienna Kunstge werbe Schule, Vienna, 1925.

Cizek, Franz, *Children's Colored Paper Work*, Schroll, 1927.

Cox, George W., *Art for Amateurs and Students*, Doubleday, 1926.

De Garmo, Charles, *Aesthetic Education*, Bardeen, 1913.

De Garmo, Charles, and Winslow, Leon Loyal, *Essentials of Design*, Macmillan, 1924.

Duffus, R. L., *The American Renaissance*, Knopf, 1928.

Ellis, Havelock, *The Dance of Life*, Houghton Mifflin, 1923.

Farnum, Royal B., *The Present Status of Drawing and Art in the Elementary and Secondary Schools of the United States*, Bureau of Education, Department of Interior, Bulletin 13, 1914.

Farnum, Royal B., *Art Education: The Present Situation*, Bureau of Education, Department of Interior, Bulletin 13, 1923.

Farnum, Royal B., *Art Education in the United States*, Bureau of Education, Department of Interior, Bulletin 38, 1925.

Frankl, Paul, *New Dimensions*, Payson and Clarke, 1928.

Frankl, Paul, *Form and Reform*, Harper, 1930.

Federated Council on Art Education, *Report of the Committee on Art Instruction in Colleges and Universities*, The Council, 1927.

Goldstein, Harriet and Vetta, *Art in Everyday Life*, Macmillan, 1925.

Gropius, Walter, *The New Architecture and the Bauhaus*, Faber and Faber, 1935.

Haggerty, Melvin E., "Education and the New World," *Bulletin of the Western Arts Association*, Vol. XIV, No. 5, 1930, p. 26.

Hartmann, Gertrude, and Shumaker, Ann, *Creative Expression*, Reynal and Hitchcock, 1932.

Johnson, Philip, *Machine Art*, Museum of Modern Art, 1934.

Kahn, Ely Jacques, *Design in Art and Industry*, Scribner, 1935.

Kirby, C. Valentine, *The Business of Teaching and Supervising the Arts*, Abbott, 1927.

Klar, Walter; Winslow, Leon L.; and Kirby, C. Valentine, *Art Education in Principle and Practice*, Milton Bradley, 1933.

Lemos, Pedro J., *Applied Art*, Pacific Press, 1920.

McGowan, Kenneth, *The Theatre of Tomorrow*, Boni and Liveright, 1921.

Mathias, Margaret, *The Beginnings of Art in the Public Schools*, Scribner, 1924.

Mathias, Margaret, *Art in the Elementary School*, Scribner, 1929.

Mathias, Margaret, *The Teaching of Art*, Scribner, 1932.

Matthiessen, F. O., *The James Family*, Knopf, 1948.

Mearns, Hughes, *Creative Youth*, Doubleday, 1925.

Mearns, Hughes, *Creative Adult*, Doubleday, 1940.

Moholy-Nagy, Sibyl, *Moholy-Nagy: Experiment in Totality*, Harper, 1950.

Munro, Thomas, *The Scientific Method in Aesthetics*, Norton, 1928.

Owatonna Art Project, *Projects in Art Education*, University of Minnesota, 1944.

Parker, Francis W., School, *Creative Effort*, Studies in Education, Vol. VIII, the School, 1925.

Pearson, Ralph M., *How to See Modern Pictures*, Dial Press, 1925.

Pearson, Ralph M., *Experiencing Pictures*, Brewer, Warren, and Putnam, 1932.

Pelikan, Alfred G., *The Art of the Child*, Bruce, 1931.

Progressive Education Association, "The Creative Spirit and Its Significance for Education," *Progressive Education*, April, May, June, 1926.

Progressive Education Association, *Adventure in American Education*, Vol. I, *The Story of the Eight Year Study*; Vol. V, *Thirty Schools Tell Their Story*, the Association, 1943.

Read, Herbert, *Art Now*, Harcourt, Brace, 1933.

Read, Herbert, *Art and Industry*, Harcourt, Brace, 1935.

Robinson, James Harvey, *The Mind in the Making*, 1921.

Rugg, Harold O., *Culture and Education in America*, Harcourt, Brace, 1931.

Rusk, William Sener, *Methods of Teaching the Fine Arts*, University of North Carolina, 1935.

Sargent, Walter, *The Enjoyment and Use of Color*, Scribner, 1932.

Tucker, Allen, *Design and the Idea*, Art Publishing Company, 1930.

Viola, Wilhelm, *Child Art*, University of London, 1942.

Whitehead, Alfred North, *The Aims of Education*, Macmillan, 1929; Mentor, 1949.

Whitford, William G., "Brief History of Art Education in the United States," *Elementary School Journal*, October, 1923.

Whitford, William G., *An Introduction to Art Education*, rev. ed., Appleton-Century, 1937.

Wilenski, R. H., *The Modern Movement in Art*, rev. ed., Faber and Faber, 1945.

Winslow, Leon Loyal, *The Organization and Teaching of Art*, rev. ed., Warwick and York, 1928.

Winslow, Leon Loyal, *Art in Secondary Education*, McGraw-Hill, 1941.

Winslow, Leon Loyal, *The Integrated School Art Program*, rev. ed., Mc-Graw-Hill, 1949.

Figure 12. John Dewey, Drawn by Donald M. Anderson. (From "In Honor of John Dewey on His Ninetieth Birthday," University of Wisconsin, 1951.)

VII

A Psychology and Philosophy for Art Education

Art education now is in a state of bewildering contrasts. Never has so much been written and said about the arts; conversely, never in history have the arts been counted so negligible among the forces that supposedly shape or direct society. Potential catastrophic destruction makes the slow achievement of art seem less significant than research in medicine, in nutrition, in biology, in new destructive and constructive forces of all kinds.

The art teacher finds these contrasting attitudes difficult to accept: on the one hand people eagerly taking up art activity, and on the other a general assumption that art cannot be a crucial factor in the present stage of world convulsion. But that is only a part of the confusion which we face in art education.

We are in a period of embarrassingly plentiful resources. Philosophy, anthropology, psychiatry, therapy, the history of the arts, social history, are all contributing interpretations of historical and con-

201

temporary art forms. A literature is growing in numbers of items and quality of thought, dealing with art in its interrelationships with other aspects of human affairs and knowledge. As for the physical plant in which art is taught, all over the country the consolidation of smaller school units, the necessary expansion of buildings, the reasonable prosperity of school districts and systems, create an improving school environment for art education.

Yet the art teacher is in a predicament. He cannot ever be all that might, theoretically, be thought desirable for him to be. When, in 1940, the Progressive Education Association committee published its *Visual Arts in General Education*, it included a statement on "The Art Teacher: His Qualifications and Preparation." [1] It could have been downright discouraging if taken too literally. For no one individual could have measured up to the qualifications soberly outlined, and by now the requirements might easily be still further expanded.

Statements on the ideal teacher such as this are seldom overwhelming in their impact, with the possible exception of a few too-susceptible undergraduates. Teachers, like other persons, go on about their business as best they can and according to their lights. They frequently know well enough that there are dark spots in their practice and their theory and philosophy—but one has to learn to live with that relative feeling of inadequacy. There is, however, the possibility that in art and art education the dark spots are not slight, individual shortcomings. Rather, it seems possible that we are so diverse in background, point of view, and emphasis that we are talking and teaching too frequently at cross-purposes to one another. More general interest in the basis of contemporary philosophy of art would advance mutual understanding among art teachers.

ART AS EXPERIENCE

In all professions there are the philosophers who are honored as having spoken the most recently accepted words of truth. In art education, to perhaps an even greater extent than in other educational branches, John Dewey has gone relatively unchallenged since the publication of his *Art as Experience* in 1934.

[1] Committee on the Function of Art in General Education, *The Visual Arts in General Education*, Appleton-Century, 1940.

Also, as in other professions, Dewey is probably relatively unread, and consequently only vaguely understood or, even worse, placed in an unjustified and narrow category loosely titled "pragmatic philosophy." It is worth making the effort to understand how Dewey's philosophy of art is the motivating power of the most valuable current approaches to art education. To attempt an analysis or a condensation of Dewey's tightly constructed philosophy of art is presumptuous. It must be tried in the hope that students will be encouraged to master the whole structure of his philosophy at first hand.

Art as Experience concentrates on developing in detail exactly the thesis of the title. Art as an activity and as a product is considered important when and as it influences human experience. Any experience that is savored primarily for its own sake, and not in terms of how much money may be earned, how much roof may be covered, how much time may be saved, and so on, is considered dominantly an experience that is aesthetic in nature.

A man for a single moment bemused by the rushing crowds in a suburban rail station, a high-school girl who is yelling, whistling, and straining arms, legs, and body in sympathy with the efforts of the players in a basketball game—both are finding satisfaction in an activity for its own sake, for the stimulation it gives their lives for that day. For Dewey, the quality of awarenes of the unique aspects of experience constitutes the "raw material" of aesthetic response.

Dewey deplores the "isolation" of art objects in museums. Sometimes artists have been bewildered by such criticism of the museum. As we have seen, the museum in America has improved in its educational efforts to make the arts more widely understood. Yet here is Dewey apparently condemning the museum. A closer attention to his thesis, however, makes possible a distinction between the museum which simply enshrines objects as masterpieces, thereby removing them from their original context, and that museum which makes a point of presenting each work of art and groups of works so that their place in an active social environment can be grasped.

An exhibition titled "Knife, Fork, and Spoon," sponsored by the Walker Art Gallery in collaboration with one of the larger American silver companies as it prepared to announce a new design in sterling silver, was organized in a scholarly manner, presented in an easily seen and readily understood format, and is being circulated to a nation-wide audience. This hardly makes for remoteness in the minds of gallery visitors toward the arts of design for table cutlery. It serves instead to illuminate a part of daily experience which for most people is likely to have been one of unseeing habit. In this instance, then, the museum serves the best interests of education in the arts by enhancing experience for its visitors, and not merely for the time spent in the gallery.

Dewey, the philosopher, is close to the Gestalt psychologists. He sees order itself as an achievement of harmony emerging from tension. The organism, the human individual, lives through a constant series of incidents in which he finds himself more or less out of step with some part of his environment. Solving his problems never returns the individual to the same status or point of view he held prior to the emergence of the problem. He has enlarged his capacities in one way or another. The simple acts of growing a lawn and putting shrubbery in front of a new house force a consideration of elements of the visual, tangible world that were probably quite unimportant to the same person when he was a dweller in an apartment house. The lawn refuses to grow under a certain tree; the homeowner reorganizes his conception either by chopping out the tree, scattering flagstones under it, or planting shade plants around it.

Some parts of this experience are certainly scientific in nature. There is an appreciable physical effort involved in doing the work. But the whole organization of the problem as to the final appearance of the plot is aesthetic. The householder wishes to preserve and to beautify his land, and to do so he finds he must see the problem as one which involves a number of elements strange to him when he began. The physical aspects of the problem are met and overcome so that an ordered, planned result may be reached.

The Gestaltist observes that in the psychology of vision, touch, and sound there is an intuitive striving to bring the perceptions of the senses into an ordered structure. A driver who may be speeding on a country road sees an obstruction far ahead of him in the traffic lane he is using. At once he "organizes" his perception. His eye does not report to his brain a series of dark and light dots on a field of visual imagery, which then simply take on a certain shape by a sort of connecting of points. Quite the contrary, as the Gestalt psychology sees it, the motorist shapes an object from his perception. He may label the shape in his thinking a wheeled butterfly, or, if he is a Midwesterner of some years' standing, he will identify it at once as a reaper. Whether correctly or not, he will have observed and given a name to a total form on the basis of his past experience or from his powers of imaginative projection of ideas.

This contrasts sharply with other modes of psychological analysis, in which various mechanisms of stimulus and response were described as the basis of human experience. According to this kind of explanation, the senses reported a whole charge of stimuli to which simple and then more complex responses were made. Experience was thought of as an immense accumulation of learned responses to stimuli. Memory was a means of storing old responses so that the same stimulus or set of stimuli would evoke the proper response.

The basic Gestalt criticism of this mechanistic psychology is that the individual creates patterns of order instantaneously from any even entirely new experience and environment. The pattern to which the individual responds may be incorrect or incomplete, but it is a pattern and it does not wait, as it were, for the complete assembling of all possible sensory data to be reported. Regarding the supposed dependence of the individual upon lines of habitual stimulus-response mechanisms, the Gestaltists note that the same stimuli may evoke utterly different responses, depending upon every small change in the detail of surrounding circumstances.

The presumably built-in human effort to organize, to create form from a total experience, was deduced by the Gestalt psychologists from what Dewey would call "raw" experience or, in their phraseology, "direct" experience. The older psychological approaches assumed similar responses to similar stimuli. Dewey, with the Gestaltists, emphasized the uniqueness of all response.

If two men stood twenty feet apart on a landscaped hillside overlooking a river while the moon rose, according to the mechanistic psychology their "pure" response would be identical, consisting of a series of tiny responses to the identical bundle of stimuli. Not so, in the Gestaltist view, for the fact that one man was twenty years old, the other sixty, the first with a girl, the other alone, would alter completely their individualized response to the total situation. Nor would this necessarily be in the conventional terms one would assume, given the situation stated. It might just as well be given to the man of sixty to feel a sense of mystic, unsolved, and blessedly eternal problems in the contemplation of moonlit skies, while the young man might be so constituted as to be aware simply of a less intense illumination than that of the sun. Should both men discern a dark, not distinct shape on the water, both would give to it a form which they would probably try to name—a barge, a cloud shadow, a suddenly rippled area on the stream—but in each case it would be an immediate effort to organize, not a passive checking in of responses until the whole thing took its own shape for recognition or lack of recognition as the case might be. Still further, if both men had an identical experience one year hence, both responses would be likely to be radically changed, unlike each other and unlike their own former reaction to the same stimulus.

In this view of the matter, the individual's experience in the world is of key significance, even to the differences from moment to moment and from day to day in the quality of that experience. By virtue of this fact, it would appear that both the philosopher and the psychologist must become exponents of democratic values in life and education; for obviously only a democratic society with democratic schools can seek to safeguard the uniqueness of the individual's response to environment and also of his expression of that response in the shape of art work, writing, discussion, or by any other means.

Art, in Dewey's scheme of things, in all its forms—plastic, musical, literary, dramatic—provides a form of expression for the uniqueness of personality. On this basis we have come to accept the principle that some experience in art is important to everyone, and that the most important value to be sought in the art work of general education is the evidence of the development of a constructive, creative personality.

Stemming from this philosophy, its logical application to the school curriculum, and its extension to the classes for adult amateurs, among artists and teachers a fear has crept in that standards in art are no longer possible to maintain. The belief is that if standards of value are to be seen largely in the individual's power of expression, then a ten-year-old's painting may be as good as that of any mature artist.

In answer to the questions raised by this fear, the majority of philosophers remind us of the era of the Hegelian ideals of art when a great work was expected to suggest an ideal or transcendent existence beyond and superior to man's ordinary environment. The hollow posturing in the "ideal" paintings forces us by reaction to welcome art forms evolved from the artist's personal and earthly experience.

Abandoning the transcendental view of art, we find ourselves still seeking some basis for creating a hierarchy of values. We have the human desire to identify one work as being a greater piece of art than another, one artist as being more important than his contemporary. We believe it to be important to have a scale of aesthetic values.

Inevitably, the philosopher and psychologist turn the problem back to the individual, his reactions, and his sum of experience. The great artist, the great work of art, are described as that artist who has grasped some fundamental significance in life, and the great work as a piece which manages to convey that significance to others. There is occasionally a superficial effort among writers and artists to dissociate art and morals; yet when one investigates this urge closely, I believe that what is meant, is that art devoted to the narrower and more temporary aspects of a moral code will be as limited as the practices for which it speaks. Today we are not perturbed by the moral alarm which would have been expressed in 1850 over a woman who would enter a crowded public restaurant alone. Obviously, a great art would have to be absorbed in more fundamental relationships of man and his environment than such an incident suggests. Herbert Read, who is not an advocate of sentimentality or literal messages in art, still uses the terms "moral goodness" to identify the human virtue or insight possessed by great art and artists.

CREATIVE THOUGHT COMES OF AGE

The emergence of the museums in education, the Federal Art Project, the initiation of extended laboratory studies in the schools—

these activities, touching art education closely, were accompanied by a spread of the creative approach in school art rooms across the country.

No more devout statement of the glories of growth through creation in art could be written than was done for *Progressive Education* magazine in the mid-twenties. But by 1934–1935, works like R. R. Tomlinson's two books, *Picture Making by Children* and *Crafts for Children,* were available to teachers. Tomlinson was a senior examiner in the London County Council Schools, and the individualistic children's work with which his books were illustrated represented a whole school system rather than the work from the classrooms of a few talented teachers.

In America in 1935, Felix Payant pulled together material from his classes and from back issues of *Design* magazine, publishing it in book form under the title *Our Changing Art Education.* The Foreword presents creative expression for the individual as replacing rapidly the regimentation of the near past. This sets his theme for text and pictures, and indicates again the pervasive nature of the creative-art movement. A couple of years later the Nicholas, Mawhood, and Trilling book, *Art Activities in the Modern School,*[2] showed the distance traveled in a few short years by the majority of art teachers. The aim was again that of the organization of art curricula, but the understanding of the creative processes was markedly advanced since 1930. Winslow brought out the first edition of his *Integrated School Art Program* in 1939,[3] and here the illustrations of child work, mostly from the Baltimore schools, the unusual coördination with the museum program, the emphasis on the integral part art can have in the whole school program, produced the most popular and useful of the organizational guides in which creative approaches and objectives are stressed.

Depression years hindered art education appreciably in the smaller school systems where actual cash savings could be made by dispensing with an art teacher, but larger cities were only slightly affected in this way. In the period of time before war came again, many excellent materials were circulated from the offices of art di-

[2] F. W. Nicholas, N. C. Mawhood, and M. B. Trilling, *Art Activities in the Modern School,* Macmillan, 1937.
[3] Leon Loyal Winslow, *The Integrated School Art Program,* McGraw-Hill, 1939.

rectors in the larger cities. These were in the form of all-over and special-area curricular patterns, of studies in particular crafts and in art appreciation, of statements of objectives and activities drawn up by faculty committees. In turn this work was reflected in the convention meetings of the regional art-education associations, which continued active while the national department was pretty much dormant.

The years 1940–1942 brought a culmination of clear thinking and summing up in art education. In the two years just before and after Pearl Harbor, a number of statements on practice and philosophy important to our present approach in art education were published.

By 1940 a committee of the Progressive Education Association got out its *Visual Arts in General Education.*[4] Victor D'Amico was committee chairman and with Marion Ostrander prepared the first five chapters for committee approval. The sixth chapter was done by Artemus Packard and Mrs. Ruth Friess. Other committee members familiar in art education were Mary Albright, Belle Boas, Rosabelle MacDonald, and Thomas Munro. Natalie Robinson Cole's *The Arts in the Classroom* is dated 1940, as is the Bryn Mawr symposium on art.[5]

The three books perform diverse and complementary tasks. The first was one of a series examining subject-matter fields for the Progressive Education Association. It especially brought to a focus the psychological emphasis on the integration of the individual through the arts. This concept was felt to be of greater importance than the former attempts to integrate the contents of various subjects. In pursuit of the theme, a helpful discussion of personality patterns was attempted, based upon the individual's successes and failures in coping with art materials.

Natalie Robinson Cole has been the most widely read contributor of distinctively personal teaching methods of the last decade. Her book deals with the experience of teaching a fourth grade in Los Angeles, where she developed a program including painting, clay work, block printing, dance, and writing. Her approach is surely that of a true descendant of the early progressives. The volume

---

[4] Committee on the Function of Art in General Education, *op. cit.*
[5] Bryn Mawr College, *Art: A Bryn Mawr Symposium*, Vol. IX, *Notes and Monographs*, Bryn Mawr, 1940.

Creative Expression,[6] which made the 1926 magazine art articles available in book form, included music, visual and plastic arts, writing, dancing, and play acting. In her work Mrs. Cole continued to use the arts as easily and naturally in classroom activity as most teachers use reading. She explores the impulse of successful art creation as it affects the child in his daily associations. In particular, she makes us aware of the worth of personal expression to the child who feels submerged or persecuted by reason of family poverty, unpleasant home life, or neglect.

The Bryn Mawr symposium brought together historian, anthropologist, philosopher, and psychologist. The accent was on the Gestalt point of view. Koffka, the psychologist, is one of the small group of men in his field, recently joined by some psychiatrists, who are interested in the art processses and who will continue to influence art analysis and production. Their thinking is often distasteful to the artist, but by trial and error, with and without help from the artist, they are bound to reveal basic drives for aesthetic action as they have for other aspects of existence.

1941: BEFORE PEARL HARBOR

The publication date for a too-little known landmark in education was February, 1941. The 40th Yearbook of the National Society for the Study of Education was discussed at the annual meeting in that month; the title of the yearbook was *Art in American Life and Education.*[7] Thomas Munro was chairman of the yearbook committee, succeeding Melvin Haggerty, who died in 1937. Committee members and the roster of contributors constituted a cross section of art education. On the committee were Alon Bement, George S. Dutch, Raymond P. Ensign, Royal Bailey Farnum, Ray Faulkner, Robert S. Hilpert, Ernest Horn, C. Valentine Kirby, Felix Payant, and Edwin Ziegfeld.

Four sections comprised the book. Numbers One, Three, and Four, respectively—"Art in American Life," "Art Education: Its Aims, Procedures and Agencies," and "The Preparation of Teachers"

---

[6] G. Hartman and A. Shumaker, eds., *Creative Expression,* Reynal and Hitchcock, 1932.

[7] National Society for the Study of Education, *Art in American Life and Education,* 40th Yearbook, Public School Publishing Company, 1941.

—were informative and excellent material for the record. Section Two, "The Nature of Art and Related Types of Experience," is a major document in its importance. Thomas Munro's writing—"The Psychological Approach to Art and Art Education," "Creative Ability in Art and Its Educational Fostering," "Powers of Art Appreciation and Evaluation," and "The Analysis of Form in Art"—should be known to all art teachers, for no more reasoned and balanced thinking on the subjects is available. Ray Faulkner buttresses Munro's theses with "A Survey of Recent Research in Art and Art Education," "Standards of Value in Art," and "Art and Its Relation to Society." "Recent Research in the Psychology of Art," by Norman C. Meier, ably completes these valuable chapters.

One's first reaction to Munro's thinking is that it is of the "common-sense" category. More slowly, it dawns upon the reader that Munro is making an inclusive and conclusive summary of the most useful points of view expressed by the artist, the teacher, the psychologist, and the child, with a sympathetic insight into the background of each. His analysis of the limitations inherent in the teaching of art "principles" in the manner of Dow; his overview of the effort to determine a basis for art values, making a good introduction to later work by Herbert Read; his exposition of the relative merits of the Gestaltists and the analysts or behaviorists; and his observations on the presence of and the development of art abilities are all among the soundest writings we possess. They ought to be republished separately.

Much earlier, in 1932, at the Fieldston Conference,[8] and before that as a contributor to the Barnes Foundation *Art and Education*,[9] Thomas Munro gave us insights into the relationships of psychology and art education which were in advance of the times and based upon a greater familiarity with European work than was enjoyed by his colleagues. Only now do we find the art-education profession somewhat abreast of his earlier work, and realize that his writing is not well-enough known nor easily available.

Art Today, by Faulkner, Ziegfeld, and Hill,[10] put into textbook

[8] Thomas Munro, "Art and Adolescence," *Bulletin of the Worcester Art Museum*, 1932.

[9] John Dewey, ed., *Art and Education*, Barnes Foundation, 1929.

[10] Ray Faulkner, Edwin Ziegfeld, and Gerald Hill, *Art Today*, Holt, 1941.

form for senior-high-school and college use an approach to contemporary design, architecture, painting, and sculpture. The material evolved from courses offered in the general college at the University of Minnesota. It was fresh, well-organized, and graced with fine pictorial examples; its revision in 1951 attests to the needs it has met, improves the pictorial content, and further clarifies the text.

The pre-Pearl Harbor year, as has been observed in cultural fields in other prewar years, continued, among other good works, to provide more background in art education. These included Minnie McLeish's *Beginnings of Teaching Art to Children,* Charlotte Major's pamphlet, *Teaching Art in the Elementary School,* Ralph Pearson's *The New Art Education,* Rosabelle MacDonald's *Art as Education,* and Harold Gregg's *Art for the Schools of America.* Not one of these books failed to enrich the thinking of art teachers. Pearson, then as now, preached the gospel of form, of structure, as the predominant aesthetic value. McLeish, Major, and MacDonald developed the theme of broadening art experience, Major with an emphasis on expression of experience, MacDonald with a greater interest in appreciation. MacDonald has stated clearly the case for a better use of the arts in the secondary curriculum.

Art in the rural schools has probably not been better taught than in Sonoma County, California, where Harold Gregg acted as art supervisor. His book is an outgrowth of that teaching, and has run into several reprints because, in addition to his more general concepts, he deals so convincingly with immediate teaching practices carried on in that farm community. As with the Cole book, description of specific experience makes it a worth-while reference.

Within the one year, there had come so many and such varied aids for the improvement of art education that even under normal conditions it would have taken years to assimilate them all. War years certainly slowed the process, but fortunately the work was neither lost nor overlooked, for today these studies are in constant use.

CHILD AS ARTIST

The gist of all the work of the first few years of the decade of the forties was that the child must be privileged to work as an artist works. Victor D'Amico had taught at Fieldston School and then as educational director at the Museum of Modern Art. Inevitably, when he compiled his experience and philosophy for book form, it was this emphasis he accepted and which formed the basis for *Creative Teaching in Art*.[11] Coming out in 1942, it performed the function of summarizing and making explicit a great deal of the accomplishment of the preceding several years; this was especially true of the art work at the junior- and senior-high-school level.

D'Amico believes that the artist is one of the most valuable members of society; that the artist's approach to living and to his work is one of creative sanity in a world not distinguished for an oversupply of that quality. Further than that, he believes that the child can, with the right school environment, be helped to create his own personality in something like the way an artist approaches his current effort in any media. Chapter headings deal with the subjects "The Child as Artist," "The Child as Painter," "The Child as Mural Painter," "The Child as Sculptor," "The Child as Potter," "The Child as Graphic Artist," "The Child as Stage Artist," "The Child as Designer and Craftsman," and "The Child-Artist and His Materials."

We know as we contemplate American public education that specific curricula and educational theory will change and be modified, but the Parkers, the Deweys and disciples like D'Amico will continue a great tradition in American teaching: the fine art of inducing student initiative, replacing the apathy of following directions with the activity of personal responsibility. In the arts, D'Amico commits himself to the thesis that the child's use of the materials and techniques of the artist can be an element of great value in personality development, provided that the child artist is able to go at his art work in just the spirit and the unhampered processes followed by the independent artist.

For D'Amico the cute craft objects, the resuscitated and gilded fir cones, the decorated glass bottles, the tie-dye scarves, are not worthwhile listing as class projects—not so much for themselves as for exactly the same reason that they annoy the serious artist. They are the product of simperers and gigglers around the fringes of art. They are pseudo-art products requiring nothing of their makers but time and a little manual skill. The text of *Creative Teaching in Art* shows no

[11] Victor D'Amico, *Creative Teaching in Art*, International Textbook, 1942.

interest in art-class products made of salvage goods, in mass production of party favors, in busy work with crepe paper embowering the school gym for the prom.

The emphasis on the substantial media of painting, sculpture, ceramics, graphic arts, and such crafts as stage design and furniture is deliberate in its omissions as well as its inclusions. Everything the student should be able to do in art is included for the creative planning it requires, for the resistance it offers technically to the student artist, for the merit it possesses as a successfully completed project. Objects and media which are negligible in any of these ways are not even suggested.

A true art experience, D'Amico believes, must have a double-barreled integrity. It must be the honest design of an individual or group of individuals approaching the work with a desire to do a fresh, unique job. And it must have a dignity and integrity arising from a considered and fresh use of the materials involved.

He deplores the vicarious nature of so much school art work: textile designs which are never intended to be transferred to cloth, "allover" patterns with no further use than their own existence, designs for ceramics, for dramatic productions, for furniture, or drawings made in the manner of block prints or etchings—all these started and completed without the slightest aim to go beyond the "designing." This remoteness from the actual materials of crafts cannot be justified. Almost as lacking in justification is the timid, time-killing designing for a craft before the students have had a chance to work with the new media. The only logical and psychologically right approach to a craft should be that of direct experience. After a familiarity with processes and material has been gained, the student may find it worth the doing to design on paper before starting a new piece.

Under the present circumstances of crowded elementary-school rooms and a minimum of art equipment and supplies, it is unfortunately true that the art work D'Amico visualizes, especially in the sculptural and crafts area, is more possible where art is taught by a special teacher, as in the junior and senior high schools, than it is in most elementary grades. In the case of complex activities like stone carving or etching, there is little or no likelihood of wishing that these crafts could be available to the sixth grade and below. Ceramic work, on the other hand, is excellent for grade children.

The principles proposed can, however, remain the same when applied to work in slighter media. Papier-mâché and tubular paper forms, though to some not as interesting a sculptural media as fired ceramic, are creatively used in the middle grades. It holds true that to "design" on two-dimensional paper is probably time thrown away for the child unacquainted with the three-dimensional quality of papier-mâché.

The primary theme running through this book, and through all of D'Amico's work as educational director of the Museum of Modern Art, is that of personality growth greatly enhanced through art expression. His insistence on the quality of that experience being made like that of the artist does create a bias in favor of the separate and alone activity, the self-expression for which our school communities provide so little opportunity in other fields.

"Self-expression" has always been a suspect term with conventional teachers and lately, too, with some keener thinkers who begin to see too strict an adherence to "self" as a limitation sometimes to be transcended. For the independent artist of our time is a lonely performer, too, cut off from his society, though not necessarily by his own wish. He does have, usually at a financial loss to himself, a freedom to contemplate, to plan, to make a product, as few other persons are privileged to do. He can, in actuality he usually must, initiate and carry through his total concept. The realization of this independence of concept is obviously favored by D'Amico for its value in child development. If it has a limitation, it is the same limitation known so well to the mature artist.

The balance we are reaching for in the professional arts would be equally desirable for the children in the arts classroom. A society most hospitable to the arts will not be one requiring nothing from the artist, but will instead ask for great things. Such a society will have come closer to knowing what the artist can and should contribute; its projects could stimulate unlimited efforts from its artists.

It is similar in the classroom; the child, like the artist, can grow advantageously through individually selected and planned work. But there is a possibility that our present emphasis tends to deny the search for community-initiated work, where art values may and do reside, if a keen aesthetic intelligence makes the proposal and shares in the direction of the work. D'Amico's teaching of mural painting and stage arts develops this aspect of art in the schools. If he reflects an attitude common to art teachers, that of jealous insistence on the designer being supreme in his field, it is simply the result of all artists' experience. When a citizen, or citizen committee, unfettered either by an artist or a person with some art knowledge, assumes the responsibility for setting up an art project and for evaluating its progress, the results have often ranged from the lower levels of mediocrity to the sub-basement of aesthetic disaster.

Nevertheless, artist and student in the arts will continue to have to work in a community and for the community. One of the most fertile fields for development in the future must be that of mutual education between the drive of the artist and the interest of the layman who is intelligent enough to be concerned with art. The artist-student will have to learn to see the kernel of possibilities in what may seem at first a rather dull project. The lay coöperator must be helped to recognize, to welcome, and to encourage the unexpected shift of direction, the new richness, which an honestly stimulated designer sees in the project under consideration.

How to evolve this intelligent and interested layman is art education's biggest question. D'Amico, in the museum as in his teaching, holds to participation as all-important. The museum, under his leadership, has invented art fairs where children and sometimes accompanying parents have been literally lured into drawing, painting, cutting and pasting collages, and operating electrical color instruments and pieces of mobile-sculpture units.

Accepting the postulate that participating in any activity is a great aid to understanding, there remain for us the questions: What activities? How shall they be conducted? Shall they be popular, appealing, colorful—and to be all this must they be a little on the parlor-trick scale to enlist the largest possible mass audience—or must they be more substantial?

The basis of D'Amico's philosophy is that of emphasizing creative achievement. Art may be gay and whimsical as well as profound, but it must offer to every student a reasonable variety of materials

216

and the technical guidance to realize one's own ideas. Art is not copying; it is not the easy adaptation of conventional patterns, the imitation of vulgar advertising and illustration, or the craft project equipped with an enclosed design.

He believes that the student of any age can more nearly realize his full capabilities by developing creatively in art. D'Amico describes better than most how we may teach creatively, achieve an environment that stimulates art production, and teach the needed skills without diminishing the personal quality each student's work displays.

CREATIVE AND MENTAL GROWTH

Viktor Lowenfeld provides a supplement and an amplification for progressive-education practices in art.[12] Chronologically, it is not out of place to think of Lowenfeld's psychological analysis of children and their potentialities in art as a supporting document to D'Amico's earlier profession of faith, to the teaching of Margaret Mathias, Belle Boas, Rosabelle MacDonald, and hundreds of their less widely known colleagues.

Lowenfeld examines the range of child groupings in the schools and tries to depict more completely and accurately than has been done before what may be hoped for in their art work. This he does in reference to children's stage-by-stage emotional development and to the gradual evolution in their use of the most commonly used art media. D'Amico makes a persuasive case for the child's necessity to develop individually as a person and as an artist. Lowenfeld charts the course of that development so that we may recognize the landmarks and progress being made by our students.

Relativism still rules. We are not looking for an absolute ideal pattern of visual forms toward which the child's earliest-drawn forms are to be directed, as was true in 1900. We are not jovially "permitting" childlike scrawls for a year or two by way of arousing interest later in the more serious business of learning to draw naturalistically. We are not even, as Lowenfeld sees it, engaged in the slow work of developing freedom of expression in visual form in order that the student may turn with strict ardor to the compelling effort of achiev-

[12] Viktor Lowenfeld, *Creative and Mental Growth*, Macmillan, 1947; rev., 1952.

ing pictorial structure, "composition," or "significant form" regardless of the incidentals of personality, place, and time.

Instead of these objectives, each characteristic of an era in art education, Lowenfeld offers a guide to the growth of the whole individual as it is mirrored in works of art. His preparation for this task is that of years of teaching and a scholar's command of the large mass of material, especially in German, summarizing the normal change of visual concepts among children of the Western cultures. Paralleling this, he is equally interested in, and selects most skillfully from, the psychological background of children as it relates to the art work of the individual.

A child of four scribbling with crayon on a sheet of newsprint is making lines and forms which are arranged in a manner as personal to that child as his voice, even as his fingerprint. Psychologically, Lowenfeld points out, art expression thrives when the personal quality, the "self-expression," inherent in the way in which we all work is recognized and encouraged by the art teacher.

In his paragraphs on "Self-Expression" and "Self-Adjustment," [13] he makes clear a distinction between the content of any individual's work and the manner of its realization. Over the past three decades, many excellent art teachers have found themselves bewildered by the doctrine of child initiative in the classroom. Often a skilled teacher will find that a class is at a point where, as a group, it can profitably determine the nature of the next work it will start. This is true of special art work as it is of other aspects of activity. But much educational literature seems, or seemed in the recent past, to suggest that the only valid educational ventures must come from the child. While the teacher knows this is practically not possible, there has been the gnawing question as to whether or not one is doing all that he might to permit greater student contribution to planning.

Lowenfeld's careful discussion of self-expression states that the all-important individual contribution in art work is in the "how" of its accomplishment. This does not mean that a succession of rigidly scheduled problems in art work will do just as well as the more flexible program of a teacher sensitive to the direction and capabilities of single class members and of the group. It does make evident that

[13] *Ibid.*, pp. 4–5.

the teacher's leadership in initiating class activity should be carefully adapted to bring out the most vigorous response from the children. A class in which each individual finds that he is able to interpret some part of his own experience in art form, and that the teacher helps him to realize his conception, is a successful art class. A class of this sort will inevitably gratify the teacher by providing its own leadership as often as there is an opportunity.

Significantly, when he comes to "The Meaning of Aesthetic Criteria" and "The Elements of Composition," [14] (Lowenfeld interestingly uses aesthetics and composition as synonymous), he discusses line, space, light and shadow, color, and unity as adjuncts of the expression of the individual. In relation to these elements, he attributes to each of them the "physiognomic" or tertiary characteristics elaborated upon by Koffka in his paper for the Bryn Mawr symposium of 1940. As he sees it, *line* has a life given it unconsciously by the artist no matter what his age, ability, sex, or skill may be. Stable, open, receiving, closed, protective, breaking through, are all qualities freely attributed to line. He is as sympathetic to the Gestalt views as is Kepes in *Language of Vision*. This pattern of thought is followed throughout the discussion on the elements of composition. He is concerned with the dynamic psychological use of the elements as revealed in the history of art epochs, and as we may see them handled unconsciously by most children and amateurs and with masterly awareness by mature and able artists. Lowenfeld sums up this section:

> In recognizing this unity of composition as the highest form of organization and economy in which nothing can be changed without doing harm to the whole, an important means of criticism is placed in the hands of the educator.
>
> . . . however, he will not succeed if he does not place the individual above rules, if he does not consider unity of composition the most *integrated outcome of personality and creation.*[15]

Beginning with his Chapter VI, "The Pseudo-Realistic Stage, the Stage of Reasoning" (eleven to thirteen years), he dwells upon the distinction between the visual and subjective types of personalities as they show themselves in art. Later on he uses the term "haptic"

[14] *Ibid.,* pp. 165, 166 in 1947 ed.; pp. 265, 266 in 1952 ed.
[15] *Ibid.,* p. 191 in 1947 ed.; p. 291 in 1952 ed.

to identify the student possessed of the subjective reaction to environment. Herbert Read, in his *Education Through Art,* gives a scholarly background for the use of the terms, which Lowenfeld illustrates by direct reference to classroom activities and products.

According to our best contemporary knowledge, close to a quarter of the population is more aware of the stimulation of touch, of kinesthesis, than of sight. Through the early years of school, the majority of visual-minded children and the lesser group of haptically oriented, as well as the group of individuals not strongly inclined either way, do not appear in their art work to be so very different. Their symbols for the human figure, whether visually or haptically stimulated, are so incomplete, so likely to emphasize one aspect of the body at the expense of all other proportions, movements, or clothing, that even the most observant teacher would need to watch several drawings in process before making generalizations about any student's approach.

It is in the years of the "Pseudo-Realistic Stage" that the diverging tendencies become more apparent. The individual is more interested in the finished product, less so in the processes. As this develops, the visual-minded student sees more clearly than before the relationship of himself, of people in general, to the environment. His use of space, of color, of line pattern, his effort to grasp perspective, all are from the point of view of a spectator, of one looking at and seeing his surroundings.

The haptically oriented child can be aided in his art expression by realizing that his use of form, color, and space is concentrated upon expressing what he feels about the subject. Stimulation, Lowenfeld shows, must be in the form of subjects which can be physically and emotionally grasped without strong reliance upon a visually conceived setting. The majority of children at the age of fourteen have a visual concept of a basketball game. The smaller number of haptic individuals would have a feeling for the tenseness of the enthralled fan, the speed of the players, the rhythmic pounding of feet back and forth across the court. They would tend to be less interested in the winning or losing of the game for its symbolic value to school pride.

Lowenfeld's elaboration of this theme is useful material for the junior-senior-high-school art teacher dealing with the transition from childhood to maturity.

Edward Warder Rannells supplies an invaluable supplement at this point in his pamphlet, *Art Education in the Junior High School*,[16] which was unfortunately issued in somewhat limited and local circulation by the University of Kentucky Press. His survey of the art experiences on the junior-high level is solid, psychologically thorough. His complete grasp of all the worth-while writing bearing on the subject illuminates his own offering. Rannells is particularly valuable in his suggestions for the kind of work, and the bases for it, which will carry the junior-high student through the period when social inhibitions and sexual development are making the heaviest impact on personality. He makes the case clearly, and with all the needed brackground, for a variety of activities, challenging in their demands and making possible all kinds of attractive byways, for the erratic, somewhat unpredictable members of the junior-high-school-age community.

ART IN THE HIGH SCHOOL

With an appropriate title, "The Period of Decision," [17] Lowenfeld devotes a chapter to the work of the senior-high student. A special vote of appreciation is in order for his extensive listings of possible stimulation to art work in the high school. Teaching aids similar to it are common, but they are usually a snare and a delusion, encouraging the teacher to seek uniform skills and finished performances from all students alike. These listings, based upon a psychology of individual differences, avoid such a dead end.

An art teacher reading D'Amico, Lowenfeld, and Rannells on the place of art in the life of the high-school student finds agreement easy. But any high-school art teacher knows at once that while we can speak ably for an approach to art in the elementary school and junior high school—which is possible and is fairly rapidly being attained—the same is not true of the senior high. What we believe in and write about concerning art in the senior secondary schools is not applicable to *the* student, as is the case with art in the elementary

[16] Edward Warder Rannells, *Art Education in the Junior High School,* University of Kentucky, 1946.
[17] Viktor Lowenfeld, *op. cit.,* p. 125 in 1947 ed.; p. 225 in 1952 ed.

grades, but to *a* student. The student in high-school art classes is apt to be only one out of ten or more of his classmates. The art work has become not a general discipline but a highly specialized interest to be elected by a few students.

None of us can speak about art for the general high-school student with the same authority that we feel about art in the grade schools. In ninety-nine cases out of a hundred we have no way of knowing what would be a productive art course for general high-school students because we have never had the opportunity of teaching such groups.

The Eight Year Plan explored some of the administrative and schedule-making schemes for making art more available as a subject to a greater number of secondary students. Yet few of these schemes, and no others currently available, forecast a time when all high-school students will be exposed to art experiences as a regular part of their curriculum.

This is true in spite of the fact that many valuable contemporary writers on the arts and education—Herbert Read in *Education Through Art,* Kepes in *Language of Vision,* Faulkner, Ziegfeld, and Hill in *Art Today*—propose as a necessity a general education in the arts for the whole educable population. Most art teachers, if quizzed sympathetically and not frightened out of their normal missionary spirit, would readily agree that all secondary students should take art.

The next step, if such a situation were to be brought about by administrative fiat, could be chaotic. The fact is that we are not ready or able to teach all high-school students in art classes. In the unlikely event that they were suddenly assigned to a required art period, there would be waged, for some time at least, a heavily unequal contest between doubtful, unconvinced students and teachers by no means sure of their objectives or of their use of the equipment available. We are lacking in practices calculated to create among these general students an interest in the visual and plastic arts. Unfortunately, in the few schools which have had general art-education courses as a requirement, there has seldom been enough time for planning, enough experimentation, enough recognition of the wholly different nature of the job from that of the customary selective senior-high art group.

222

EDUCATION THROUGH ART

Does that mean we must abandon Herbert Read's formula, as expressed in his *Education Through Art*,[18] when our boys and girls enter high school? Read, on his title page, uses a typical Bernard Shaw aphorism: "I am simply calling attention to the fact that fine art is the only teacher except torture."

Presumably, then, taking Shaw literally, art teachers would say that most students in high school get on without being taught at all, since the large majority of them never have a class in "art." It is time that public-school, college, and professional-art-school teachers faced this contradiction in their philosophy and practice, for it has been a generally acknowledged belief among us for many decades.

Herbert Read is perhaps the most thorough and helpful scholar of our age to consider at length the place of art in society and the task art education has started to tackle. Like such men as Gibbs in the sciences, Frank Lloyd Wright in architecture, Dewey in philosophy, he produces so lavishly, extends our powers of concentration and understanding so greatly, that it will take us time to catch up to and implement the major results of his labors.

Education Through Art is a synthesis of his own thinking on the subject with a generously annotated guide to the growth of that thought through his readings in aesthetics, philosophy, art, psychology, and education. Read insists, without apology or equivocation, that education for all people must be aesthetic.

Certain observations come immediately to mind as we consider this dictum. One is that Read, like Dewey, believes existence itself is only possible on an aesthetic level. To my mind, we are all guilty of the use of the word "aesthetics" without supplying for ourselves and the public a recent and better definition of it than appears in the dictionary. Since Hegel's time aesthetics has been considered the "science of the beautiful." Our recent usage of the term seems to say that aesthetics is the study of the linked process of perception, conception, and creation on the part of the individual within his environment. "Aesthetic" as an adjective could then refer to a perception, a conception, or a creative act which was making forms out of experience. Dewey's analysis would imply that any human awareness

18 Herbert Read, *Education Through Art*, Faber, 1943.

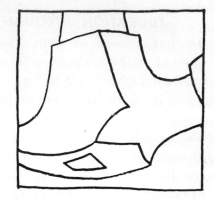

Figure 13. "Three-Dimensional Subject Space Relationships." (From Ralph M. Pearson, "The New Art Education," rev. ed., Harper, 1952.)

Figure 14. Left, "My House," by Extre-averted Sensation Type; right, Same Subject, by Introverted Sensation Type (An Hysterical Boy with Stammer.) (From Herbert Read, "Education Through Art," Pantheon, 1945.)

of the environment through the senses which is consciously received and evaluated becomes some sort of form which is the basis of aesthetic emotion.

An individual may stand on the curb of a busy street. If his awareness of the traffic is simply that of keeping caution alive while he thinks of the work he must do, the shopping intended, or the nearest bus stop, then an aesthetic reaction is not prominent, or it may be unconscious, stored up and revived to thorough consciousness and evaluation, hours, even years, later through some incidental association.

But if another individual on the same curb becomes consciously aware of the glitter of chromium plate visible in both lanes of traffic, sees the sharp points of sun glint, contrasts it with the color of summer clothes on the sidewalks and the relative drabness of the masonry walls hemming in all this activity at the top of the man-made ravine—then he has had an immediate aesthetic perception and formed a concept which in turn could give rise to a creation in the form of a verbal description, or even ultimately in a formal work of art in any one of several media, writing or painting, music or dance.

We must accept Read's *Education Through Art* on that basis. He writes: "Education is the fostering of growth, [and] growth is only made apparent in expression—audible or visible signs and symbols. Education may therefore be defined as the cultivation of modes of expression. . . ."[19] The nineteenth-century understanding of art as being inseparable from a "sense of beauty" is no longer valid. Too many of our fellow citizens narrowly insist that art and beauty are restricted to the activities of "ladies": home decoration in the vein dictated by current good taste. Some will agree that there is beauty in the lines of a new car or in a physically well-favored and well-dressed young woman, but they will be dubious about these forms of beauty being related to art or to that still more formidable term, aesthetics. For the art teacher, however, aesthetic perception comes to mean a heightened, significant awareness of environment experienced through whatever complex of personality and background the individual may possess.

Let us return to Read's thesis. He says education must be aes-

[19] *Ibid.*, p. 11.

thetic. Obviously, we can observe that education *is* aesthetic. No one in our society could grow up to the state of a reasonably responsible adult unless he progressed in the quantity and quality of such experience; every part of our surroundings contains signs and symbols of expression.

What Read implies is that formal education, education in schools as well as the casual education of every waking hour, must be aesthetic. In a sense, this is so. The art forms of writing, speaking, picture making, music, movement in drama and dance, constitute the only available tools of the teacher. What has been lacking since schools for the millions began has been a broader view of the educable potentialities of the individual. In 1790 it occurred to men like Thomas Jefferson that the chief difference between an educated and an uneducated man was the power to read. Ever since we have concentrated on the learning of this single means of communication, of expression. What Bernard Shaw certainly meant, and is for that reason quoted by Read, is that we are in fact educated by all our senses and by the creations of artists dependent upon and appealing to the senses. Possibly Shaw had the more limited notion of mass man being educated by contact with the finished works of fine arts created by professional artists. But Read demands positively that all mankind be educated, not alone by his contact with superlative works of the fine arts, but by actual, personal experience in the processes of creating art forms. We must teach so that all of our students are daily more aware of themselves and of their unique powers of conception and creation in one or many art forms.

Do we then set about to turn the schools over lock, stock, and blackboards to the art teacher? Is that the impossible admonition we are to take from Herbert Read's exhortation? The likelihood of such a revolution is happily remote.

Yet there is in process at the present time in American life a synthesis of many forces which is already, though rather unconsciously, creating a more aesthetic way of life. Education of the formal variety can give this synthesis strength; pull it into a more conscious focus; make it a more potent force in daily schoolwork. Naturally, the teacher in the arts will have to be a leader in this movement. To do so he must first sharpen his own awareness of what goes on.

CONTEMPORARY RELATIONSHIPS IN THE ARTS

The classroom art teacher whose immediate problem is initiating and guiding the activities of a class of twenty-five children may wonder how the relationships of art to such fields as anthropology, optics, regional planning, or social history has any more than theoretical importance to the work at hand. Or he may reflect that art education has always presumed to have some interest in the objects of everyday living, and that there is nothing new in the relationships which are to be discussed here. My wish is not to attempt any new or novel theme; it is only to make more explicit, if I can, the pervasive nature of the arts, and hence the importance of education by way of the arts.

Lewis Mumford, among others, has described the art of impressionism, of Cézanne, of cubism, as being characteristic of the late nineteenth and early twentieth century because the men and movements were concentrating on the analysis of certain phases of pictorial art. Mumford sees most human creative activity of that period as being analytical, splitting the whole into smaller parts the better to know its composition and function. The corollary to that thesis is that we now need the equally necessary effort to synthesize, to bring together some of the things we have discovered or defined, to the advantage of all the fields concerned.

Synthesis of the values of art with philosophy, with literature, with the sciences—as well as a larger concern with art in business, in education generally, and in government—is in process now. And it is a larger, more significant trend than anything we as art teachers have heretofore described as "art in everyday life."

In a sense there may be nothing particularly new to art history in noting that the artifacts of a South Pacific culture bear definite relationships to the total social structure, or that an unusual amount of work and thought has recently been done on the influence of visual perception upon the visual forms created in pictorial arts. As to the former proposition, art has always been acknowledged as the chief clue to the culture of the past; and for the latter, visual perception is obviously indispensable to pictorial art.

It is not only that art is important in many human activities; it always has been. It would be possible for thinkers in many professional fields to drag some mention of art into their surveys merely as a proof of their breadth of culture. Many writers and critics prior to 1920 did give every indication of referring to art, when they did so at all, in just that way. However, there is now in evidence an informed conviction in the way we find philosophers, anthropologists, sociologists, and others describing the arts as major elements in human experience.

Perhaps the new element we face in the arts and in art education is simply that all human knowledge and the accelerated tempo of research describe art as indispensable to human existence; demonstrate that art on this earth ranks with science, politics, or what we call business.

Sometimes, if we would be honest, we are frightened by accepting that statement as the full truth, for most of us have been raised in the arts as in a privileged garden, in a somewhat rare and precious atmosphere. Art as ubiquitous as commerce loses its rarity, certainly its quiet exclusiveness. Does it have to sacrifice, to forget quality? Will art become, not a fine expression of humanity, but only a record of its having existed?

Does the notion that art is achieving a synthesis with other disciplines and a currency among millions of people in our democratic society necessarily create a monster? Might art teachers rather not welcome this growth, aid it by the enlargement of their outlook, and teach with a more vigorous, less fragile outlook upon what constitutes the aesthetic attitude for themselves and their community?

I prefer to begin this survey of movements toward synthesis as I see it by discussing the ideas which broaden the definition of art, which blur the distinctions between "fine" and "practical" arts, and which start out with the life and society of all the people in whatever culture we are examining as the basis for identifying and evaluating the arts of that culture.

John A. Kouwenhoven in 1948 brought out the book *Made in America*.[20] In it he discussed at length what he terms the "vernacular" tradition, using as example such things as locomotives. He pointed out the distinctive contrasting qualities existing in English and American locomotives of the early years of railroading. The

[20] John A. Kouwenhoven, *Made in America*, Doubleday, 1948.

English from the first built rigid-frame locomotives, and the Americans built them as flexibly as a linked chain with something of the puddle-jumping characteristics of the twentieth-century Model T Ford car. The American engine had a longer route over a more varied country and on roadbeds which were only slightly better than the original deer or buffalo trails, hence the need for wheel mounting which made the front pair a kind of independent feeler for the weight-carrying set of four further back under the boiler. With this arrangement hills, valleys, and curves could be negotiated. All the wheels on the English machine were in a rigid iron frame. Doubtless their right-of-way mileage, being much less, was built more carefully with more lasting and level roadbeds. The locomotives reflect the contrasting national tempers and environments of the time.

Through the use of such a case study, Kouwenhoven contrasts this interrelated design problem—one which involved finance, transport, topography, industrial development—with that part of the culture of the time which was officially labeled "art." The gist of his thesis is that the official and the vernacular design activities, being kept apart, failed to enrich each other, and that we cannot and must not for the future maintain high walls between fine and practical arts.

Kouwenhoven acknowledges the debt he owes many predecessors in his discourse upon the "vernacular" in art; he is not, of course, the first to discover it. The decade of the 1920's was avid in its resurrection of the antiques of the nineteenth and eighteenth centuries, of Currier and Ives prints, of primitive hand-built furniture, of Pennsylvania Dutch chests, and so on. The difference between this interest of the 1920's and the present scholarly interests of Kouwenhoven, Pevsner, Giedion, and Mumford is that in the first instance we have a search for the quaint for the sake of its delicious quality; and in the second we come upon a dominating interest of our day, the effort to understand the near past and perhaps our own future through the total arts of the society.

True, Albert Pinkham Ryder was producing his magnificent paintings in 1876, and he is a gem in the history of American art. It is also true that the exhibit of the Philadelphia Centennial of 1876 was only a little less horrendous in its exhibit pieces and infinitely worse in its architecture than the British International Exhibit of 1851. Nevertheless, both Ryder's paintings and the Exposition are aesthetic land-marks in our background; nor are they so merely to contrast "good" and "bad" as an aid to forming superior aesthetic judgment for the future.

If we find an 1876 bedstead equipped with a six-foot-high, ma-chine-carved, and veneered headboard less functional than a pres-ent-day Hollywood-style bed, we begin to make this distinction not simply as a matter of what is superficially in style, but because we are being led to see design as related to, and actually making possi-ble, a way of life. The six-foot headboard is too big, too heavy, too much work to dust, and no compensation for its somber domination, visually, of the room in which it stands.

We are not without tendencies, in this day, to make a display first and to achieve usefulness only incidentally. By the year 2000, some of our lamps, automobiles, and clothes will be seen in their proper perspective as comparatively ugly and unfunctional objects with which to live.

The point we must keep in the forefront of our consciousness in art education is that the whole man-made physical environment is aesthetically designed, whether it be the current issue of a weekly magazine or the new building of the United Nations. All the objects man makes have degrees of quality or lack of quality which reflect the life we lead and the personality, group and individual, of those who are doing the making. To dwell upon this point does not absolve the teacher of art from seeking and encouraging qualitative work, but only puts the effort in a somewhat larger social framework than many are accustomed to consider as the realm of the arts.

To group, as units in our aesthetic expression, everything from pre-fabricated houses and steel kettles to motion pictures and paintings does not mean that the art teacher abrogates his own good judgment either of the completed object or the manner of its design and pro-duction. A junior-high-school teacher may never come closer to auto-mobile design than to drive a car, but he does possess a greater critical concern with the quality of design than do most people. Part of his job is to provide his students with a basis for such critical evaluation.

The most valuable result of broadening the scope of the arts will be that of encouraging aesthetic awareness and judgment of those human products familiar to all, whether they live in the largest city or the smallest village. With this as a beginning, there will be less reluctance on the part of many persons to follow their interests into other art forms as spectators or as performers.

TWO FORMS OF AESTHETIC JUDGMENT

Mankind has done curious and wonderful things in shaping the environment, and much of this impulse has been aesthetic; that is to say, man has carried out a conception based on nature's raw materials and realized by the work of man. In 1787, when the Northwest Ordinance was passed, if the men who signed that document had been asked to define their ideal art form, they would probably have chosen a portrait of one of their leading citizens, replete with romantic, splendid symbols of office and rich red-velvet robes and drapes partly revealing bits of classical architectural stage properties. Their art preferences pictorially were romantic to the last degree; nowadays we would call them pompous.

The same men, however, when called upon to devise a method of opening up the western territories beyond the Appalachians, passed a bill dividing a huge plot of ground into as rigorous a geometrical pattern as was ever imposed on a section of the globe. Ever since, this rational "gridiron" of sections and townships has been a convenience for identification and bookkeeping, and on the other hand has created some of the most preposterous planning of roads, streets, and even farm divisions and cities that can be imagined.

The desire in the eighteenth century for a geometrical order of man's life was arbitrarily imposed on the endless variety of nature. It was an aesthetic judgment carrying seeds of value and great inconvenience alike. Now, almost two centuries later, the science of soil conservation, through the "contouring" of hilly land, is creating with increasing speed a drastic change in the appearance of large parts of our agricultural land. While the genesis of contouring is scientific, its visual results will be infinitely pleasing to the eye, revealing and emphasizing the organic structure of hills and valleys. On the fringes of the cities, over seventy years ago, the aesthetic desire for something other than the rigid checkerboard of streets created the suburban areas, where thoroughfares follow, in something like the effect of contouring, the gracious curves of the landscape itself.

The appearance of the land is an example of man's planning. Just as much as the official portrait of 1780, it reflects the vision of the men of that day. It is difficult, really impossible, to separate wholly the sociological, aesthetic, and scientific influences which determined the designs we live with and on. Certainly a sharpened aesthetic perception will contribute largely to the other aspects of man's organization of nature, of his tools, of his structures, of his means of communication, as well as of those activities more commonly known as the arts.

THERAPY AND THE AMATEUR

The forms of art in the twentieth century are multifarious, and we are aided in teaching every time we extend our ability to identify the aesthetic content in an act or product previously overlooked.

Equal in importance to this stepping over the narrow borders of the "fine arts" is the matter of reëxamining the act of aesthetic creation as it is illuminated these days by the researches of psychologists, optometrists, psychiatrists, and therapists. The tendency of many artists and teachers will be to bring up their heaviest artillery for the attack on "art as therapy," or on the leisure-time, hobby-hour angle of popular art activities. The artist is apt to include most of the psychiatrists' observations on the arts in the same category as the papers given on alternate Wednesday afternoons for the local study club: good tries, worthy enterprise, but little knowledge or interest in the subject.

The artist is more than shy of acquainting himself with the psychology of the act of creation. He is pathologically antagonistic. He believes that art is infinitely more than it seems to be in the thinking of the men of medicine. And he is apprehensive of some of the people who are busy toying with art supplies in the interests of their personal therapy. The amateur today may become a major influence on the arts; unless he increases the seriousness of his interest beyond an initially therapeutic stage, the influence will be unfortunate. There is a problem here to which we must return, after we have considered the general setting of art as an aid to therapy, occupational and emotional.

The art of painting and many crafts are activities which attract more thousands of people each year. In this aspect these arts rank with other hobbies and recreational activities where the individual concerned is doing something, participating rather than watching. Two hundred years ago, the aristocrat was a person of "accomplishments." The common man worked for his living too much of the time to afford similar activities. Now we take for granted increased leisure time for most of the population, and many people seek to acquire an accomplishment, an interest outside their means of livelihood. Arts for all these people is therapy only in the broad sense that any constructive or contemplative activity is therapy. Modern life did not invent the rhythm of work alternating with festival, with travel, with play of one sort or another. Such a rhythm is therapeutic primarily because it is a natural way to live.

A rational attitude to take to the amateur, the hobbyist, is that he is engaged in the therapy of intelligent activity. There is no more need or excuse for the art teacher to assume the role of the clinical psychologist toward his adult class or his social-center group than there is for the gym coach or the drama director—and, on the other hand, there is no less need for him to be somewhat aware of basic psychological implications in the work done and the manner of its doing.

Quite possibly, if there is a tendency among the public to believe that painting is a more appropriate therapy than other interests for an emotionally off-center individual, it is partly because some art teachers have overemphasized this contribution. Purposeful activity is good therapy. That includes all varieties of arts, but it does not and should not be taken to indicate that certain arts are of more therapeutic value generally than sports or woodwork or typing. What counts most is the individual concerned and the nature of his needs for activity.

The arts and crafts used in the practice of occupational therapy must meet one or the other of two requirements. The first necessity is for a battery of craft processes which will help to reëducate and exercise various muscles. The other demand is for activity which will mitigate the emotional strain of hospital life, of convalescence. The emphasis among therapists has been upon learning only the skills needed to do fly tying, leathercraft, simple weaving, chip carving, bookbinding, and other crafts. In the schools and colleges training the therapists, a variety of course organizations are found. In many instances, art departments provide the specific craft classes. In other cases, craft classes are conducted by faculty members trained as art teachers or by therapy graduates with particular skills and interests in the crafts.

Members of the art personnel observe that the therapy group has a minimal interest in what we call creative activity. There is among therapists an uncritical willingness to accept and to use freely patterns for design on leather or other materials; in some schools part of the training insisted upon is that of preparing therapy students to make a large collection of "designs" as part of their equipment in the field. To the art teacher, crafts done in such a spirit seem questionable. If the element of personal achievement in design as well as in the craft's manipulation is not present, why do the work at all?

This point of view ignores two important considerations which the therapist must face. One is that a great deal of the work done by therapists is with patients who may be under their direction for short periods of time, ranging from a few days to less than a month. This time consideration becomes increasingly more stringent since hospital beds are so limited in number all over the country. The growing practice of returning patients to at least limited normal activity as soon as possible also changes therapy practices. As a consequence, for these short-term patients the therapist feels obliged to provide materials which will guarantee a fairly satisfying product in a short time. A billfold project, already cut, complete with a Pilgrim-ship design prepared for tooling, and with holes punched for lacing, probably will entice some patients into a craft where anything more complicated might not.

But too frequently the therapist has taken the position that all patients need and indeed insist upon this same kind of ready-made, prefabricated craftwork. There is a middle ground, and the best compromise between the creative artist and the therapist involves the use of simple devices for inventing or stylizing common design motifs in such a manner that the patient can bring as much or as little creative zest to the designing as he wishes. The important factor for increasing the quantity and quality of creative work in crafts for therapy is nothing more than therapists trained to recognize the value of individual initiative where the patient is able to exercise it.

The other situation where the artist's concern for the creative aspects of the craft must be modified when applied to therapy is in that branch of the work meeting the needs of reëducation of muscular and nervous controls. The first requisite is to devise activity employing the muscles which must be revived. All other values must wait upon that.

The therapist denying any value in creative design is deliberately narrowing the range of his effective operation. Doubtless most patients, if asked, will timidly back away from designing when first approached with the possibility. On the other hand, by the time they come to the end of their work, many patients would be increasing in interest and activity. A normal adult can take only a limited interest in jobs for which somebody else has done all the planning. Crafts in therapy as well as general art activity for the amateur give rise to some hope and to a still greater fear in the mind of the artist.

The fear of the artist is that the amateur's art experience is limited largely to a desire to learn technical excellence, but to express with that skill only the most commonplace, the most hackneyed, conceptions.

The hope lies in the fact that from the immense group of amateurs here and there in every community where encouragement keeps them going, some of the best will show qualitative as well as technical growth in their work. All the teachers in recreational areas, the arts and crafts, drama, writing, music, have a responsibility beyond getting amateurs started in one of the arts; the neurotics claiming great art enthusiasms are not much aided by superficial attempts at one thing and then another. The activity-flitter appears to be compounding neuroses by the speed with which old enthusiasms are dropped and forgotten in favor of the latest fad.

To find and to earn the rewards of progress as a person with something to say and a way to say it, the individual must stay with an art expression for a considerable time. For anyone, amateur or professional, there are no short cuts to a satisfying experience as a performer.

TESTS AND MEASUREMENTS IN ART

There are no short cuts, either, in the way of tests and measurements to determine aesthetic powers or sensitivities. Thomas Munro has indicated that while we may be able, with the help of the psychologist, to identify gradually some of the component abilities necessary in the arts, we have a lot of work to do before we can say that one person has more or less art ability than the next. Because it is possible to determine with fidelity various reactions to red color, does not give us any real clues to total aesthetic responses, or to degrees of ability to produce in the arts.

More vigorously than Munro, E. W. Rannells has written a conclusive critique of existing tests in aesthetic fields. He deals as follows with the assumption that art elements can be separated out of their context: ". . . it is a fallacy to assume that an element of art taken separately as a variable, will produce an art response. . . . Nor is it true that a work of art can be the sum of its parts. Every work of art, and every experience of it, is more than an assemblage of separable parts. . . . In short our test makers have been employing the methods of an outworn 'faculty' psychology." [21]

Rannells further shows that some test aspects have been unconsciously slanted to determine the student's ability in a particular interpretation of art work. As a case in point, the kind of neatness and precision often required of an artist working in advertising may be indicated as present in testing a boy or girl whose ability to design creatively is nil. He exposes, too, the frequent lack of adequate validation by the proper means of thousands of test samples. A test tried at random among a hundred or so subjects, who are then never followed up to determine their conformity in later practice to their test scores, does not encourage faith in its conclusions.

Finally he notes, as has Munro, that the test makers would seem to have only the most meager interest or background in art, and that their test instruments fail miserably in not being aware of a tenth of the aesthetic qualities they are supposedly measuring. When the art

[21] Edward Warder Rannells, "Psychological Testing in Art," *Art Education Bulletin,* Eastern Arts Association, September-October, 1948.

teachers, guidance directors, and psychologists who make tests start with a better concept of art values, their success in identifying aspects of art abilities will increase and their claims of achievement will probably be more moderate. Any valid testing instrument will need to have met the criticisms Rannells has made.

PAINTING AND PERSONALITY

The general beliefs of psychiatrists today in regard to the arts seem angled more toward analysis of the basis from which the individual projects a piece of art work than an interest in the quality of the experience or of the finished art product.

Why does any individual create as he does? Why does a lonely four-year-old paint in dark blues and grays with brown strokes for outlines? Why do some persons continue early play with art media into adult seriousness and become artists?

Psychology proposes some answers to these questions. The answers fall roughly into two categories. The first is that of explaining the variations in art work as observed in the products of children and of the adult amateur; this continues the work started years ago by the educational psychologists in their study of child drawings. The second and much rarer category of art inquiry is directed at the motivations of the mature artist.

The first area has resulted at its best for the art teacher in the work of Viktor Lowenfeld. More narrowly, the use of art work as a clue to personality structure and particularly to upset emotional patterns has become important. The two-volume study by Alshuler and Hatwick, *Painting and Personality*,[22] is an important work in that direction.

The study aimed to follow closely the "free painting" of a group of children between the ages of four and seven, and to keep a record at the same time of the relevant data from the children's home and school lives. The school system in which the study was performed provided the room and materials, which the children used freely during regular hours each week. Instruction from art teachers, except for the mere handling of materials, was not desired. The children were encouraged to paint freely and often, in the same way

[22] Rose H. Alschuler and LaBerta Weiss Hatwick, *Painting and Personality*, University of Chicago, 1947

they might talk at random among themselves; there was no intrusion of aesthetic judgment upon the products.

The dominating interest was that of tracing the influence of the individual's social-emotional adjustment in school and at home, as it portrayed itself in painting. As does Lowenfeld, the authors note certain tendencies in subject preferences, in color usage, in sex differentiations; but their chief focal point is the life of the individual child and the correspondence of clearly defined patterns in painting to his dominating life experiences.

Their conclusions are presented with a reasonable, not rash, air of certainty. The common forms taken by children's paintings are described: the random circling lines, the early efforts to manage rectangular shapes, the irregular linear patterns, including the rhythmic and the more jagged. As with forms, the significance of color usage is discussed at length. In all the recorded observations, those carrying on the study were convinced that each child projected definite emotional states of mind into this free use of paint. For instance, the production of paintings in a high-value key, using large areas of yellows, oranges, reds, and yellow-greens, and making use of darker colors only in smaller areas and for linear accents, was to be observed almost uniformly from children who were well pleased with themselves and their world, at least for the moment. The commonly observed gesture of rejection of one's own work, that of smearing over an almost finished painting with a dark color, usually brown, purple, or black, was found to indicate, when repeated often in a few days, some pronounced emotional distress. Often the child smearing his work was himself feeling rejected in the home group by the arrival of a baby, by repeated quarrels between father and mother, by being brushed aside in a dominantly adult household.

In several dozen carefully documented case studies, the child's life story and his expression in the free-painting period were studied comparatively; the conclusions individually and generally drawn are invaluable to the teacher of art. Concerning the emotional connotations given to the use of colors, there will be variations of belief; and it is probably better for the artist and teacher to agree that color does have powerful emotional implications for most of us, but that too refined a system of values can never be universally pronounced.

While some persons consider yellow-green an almost poisonous color, others more immediately attach to it the emotional promise of spring and fresh growth. There is nothing too dogmatic in this study about color impact, but a great many readers leave it with the impression that psychologists claim too much insight into personality difficulties on this basis. The cumulative evidence of these case studies is that for children of the age level investigated, almost no other form of expression is as revealing as paintings, but that each child and his work must be considered separately with a minimum of generalized preconceptions.

A critical problem for the art teacher which this study presents, other than the use of art forms as diagnostic material, is the emphasis on the value for the psychologist of the art product which is "free" expression, that is, untrammeled by art instruction. One's first thought is that the psychiatrist is always after "free" expression in any form, verbal, visual, in motion, or on paper; and, of course, the need for relatively uninhibited responses for analytic purposes is fairly obvious.

For the purposes of aesthetic education, this use of free expression need not lead the art teacher to think that the school of "let the child alone to create" ought to return. One other reaction to this kind of study on the part of artists is that the psychologists and the psychiatrists are standing on tiptoe on an unbalanced chair to reach for their deductions. Since artists are not likely to be adequate as psychologists, it is as well for them not to attempt to become amateurs in the field of analysis. But to deny validity to the researches of the psychologists using art works is equally as wrong-headed as for the art teacher to indulge in pseudo-psychiatric séances.

To try to understand what it is the psychologist looks for in a work of art is not to abandon art values. The art instructor who rides a new hobby, who feels compelled to turn up with a new medium or article of bric-a-brac every so often, has in recent years been guilty of relegating children's art to the place of a symptom instead of a creation. It is this exaggeration the conscientious teacher should wish to avoid.

Art work has a cumulative value in the growth of the individual which can approach a maximum only through guidance, through the most skillful of instruction. At the same time the art product should be sufficiently personal, self-initiated, to offer useful insights into the personality of the student. To emphasize this aspect of art tempts the art teacher to try more than he is prepared for in mental therapy, thus quite likely destroying greater therapeutic qualities inherent in helping the student make aesthetic progress. If a piece of student art work makes evident serious abnormalities, school and medical authorities should be consulted by the art teacher for their more adequate evaluation.

PSYCHOLOGY AND AESTHETIC CREATION

Artists fascinate even the twentieth-century American. We are supposed to be a relatively unaesthetic country devoted to the triumphs of industry and science. Our greatest hope is said to be that of carrying on the routine tasks of living in a semiautomatic fashion. Contradicting these easily tossed-off aphorisms is our immense and intense patronage of the movies, sports, television, music; the tone of printed matter, from comics to philosophy; our national admiration for Dimitri Mitropoulos, for Elizabeth Taylor, and even for Bernard Shaw. Our popular heroes are not often of a contemplative turn of mind; many of them are vulgar to their toes with a passionate taste for the adulation of the millions; but their performances are those of the artist, and the people applaud them as such.

Unusual as such an observation may seem, the fan magazines of Hollywood and the 1940 Bryn Mawr Symposium on Art have something in common. Both are preoccupied with the workings of the heart and mind of the artist. The fan magazine is busy manufacturing legends about an earthbound industrial monster among the arts. The Symposium attempted to analyze the raw material out of which the legends emerge. From the deliberative academic studies and from the legends, too, we get a cross section of ideas about the artist, about his reasons for becoming an artist, and about his approach to his work.

Most of the serious studies refer to Freud's early effort to analyze the artist. He believed the artist to be more able than other persons to modify the impact of internal emotional conflicts through the creation of works of art. In the work of Thomas Munro, Herbert Read,

240

Otto Rank, and Karl Koffka, we find various references to the psychological structure of the artist personality. In different ways each names that part of the human individual which makes instinctual responses as the root of aesthetic response and creation. This element, by Freud named the "id," is described as that quality impervious to time, to change, to reason, to conscience, which causes the individual to react distinctively and immediately to his environment. To complete the use of the Freudian terms, the ego serves as the individual's conscience, his guide for the id to rational thinking and behavior. The superego represents the highest possible degree of knowledge and reality. And the tension in human life is injected in the clash between the instinctive responses of the id and the modifications of those responses by the ego and the superego.

According to this theory, then, the artist is one whose energy is devoted to working off these conflicts in the form of doing work in an art medium. The nonartist subjected to the same tension either turns to creative activity in other work or resolves his tensions in other ways—sports, drink, gossiping, dope, or the movies. Those who find nothing very satisfying are the large group of neurotics our society produces.

Medical records, court proceedings, and ordinary observation suggest that the number of partially neurotic persons is large, that is, the number of people whose nervous conflicts have reached a point imposing a real handicap on normal living. More optimistically, possibly a large proportion of the population either finds the instinctual drives easier to curb than does the artist or are luckier in being oppressed with a less rigorous set of requirements by the ego and superego.

Thomas Munro notes that one of the efforts of modern education is to build up a minimum of negative inhibitions and a maximum of permissive drives within the realm of constructive citizenship. When this is successfully accomplished, he questions, does the artist vanish for lack of a conflict pattern within which he needs to function?

Otto Rank advances the theory that the artist possesses a "will to Form" that is only incidentally a sublimation of conflicts. He notices that most artists when really at work go far beyond sublimation, for instance of the sexual impulse. They demonstrate what amounts to an antisexual concentration on their work. He connects this will to create with a desire for immortality. And for the contemporary artist of our liberal Western society, he believes the motivation is also that of striving for the achievement and recognition of a distinctive individuality.

The most explosive of Rank's conclusions is that, since contemporary art is devoted to the development of personality, there may come a time when the greatest of artists will renounce the "work of art" as a goal and bravely establish the creation of a fruitful personality as his true goal, the usefulness of the personality to be in "life and the formation of life." [23]

This seems to me based on the narrow view of contemporary works of art as the isolate fragment, the separate object made for museum contemplation; for that is the only kind of "work of art" that might be thought necessary to renounce in living a fuller creative life in a larger social context. Perhaps Rank's idea gets us back to the dream of a society in which "art" is no longer separate and in which art or aesthetic qualities distinguish all physical creation. Perhaps Rank's view of the evolution of the creative personality and Kouwenhoven's view of the "vernacular" in art indicate a possible fusion of social and aesthetic values which will encourage creative personalities who might have been painters in the 1940's to become free-lance designers in the grand manner in the 1980's, impartially turning out toys, motion pictures, or trunk-line highways, unburdened personally with a sense of incongruity in so great a diversity or with any sense of guilt in not yearning to produce a private and highly precious art form like a painting. A development in society that made possible a far greater number of able and independent designers would be a sign of health, of independence, in government and economic life. Many young people of creative abilities might better be doing such work than the more private activity of independent painting.

There is an exception to be made in this projected future. In a free society there always will be some lonely, contemplative artists; their work will always have a value whether their medium is paint, film, words, or music.

[23] Otto Rank, *Art and Artist*, Knopf, 1932, p. 431.

When we return to thinking of art education for all students, we are obviously dealing with persons who lack the intensive compulsions of the mature artist. If that is so, when we teach art to all students are we working against the grain of the psychological structure of most individuals? Our best belief now is that we are not.

First of all, there is good sense in the empirical observation that a majority of children to the age of twelve can express themselves effectively in one or more art forms. Second, where all children are taught by a good art teacher, their ability to use art expression is increased and lengthened. Even when, as they leave the period of greatest art productivity, they direct their major interests to other subjects, if their art background has been good they retain a degree of creative individuality.

Finally, much recent research indicates that the conflicts of personality growth are with most of us most of the time. Here we can return to Dewey's calling any significant experience aesthetic in nature. Keeping that in mind, we can assume that any dozen eighteen-year-old students are involved with their own adjustments to conflicts. One of them will turn his conflict-generated energies to art, another to learning a trade, a third to a precocious attention to moneymaking, and all of them to a more or less constant preoccupation concurrently with the opposite sex. In all of these reactions there are, says Dewey, inevitable aesthetic qualities and motivations. Education in the arts, education of a creative nature, will aid all these students in building constructive life experiences, in avoiding long-continued and self-multiplying frustrations leading at last to helpless or socially dangerous neuroticism.

We do not yet seem to have an answer to the question why a small number of people continue work in the arts as their mature expression, nor why some few of these artists have that consuming energy and insight which constitute a genius. For now, we must be content with the reasonably well-established fact that all of us possess some of the motivations of the artist, and that we can and do give aesthetic shape to our lives even in the activities not ordinarily associated with the arts.

The artist may indeed be the product of his own peculiarly sensitive reaction to the environment and to the impact of his emotional

243

conflicts. Quite contrary to the fear that education may some day eliminate a large part of our fears and forebodings, we will probably discover that these distresses and the aggressions they give rise to can never be altogether overcome. The best hope is that we may learn to use the tensions we generate, large and small, individual and collective, as motive power for constructive projects.

Bibliography

Allen, Arthur B., *The Teaching of Art to Infants and Junior Children*, Warne, 1937.

Alschuler, Rose H., and Hatwick, La Berta Weiss, *Painting and Personality: A Study of Young Children*, 2 Vols., University of Chicago, 1947.

Anderson, Maxwell; Carpenter, Rhys; and Harris, Roy, *The Bases of Artistic Creation*, Rutgers, 1942.

Barr, Alfred, "Letter to the Editor," *College Art Journal*, Fall, 1950 (on dates of exhibitions of primitive arts in European and American museums).

Bartlett, Francis Grant, and Crawford, Claude, *Art for All*, Harper, 1942.

Bender, Laurette, "Gestalt Principles in the Sidewalk Drawings and Games of Children," *Pedagogical Seminary*, Vol. 41, 1932, pp. 192–210.

Biber, Barbara, *Children's Drawings from Lines to Pictures*, N.Y.C. Bureau of Educ. Experiment, 1949.

Bogoslovsky, Boris Basil, *The Ideal School*, Macmillan, 1936.

Bryn Mawr College, *Art: A Bryn Mawr Symposium*, Vol. IX, *Notes and Monographs*, Bryn Mawr, 1940.

Cane, Florence, *The Artist in Each of Us*, Pantheon, 1951.

Chandler, A. R., and Barnhart, E. N., *A Bibliography of Psychological and Experimental Aesthetics*, University of California, 1938.

Cheney, Sheldon, *The Story of Modern Art*, Viking, 1941.

Cole, Natalie Robinson, *The Arts in the Classroom*, Day, 1940.

Collins, Mary Rose, and Riley, Olive L., *Art Appreciation*, Harcourt, Brace, 1932.

Committee on the Function of Art in General Education, *The Visual Arts in General Education*, Appleton-Century, 1940.

D'Amico, Victor, *Creative Teaching in Art*, International Textbook, 1942, rev. ed., 1953.

Dewey, John, *Art as Experience*, Minton, Balch, 1934.

Dewey, John, and others, *Art and Education*, rev. ed., Barnes Foundation, 1947.

Dorner, Alexander, *The Way Beyond "Art": The Work of Herbert Bayer*, Wittenborn Schultz, 1947.

Dunnett, Ruth, *Art and Child Personality*, Methuen, 1948.

Edman, Irwin, *Arts and the Man*, Norton, 1939 (now available in Mentor reprint).

Eng, Helga, *The Psychology of Children's Drawings*, Trench, Trubner, 1931.

Evans, Joan, *Taste and Temperament*, Macmillan, 1939.

Faulkner, Ray, *Teachers Enjoy the Arts*, Committee on Teacher Education, American Council on Education, 1943.

Faulkner, Ray; Ziegfeld, Edwin, and Hill, Gerald, *Art Today*, rev. ed., Holt, 1949.

Gibbs, Evelyn, *The Teaching of Art in Schools*, Greenberg, 1936.

Giedion, Siegfried, *Space, Time and Architecture*, Oxford, 1941.

Goitein, Lionel, *Art and the Unconscious*, Basic Books, 1948.

Gregg, Harold, *Art for the Schools of America*, International Textbook, 1941.

Iglehart, Robert, "Theories of Design: An Evaluation," *Art Education Today*, Fine Arts Staff, Teachers College, Columbia University, 1941.

Jacobson, Egbert, *Basic Color: An Interpretation of the Ostwald Theory*, Theobold, 1948.

Katz, David, *Gestalt Psychology: Its Nature and Significance*, tr. by Robert Tyson, Ronald Press, 1949.

Katz, Elias, *Children's Preferences for Traditional and Modern Paintings*, Teachers College, Columbia University, 1944.

Kaufman, Edgar, Jr., "Industrial Design in American Museums," *Magazine of Art*, May, 1949, p. 179.

Klar, W. H., *Art Education in the High Schools*, Federated Council on Art Education, 1936.

Koffka, Kurt, "Mental Development: Powell Lecture in Psychological Theory at Clark University," *Pedagogical Seminary*, April, 1925, pp. 659–673.

Kohler, Wolfgang, "An Aspect of Gestalt Psychology," *Pedagogical Seminary*, May, 1925, p. 691.

Kohler, Wolfgang, *Gestalt Psychology*, Liveright-Black and Gold Library, 1947.

Kootz, Samuel M., *New Frontiers in American Painting*, Hastings, 1943.

Kouwenhoven, John A., *Made in America: The Arts in Modern Civilization*, Doubleday, 1948.

Larkin, Oliver, *Art and Life in America*, Rinehart, 1949.

Lee, Kathryn Dean, *Adventuring in Art*, Appleton-Century, 1939.

Levy, Florence, *Choosing a Life Career in the Design Arts*, Federated Council on Art Education, 1936.

Lowenfeld, Viktor, *The Nature of Creative Activity*, Kegan, Paul, Trench and Trubner, 1939.

Lowenfeld, Viktor, *Creative and Mental Growth*, rev. ed., Macmillan, 1952.

MacDonald, Rosabelle, *Art as Education*, Holt, 1941.

McLeish, Minnie, *Beginnings of Teaching Art to Children*, Studio, 1941.

Major, Charlotte, *Teaching Art in the Elementary School*, Service Center Committee, Progressive Education Association, 1941.

Malraux, André, *The Psychology of Art*, Pantheon, 1947–1948.

Meier, Norman Charles, *Art in Human Affairs*, McGraw-Hill, 1942.

Moholy-Nagy, L., *The New Vision*, Norton, 1938.

Moholy-Nagy, L., *Vision in Motion*, Theobold, 1947.

Munro, Thomas, *Scientific Method in Aesthetics*, Norton, 1928.

Munro, Thomas, and others, *Art and Adolescence*, Fieldston Conference, Bulletin of the Worcester Art Museum, July, 1932.

National Society for the Study of Education, *Art in American Life and Education*, 40th Yearbook, Public School Publishing Co., 1941.

Naumburg, Margaret, *Studies of the "Free" Art Expression of Behavior Problem Children and Adolescents as a Means of Diagnosis and Therapy*, Nervous and Mental Disease Monographs, No. 71, Coolidge Foundation, 1947.

Nicholas, Florence W.; Mawhood, Nellie C.; and Trilling, Mabel B., *Art Activities in the Modern School*, Macmillan, 1937.

Ogden, R. M., "The Gestalt Psychology of Learning," *Pedagogical Seminary*, Vol. 38, 1930, p. 280.

Payant, Felix, *Our Changing Art Education*, Keramic Studio, 1935.

Payant, Felix, *Create Something*, Design, 1939.

Pearson, Ralph, *Experiencing American Pictures*, Harper, 1943.

Pearson, Ralph, *The New Art Education*, rev. ed., Harper, 1953.

Perrine, Van Dearing, *Let the Child Draw*, Stokes, 1936.

Perry, Kenneth Frederick, *An Experiment with a Diversified Art Program*, Teachers College, Columbia University, 1943.

Pevsner, Nikolaus, *Pioneers of Modern Design from William Morris to Walter Gropius*, Museum of Modern Art, 1949.

Powell, Lydia, *The Art Museum Comes to the School*, Harper, 1944.

Prescott, Daniel Alfred, *Emotion and the Educative Process*, Committee on the Relation of Emotion to the Educative Process, American Council on Education, 1938.

Rank, Otto, *Art and Artist*, Knopf, 1932.

Rannells, Edward Warder, *Art Education in the Junior High School*, University of Kentucky, 1946.

Rannells, Edward Warder, "Psychological Tests in Art," *Art Education Bulletin*, Eastern Arts Association, September-October, 1948.

Read, Herbert, *Education Through Art*, Faber and Faber, 1943.

Read, Herbert, *Art and Society*, rev. ed., Pantheon, 1945.

Richardson, Marion, *Art and the Child*, University of London, 1948.

Rothschild, Edward F., *The Meaning of Unintelligibility in Modern Art*, University of Chicago, 1931.

Rugg, Harold, and Shumaker, Ann, *The Child Centered School*, World, 1928.

Schultz, Harold A., and Shores, J. Harlan, *Art in the Elementary School*, University of Illinois, 1948.

Shaw, Ruth Faison, *Finger Painting*, Little, Brown, 1934.

Tannahill, Sally, *Fine Arts for Public School Administrators*, Teachers College, Columbia University, 1932.

Tomlinson, R. R., *Picture Making by Children*, Studio, 1934.

Tomlinson, R. R., *Crafts for Children*, Studio, 1935.

Tomlinson, R. R., *Children as Artists*, Penguin, 1944.

Walker Art Center, "Knife, Fork, and Spoon," *Everyday Art Quarterly*, Spring, Summer, 1951.

Wilenski, R. H., *The Modern Movement in Art*, Stokes, 1934.

Winslow, Leon Loyal, *The Integrated School Art Program*, sec. ed., McGraw-Hill, 1949.

Zaidenberg, Arthur, *Your Child is an Artist*, Grosset and Dunlap, 1949.

Figure 15. Drawing by Senior-High-School Student. (From National Art Education Association, I. L. de Francesco, ed., "This Is Art Education 1952," The Association, 1952.)

VIII

Art Education: The Shape of Things to Come

This concluding chapter is intended to present the reader with an appropriate summation of the development of art education, and to indicate with clarity some prospects for the future. I do not believe the way ahead is at all certain, though there are indications that our educational efforts in the arts may become more stimulating and venturesome than ever. The desire to broaden the relationships of the arts, the psychological studies of art forms, the recognition of the social content of the arts, and the social responsibility of the artist seem very important today.

General education at all age levels is seeking more and better art education, and this expansion of art in general education is constructively influencing professional art education. From a less clear vantage point we see school financial resources, school administrative procedures, complicated curricular patterns, the difficult process of school-district reorganization, the reluctance of artists and school people to seek mutual understanding, as interferences to the full realization of art contributions to American education.

"COMMUNICATION" AN EFFORT TOWARD AESTHETIC INTEGRATION

One of the more influential forces in elementary and secondary education seeking broader aesthetic patterns is the field of inquiry and studies known as the "communication arts."

In education we constantly seek better tools with which to accomplish our purposes. Sometimes the use of the latest tools obscures the job we are supposed to be doing. The tools are such new, shiny instruments, such a pleasure to operate just for themselves, that they distract us from the business at hand.

The communication arts as a pedagogical movement has its effect on art and art education in that its self-established task is to integrate the artificially separated areas of expression which we generally consider aesthetic, that is, writing, speaking, music, and the fine arts. Its adherents are apt to dwell upon "communication" as a sacred instrument, showing little concern about having anything worth while to be communicated through the means developed. Those who use the term sensibly stress the common employment of all art forms in human communication, and hence the need of understanding a variety of media.

The visual and plastic arts can be important in this thinking. Since the communications enthusiasts are dominantly teachers of English literature and grammar who are anxious to deliver their subject from the criticism of narrowness, a problem is posed to the arts in this way. Unfortunately many English teachers, like the majority of the population, think of the visual arts as a secondary and less intellectualized form of narrative. This point of view is painfully clear in the critical attitude of English-education magazines on the subject of the motion picture.

If a movie is somewhat faithful to the literary work on which it is frequently based, faithful, that is, in a literal and chronological way —better yet if the movie is based on a literary masterpiece—then the picture is esteemed a success. Any further consideration of dramatic excellence is likely to be based on the resemblance of the film to a stage drama. The whole point of film as a distinctive visual medium capable of dramatic development independent of the stage, the novel, or even of the written play is often missed by the English faculty.

This attitude indicates one of the contributions possible for art teachers and English teachers concerned with the arts of communication. They can be missionaries among their colleagues for the gospel of visual-art forms as related to verbal and written literature, but as having their own distinctive form and mission.

Shakespearean plays made into motion pictures are likely to be simply excellent recording accomplishments, not the fullest exploitation of film. There is nothing aesthetically immoral or perverse about such a project, unless because of Shakespeare's eminence on the stage it is taken for granted that he must be counted supreme on film as well. Films like the documentary *The River,* or the Marx Brothers' *A Night at the Opera,* are masterworks in their medium in a fashion impossible to a filming of any Shakespeare.

Communication needs to be understood as a broadening of the base of meaning. Meaning is not transmitted only in words. Eyes see more than words, ears hear more than words, bodies communicate emotions without words. Naturally, we experience through all media and as much as possible concurrently. It is necessary to overemphasize the possibility of constructing a pattern, an order in experience, without words because we are so accustomed to accept words as the basis of any really important communication. The Cossacks on the Odessa steppes in the film *Potemkin* burn into our experience the cruel viciousness of oppression. Words may have been used in a subtitle, but we do not need them. Words told us this act was done by such people at a certain time to other persons. But we see, we remember, reasonless brutality perpetrated by military order, making mechanical horrors of the soldiers who cripple and kill defenseless people.

Using the communications-arts interest as an example, we can re-iterate the art teacher's need to clarify his own grasp of the unique properties of the visual and plastic arts. If the members of the arts community are active in broadening and clarifying their own concepts, they can see aesthetic relationships in still broader fields of community life. Summarily, the artist-teacher has to know more about the arts of the past and present, and has to know more about the arts through his own performance on a professional level, to become competent enough to see fruitful relationships of his field with other areas.

SOCIAL RESPONSIBILITY IN ART

We have noted that the visual arts communicate in their own right, possessing a semantic order of their own. Creators of work in the visual arts have a responsibility for their acts, aesthetically and socially; this is the expressed conviction of Paul Rand, John Atherton, Herbert Bayer, and others designing advertising and industrial products. In this respect they see eye to eye with the men of science whose keen analysis of the social implications of atomic power has led rather than followed public reaction.

Thus it becomes the responsibility of art education not only to help students recognize the distinctive characteristics of visual art forms. That is only one part of a larger obligation. The second part is that of developing a responsible attitude on the part of the designer as well as the "consumer" of art. Responsibility in this sense is not meant in the limited definition of censoring drawings, movies, paintings, advertising, interpreted by someone or some group as immoral, obscene, or subversive. There are obscene products so evident to all that suppression can be agreed upon virtually without dissent. On the other hand, democracy is not well served and the arts suffer when charges of immorality are hurled by one group against another group sponsoring a work of art which deals with an aspect of society not welcome to the objectors.

The artist's responsibility must come in the integrity he displays in the use of his personal ability. For instance, Paul Rand [1] believes that the fear of social inadequacy is a morally bad theme on which to base an advertising campaign: "Buy this automobile or use that toilet soap, and avoid otherwise inevitable social disgrace." Rand insists that the artist ought to share the responsibility for helping in any way with a campaign. He has become well known as the creator of a familiar figure in a nationally circulated liquor advertisement. He emphasizes gaiety and liveliness, creating a mood he believes appropriate but not apt to engender unfortunate personality tensions. The reformer who believes in legislation against strong drink, or at least against advertising it, would criticize Rand for doing any work at all for a liquor account. Rand contends, not that all artists should attempt to please everyone and antagonize no one, but that artists should respect their own basic social philosophy and refuse to let their practice of art be hired for purposes which they think injurious to public morale.

The art teacher can easily teach technical proficiency. He can encourage the development of personal expression. And finally, he does, whether he intends to or not, encourage the expression of a philosophy of the arts and of life. That philosophy differs from teacher to teacher and from artist to artist, as Rand differs from the advertiser of cosmetics who plays upon adolescent fears of social ostracism.

The artist, teacher, and art student must grow up to the fact that visual arts, like every other form of human expression, can be and should be used to create important ideas, ideas which often may be fresh enough and so vigorously expressed as to arouse intense opposition. Art is no more conformist than is atomic power. Art education, if it deserves the name, is bound to create some intellectual and emotional seething, and an examination of personal and social values, as part of the privilege of personal expression and the attainment of a craftsman's skills.

Part of the public mystification with modern painting may be explained by the fact that the artist is purposely expressing an unpalatable idea in a self-defensive, obscure form. There is nothing original in this observation, but, though it has been made by many

[1] Paul Rand, *Some Thoughts on Design*, Wittenborn Shultz, 1947.

able critics, it has been pushed aside by the still-potent dictum—even among artists whose own work is a living refutation—that the "meaning" of a painting is only to be found in its "abstract" elements of color and form. Certainly, the paintings of Max Ernst, Mark Tobey, Morris Graves, Hyman Bloom, Matta, de Kooning, and scores of others possess mature reflections upon the present state of existence. Some of these are no more obscure than they must be to be pictorially achieved. Others may be unconsciously difficult to the observer as a protection for the artist from abusive and condemnatory comments he would get on a more open statement of his convictions.

One may reasonably question the value of such veiled expression. Two answers might be made. One is that it is not the nature of all persons to make blunt, forthright expositions of an idea or point of view. This is true of businessmen, of politicians, of medical men, as well as of artists; and it begins to be understood that an extended, or seemingly obscure, treatment of an idea may be made because the idea is complex, requiring such a presentation.

The other answer is to be found in our social system of checks and balances. While we are working toward freedom of speech and freedom of expression by individuals, we have by no means achieved it. Only very young artists are almost unaware of social pressures in their work. The professional artist, like the writer, has social pressures all about him. War eras in particular give rise to bitterly cynical and satirical views of human affairs which are apt to destroy the artist altogether if his expression of them in words, paint, or speech prove wholly distasteful to a large part of the populace. A pronounced aspect of modern art in all media is this need to satirize our present confusions and groping efforts to restore some order to our planet, but a curious twist of the most satirical pieces in the visual arts is that they anger the public because they are enigmatic in form. They suggest a satirical intent, without making clear to any but the initiate the object of their attack.

The art teacher must know of these complexities in art expressions and take the responsibility for their interpretation. What he finds abstruse he might better put aside rather than blight his students' development of insight and expression by his casual disapproval of the new and unknown. No more than the English or social-studies teacher can the art teacher ignore his responsibilities for a broad interpretation of the arts as documents of human importance.

THREE WAYS TO PERSONAL GROWTH IN EXPRESSION

American people incline to the notion that their "inalienable" rights include anything that is good. Our first approach to art and art education did not go much beyond the assumption that art was good for American citizens. In the process of learning how to domesticate art, we have discovered its great value as a means of individual expression. In art education this aspect of art supersedes, for the time being, the value of art objects as creations to be studied, admired, treasured.

We had no definite guide at first to tell us what to expect of art that was primarily individualistic. Because of this lack, a quantity of bold and generally undisciplined work seemed to be the right way for children and adults to free themselves from the clichés of picture making and arrive at more personal images. Experiment with materials, freely carried out, seemed the only avenue to independence of expression.

Once it was established, through experience in the schools, through psychological studies, and by noting the increase in numbers of amateur and professional arts students, that art expression was valuable to millions of persons, possibly to every person at some time of life, then the closer study of art processes followed.

Well before the psychologists' studies of perception became interesting to art education, two men—Vernon Blake and Kimon Nicolaides—urged the study of process in the creation of art forms. Blake's study, *The Art and Craft of Drawing*,[2] was a philosophy of that craft and an early study of perception as observed through the works of the drawing media. Blake honored the Oriental traditions, the ink and pen work of Leonardo, Claude Lorain, Rembrandt, and the modern work of Matisse and Cézanne, as being all of a qualitative and distinctive nature, each in an idiom of its own.

Kimon Nicolaides became a national influence, again in the great productive year of 1941, when his wife and students issued *The*

[2] Vernon Blake, *The Art and Craft of Drawing*, Oxford, 1927.

Natural Way to Draw [3] after his death. The book described and illustrated his teaching methods of having students use the drawing medium to express their visual understanding of form through contour lines, gesture, mass, and scribble forms, and through personal combinations of these form approaches. The results of this kind of experiment were found to free the individual to seek his own best use of media in construction form as he felt it and saw it (Figure 16, page 256).

Today the newcomer to an art class is taught to study himself and the art media available. From the interaction of these two elements, the emergence of a unique expression is hoped for. The process of individual perception and the aesthetic concepts dependent on this process are the subject of Gyorgy Kepes, Hoyt Sherman, and Schaeffer-Simmern in their work of the last ten years. What these men add to the materials of art education is of sufficient importance to make them almost the "primitives" of a new area of inquiry.

Kepes is the strongest American voice of the Bauhaus transplant to American schools. His *Language of Vision* [4] has become a text in dozens of art schools and is easily the most influential single volume in art education in the 1940's and early 1950's.

As Siegfried Giedion puts it in his introduction to the volume, Kepes has successfully analyzed the optical revolution of the twentieth century in usable terms, though he is not always easily understandable. He swings us from the old emphasis upon "objects" to one concerned with "visual, tactile relationships." In three sections, Kepes deals with "Plastic Organization," "Visual Representation," and "Toward a Dynamic Iconography." First he describes and diagrams the intrinsic nature of any plastic image; the tensions created in it by line, shape, and color; and the variations a plastic image assumes in the eyes of its beholders because of each one's psychological and physiological structure.

Then he dissects for the student the multiplicity of physical, visual qualities of the earthly environment which can be visually represented, and shows how paint, plaster, photography, and other media have been used for the purpose. His use of illustrative material excellently serves the aim of enlarging our views of the potentialities

[3] Kimon Nicolaides, *The Natural Way to Draw*, Houghton Mifflin, 1941.
[4] Gyorgy Kepes, *The Language of Vision*, Theobald, 1944.

Figure 16. "Student Gesture Drawings."
(From Kimon Nicolaides, "The Natural
Way to Draw," Houghton Mifflin, 1941.)

Figure 17. Depth Representation by
Slanted Lines in Combination with Rectangles, Drawing by Twelve-Year-Old.
(From Henry Schaefer-Simmern, "The Unfolding of Artistic Activity," University
of California Press, 1950.)

of visual representation. (See Frontispiece.) With the Moholy-Nagy and Josef Albers interpretation of the Bauhaus curriculum, Kepes takes a place as one of the foremost spokesmen for the kind of art education the Bauhaus initiated in 1919. His analytical description of the visual techniques employed by Picasso, Cassandre, Rand, Malevich, Leger, and Kauffer is thorough and convincing. He goes far to dispel artificial fences between painting and design for the printing presses. No reader who understands Kepes will discard contemporary art forms as trivial or meaningless. Art teachers by the thousand have through Kepes enriched the scope of their teaching by a larger understanding of what the contemporary artists are doing. Kepes achieved for the field of art education what the art historian had not quite been able to do.

Different from the work of Kepes, but equally concerned with the development of visual imagery, is the work of Schaeffer-Simmern.

He believes that the "unfolding of artistic activity" [5] is one that must be accomplished from within. In his view, the art teacher can aid the student by suggesting materials, by encouragement in solving technical difficulties. But he would seem to suggest that while the individual can draw by looking at still life, human models, or landscape, and may be able to reproduce the visually present subject, ultimately he becomes creatively productive only when he is able to call forth freely, from memory, a visual "configuration" to serve his expressive purposes.

To support his thesis, Schaeffer-Simmern presents several case studies. In each case he changed media frequently for the student, but permitted, really encouraged, the repetition of the same pictorial motif through a whole series of works. A person whose only pictorial effort might be a stereotyped house in the shelter of two hills would be left undisturbed by the teacher as far as his subject was concerned. He would be urged to try different media, and as he became more at ease in the classroom he would be slowly and not too obviously prodded to enlarge upon his motif, to add detail, to make his house in the hills a more specific and personal picture (Figure 17, page 256).

Schaeffer-Simmern declares that only this way does the individual

[5] Henry Schaeffer-Simmern, *The Unfolding of Artistic Activity*, University of California, 1947.

develop resourcefulness and a true independence in the use of pictorial, graphic, and sculptural media. It is his contention also that the visual configuration most persons are able to master in their understanding and ability to represent by their own hand is much more limited than has been generally thought. He says that most people cannot go beyond simple overlapping forms in essentially a flat plane, or in a limited number of flat planes parallel to the picture surface. This would presume that the intricacies of visual perspective, of atmospheric depth, are recognized by viewers as similar to observed fact, but that they cannot understand the visual mechanics necessary to make an image showing these qualities. Schaeffer-Simmern draws the natural conclusion that richness in art forms must come from the materials and the individual interpretation of the definitely limited configuration.

The tendency in art teaching inspired by Kepes would be to move with all students from one medium and visual phenomenon to another in something of an analytical progress. Schaeffer-Simmern would propose progress in interpretation and materials, but would forbid moving from one visual subject or inspiration to another until the student decided to do so of his own free will. I believe that teaching experience will reveal students who respond to Schaeffer-Simmern's kind of progress and others who blossom, developing unknown capabilities in a sequence of fairly rapid experiments in many themes as well as materials. We can use the clarification of thinking that the contrast of these processes illuminates.

Still another approach to aesthetic construction is that investigated by Hoyt Sherman.[6] His work is based on the observation that visual perception and the creation of form are virtually instantaneous; that whatever the individual says about his visual perception, or whatever he transposes to a visual art form, is bound to be a dilution, a working over of the first powerful impact of perception.

Sherman has created a fairly elaborate apparatus to experiment within his framework of ideas. As he works it, the physiological extension of peripheral vision and the creation of visual form in drawing, painting, and modeling are approached simultaneously.

The studio is equipped with screens for projection, a lighting sys-

[6] Hoyt Sherman, *Drawing by Seeing*, Hinds, Hayden, and Eldredge, 1947.

tem that can be flexibly controlled, projection machines, a phonograph, a small stage in the front of the room, and broad steps facing the platform on which drawing easels are placed theater-style. Students come in, find their work place, and then the room is completely darkened. It is important that the darkness be unbroken by the slightest pinhole of light. After a few minutes a slide is shown on the screen for a tenth of a second. The student draws on his paper the image which appeared to him on the screen. The drawing is done in the dark freely and rapidly on a scale large enough to make it a free-arm-movement exercise. The process is repeated as often in the class hour as seems worth while, since concentration of the sort required is not unlimited.

Slides used in the beginning of the six-week session are simple masses of black on white. Later the slides are more complex, using gray values and more involved linear patterns together. Before the close of the sixth week, still-life setups are placed on the platform or a dancer may execute a few simple turns. With these subjects as with the slides, the students will have only the tenth-of-a-second light in which to see and grasp the image presented.

Two major accomplishments are claimed by Sherman for the process. One, and this has been verified by careful tests in the School of Optometry at Ohio State, the great majority of the participants improve the acuity and range of their peripheral vision, that is, the span to which the individual's eye is capable of adjusting. The second accomplishment is more important to art teachers. The claim is asserted that students develop a freedom to tackle pictorial art and a power to organize pictorial form instantly. Examples of student work are available which demonstrate a marked skill in transferring an instantaneous vision into a freely handled and personally interpreted painting.

The question first arising about this investigation is whether or not the students' drawings done in this environment are a personal expression at all. Sherman believes that art is an interpretation of experience through the individual's vision. He sees his devices freeing inhibited students and inducing them in six weeks' time to work with speed and emotional assurance. His conviction is that, in addition to the physical improvement of vision, the student has started to form the kind of swift-organizing vision which Sherman believes is the distinguishing characteristic of all great artists.

Contrasted to Schaeffer-Simmern, this system would seem to ignore the art form that is projected from within and which uses experience, to be sure, but experience digested, transmuted by contemplation, by memory. Sherman would likely not argue the fact, but would point out that the experience mulled over in private could, in its original inception, have been made more vivid, reached a more significant organization, by an individual who had worked with the "flash" technique. Some of the dissenters to Sherman's work believe that it puts too great a premium on vision solely and that the sum total of experience, tactile and emotional as well as visual, goes to make up the stuff projected in a work of art.

If the professional in art today faces a period in which general education in the arts probably will expand greatly, then the techniques exemplified by Kepes, Schaeffer-Simmern, and Sherman are of the greatest significance. They are so, not merely for their intrinsic values, but for the shift of direction in art teaching they portend.

In the 1920's, during the years of intense enthusiasm and achievement of progressive education, the only tool art teachers had for determining art qualities was the broadening of Arthur Dow's principles and elements of composition. These applied to the work only. While a teacher was hoping to expand his students' abilities to grow, to express themselves in distinctive creations, he had at the same time to urge the student to see his work as a "qualitative" arrangement of lines, values, and colors and as embodying principles of radiation, symmetry, transition, and so forth. It was clear to good teachers that personal creations could not issue from unimaginative following of rules, but this use of the components of art forms did, contrarily, presume that rules could be found that would work.

The flights into the wild blue yonder in visual perception, starting with the impressionists and succeeded by the Fauves, the expressionists, the cubists, purists, dadaists, constructivists, and surrealists, were ripe for analysis and wider use when the Bauhaus started after the armistice of 1918. Kepes capitalized on all of that background and upon the further clarification and Americanization of the Bauhaus work as it developed under Moholy-Nagy in Chicago.

We can still find Dow's composition approach a stimulating portion of our background, but today the full toolbox available provides a greater range of equipment.

The nature of physiological perception and its expression through art forms is seen to illuminate the analysis of art composition and to go beyond it. We need no longer try to see identical form qualities in a stone carving of an Egyptian scribe and in a mobile by Calder. Instead we see that each is a three-dimensional object brought into existence by cultures using altogether different forms in space to represent social ideas and values. And the art of the individual, like that of a whole culture, depends not upon a fortunate, a "qualitative" grouping of elements and principles, but more upon the forceful personality by means of which the work comes into existence.

When we come to the directions implied by Sherman and Schaeffer-Simmern, we encounter the fact that our culture no longer possesses any one narrow and comfortable form organization in art. Our characteristic is that we are trying at great speed to analyze and to understand for our own use the perceptions and social dynamics that created the Sphinx, Chartres Cathedral, the TVA dams, and the strobo-flash camera. As this leads to confusion aesthetically, it results in confusion compounded in the individual art student. For some individuals the Schaeffer-Simmern pattern of thought offers rescue, not by the route of *Language of Vision* with its direct ascent of the mountaintop where the riches of our day will be visible all at once, but by the quiet reassurance that whatever the individual can produce, however slight, immature, or provincial, is inimitably his own and valuable as such. With it, growth can be expected and enlarging horizons will offer themselves constantly, but no more rapidly than the student desires or is ready to comprehend.

Sherman's chart for aesthetic development is neither a map to the mountaintop nor a proposal to contemplate one's humblest first efforts as the most likely point of departure on an unhurried path to more satisfying experiences.

Essentially, Sherman, like Schaeffer-Simmern, assumes that the overall survey of art forms, their roots in perception, in social values, the analysis of their visual and tactile values in space and even in time, may be too overwhelming as a basic study for the beginner.

So his flash technique is planned to re-create in the relatively mature student something of the innocent vision of the young child and, as well, the young child's easy and uninhibited expression in plastic media. The flash experience, if we believe in its operation to date, serves the student by giving him a means of releasing himself from the crippling of aesthetic expression most people permit or accept during the years of adolescence. Sherman's faith in his procedure is that the individual, after he had worked for a while in the darkened studio, would have a richer and more personal experience in plastic arts as a basis for further development than he would have simply in drawing whatever he can in whatever stilted fashion he is able.

No one is apt to believe that the one way to expressive competence has been marked out for all students. That a variety of routes has been proposed and tried out with considerable success is what art teachers can observe. The public-school art teacher, the art faculty of the humanities college and the teachers' college, the teacher of general art-education courses in the university—these are the people who will make what use they can of these methods and who must avoid the fixed routines and the unthinking repetitions which make a "system" a straitjacket.

I emphasize the teachers of general education in the preceding statement, for I believe that the immediate future of the arts and art education in this country will be theirs to create. The professional art courses in art institutes, independent schools, and colleges and universities have never been more diverse and, at their best, more adequate in the professional preparation of artists and art teachers. The single most glaring shortcoming of the professional schools, as well as of the editing of the professional art magazines in their coverage of the New York sales galleries, is their intellectual removal from the thinking of the bulk of the American population, numerically and geographically. Possibly this is unavoidable, though many schools are aware of the problem and are working at its solution, following in some respects the work the museums have been doing in reaching their large public following. No small part of the problem is caused by the fact that most important art schools are located in the largest cities. University and college art departments are often a little closer geographically and perhaps socially to an aesthetic environment more nearly average for America.

It is, however, the art teacher in the general-education curriculum, elementary, secondary, and college, who must leave the large city, the specialized environment of the professional art course, the large museums; and who must meet, interest, and instruct a public lacking most of the advantages experienced by the art teacher in his years of formal study.

What these teachers have done already has been remarkable. What they can accomplish in the future will depend upon the communities employing them and also upon the art community which is responsible for sending them forth.

SCHOOLS OF ART AND GENERAL EDUCATION

Art education in the elementary and secondary schools is still an untapped resource for the large art schools and museums. The art teacher in the public schools feels cut off from the arts and the interest of artists when he begins his work. There is not much hope of interest on the part of the art magazines in the work he will be doing. They are dominated by sales and advertising interests or by special relationships to the colleges, to art historians, to museum organizations, or to commercial art activities. Magazines dealing exclusively with school art do so on a level which shows them as uninterested in the larger bearings of the arts as the metropolitan artists are in the problems of art education. Parenthetically, since this chapter was written, both the "School Arts" and "Junior Arts and Activities" magazines are beginning to disprove the foregoing statement.

Only the large art schools supporting progressive art-education units have the connections and the possible motivations to explore the national aesthetic scene, to catalogue our resources, and to begin a more serious development of this human and aesthetic wealth than has yet been attempted.

For such an enterprise, art-education graduates can be the hardworking diplomatic corps of the urban art centers to the rest of the country. Today they are, as it were, unaccredited. Their professional alma mater does not have any organized plan of keeping in touch with their work. Here and there in the country, the professional art schools and departments in universities are inaugurating activities to keep their graduates who are teaching somewhat in contact with the school.

The next step, and one which could be far more significant, would be that of keeping the art school aware of the problems and experiences encountered by its graduates. A comprehension of the aesthetic climate in which most art teachers work is not often evident in art departments, and it must come before the art school can be more valuable to general art education. I am not making a plea that each graduate should by turns be the adaptable and guileless young art teacher, willing to go along with the most absurd provincial prejudices in the arts, and then turn into a Bohemian Mr. Hyde who preserves Dr. Jekyll's serene poise by indulging for him in aesthetic orgies at the metropolitan art centers. Neither do art graduates benefit by pep talks exclusively designed to instruct them in the uses of conformity. When an art-school teacher of educational methods misuses an acquaintance with the difficulties of young teachers' adjustments to community life as the basis for a "do's and don'ts" list, it is apt to serve just one purpose: the discouragement of the best students from teaching at all.

What the art school could learn from its graduates that would stimulate more effective undergraduate preparation is the status and practice of the arts in the area it serves. How have children's drawing and painting subject interests changed in the years of the depression, war, inflation, cold war, and atomic energy? Have attitudes toward contemporary painting changed or remained the same as the national magazines increase their use of visual experimentation? What furniture and picture reproductions are selling in the local stores? What are the trends of the reactions the teacher notices among his student groups, participants in night-school adult classes, to the examples of all kinds of art work he may be able to show them in prints, originals, or photographic clippings? Some art-school-faculty personnel can take the lead in formulating these questions, in planning means of getting valid answers, and, most important, in using the knowledge gained to good effect.

The art school through its graduates and also through its undergraduates can reach the community institutions which have in the past aided art development: the library, study clubs, social organizations, vocational school, local historical and natural-history museums, labor unions, business and luncheon clubs, and the church social groups. In varying degree these organized citizens are as important to the arts in any town as the coöps, the Grange, the Farmers' Union, and the Farm Bureau are to agricultural progress. But we do not know what these groups can do because they are seldom asked to extend themselves beyond their usual routine.

To know does not mean to accept without reservation or desire for change. Expressionism and cubism have changed painting for good; most Americans know nothing of either of these movements and their aesthetic prejudices would show this clearly. As art schools become more aware, through studies, of the real level of art understanding, it would not mean that undergraduate students retreat to the impressionism of Childe Hassam. It could mean that a larger proportion of students would be impelled to put their knowledge of contemporary imagery and symbolism to such use as would be more widely understood. Moholy-Nagy was certainly one of the greatest advocates of extending the technical possibilities of the arts. No one could boast a more thorough acquaintance than he with the visual-symbol, advance-guard movements of this century, and no one was more eager than he to increase the public acceptance of new art forms. He saw public education as a liberating force both for the artist and for the general populace. We will be taking his leadership seriously when we have built up a technique for integrating the work of the professional art school with the work of the public-school teacher of art. We can recognize some success in the venture when graduates are eager to start their first year of independent teaching and are no longer fearful of leaving the studios because they dread meeting a public profoundly uninterested in their work, and because they anticipate how little they may look back to their art school for vigorous and well-directed backing.

Many schools are now on the verge of giving young teachers some kind of support. How the problem is to be tackled cannot be standardized. It cannot be done without making more college faculty time available for directing imaginative studies, for travel, for extension activities directly relating the best professional activity of the college or university to the local communities through the medium of its own professional art faculty.

The impressive enlargement of college and university art faculties since 1940 can be a tremendous stimulus in making more democratic our national participation in art. Departments everywhere have grown numerically. Increasingly, artist-teachers have been drawn to the faculties. As art staffs have grown, it has been more possible to bring to the campus artists of ability and prestige in specific fields: painting, sculpture, ceramics, graphic arts, metalcraft, industrial design, architectural design, textile design, commercial arts. The vigor and the achievement possible to these art-faculty members, the kind of technical plant they set up, need to be reflected more directly in the work of their art colleagues of the elementary and secondary schools. It is not necessary that the community schools be dunned to set up overextravagant plants in art, but that their art faculties find the work they do with young people of concern to the college staff. They in turn need to be urged to make use of the college plant and personnel; and not only for a brief term as graduate students, but for constant study and progress in their work in the arts and in education.

For the professional art department the tie with the art teachers of the surrounding area may in moments of stress be a practical association of great value. This country in the arts exhibits extremes of ignorance and infinite subtleties. There are valid reasons for the schools of art to expect staff members to continue their creative and research work to the most rewarding end products. Much of this work will not seem immediately worth while to the taxpayer or alumnus supporting the school.

If in fact the school is also studying, and in noticeable ways aiding art education in large and small communities, then the more complex and less understandable work can be assumed to have a potential future relationship to the arts in general society, just as independent scientific inquiry is the most fertile ground for the growth of useful applied research.

ANTICIPATION

All institutions devoted to education in art need more money. In these days of uncertain financial standards, it would be safer to say that art institutions need a greater proportion of the national income. The sum total of all funds now spent on public education in the arts is so small that large proportionate increases will represent only the minutest fraction of the national income. How additional moneys can be raised need not concern us in detail. It will be available because more people want to work in the arts and to know the arts. They will support extensions of art education whenever they are proposed on a sound basis by a responsible group or leader. Many more activities than those already carried on would by now be in progress if it had not been for the immense burden of defense spending. But even that will have to shrink someday. Progress has been steady in the last hundred years and, barring nation-wide catastrophe, we are ready for more art ventures reaching more people than ever in our history. What are some of the things we may reasonably anticipate in art education?

ANTICIPATION: THE MUSEUM

We need not repeat what has already been surveyed earlier. And many excellent works have recently been produced more fully describing the educational work and significance of the American museum of art. I should like to make some speculations on those educational activities the museums are most likely to continue and initiate in the near future.

Let us hope that the expansion of our art background will move toward a greater knowledge of the arts of India, Africa, and finally China and Russia. Only if international tensions reach a state of at least moderate relaxation can all these hopes be realized; but when the international situation permits, we may expect excellently prepared material in our metropolitan museum circuits stressing the arts of the One World. As it becomes possible for the museums to organize historical exhibits of the arts from hitherto little-known parts of the world, we will expect to see some of the surveys followed by exhibitions of contemporary work from the same places.

Indicative of a state of international amity and constructive living would be periodical exhibitions of models, maps, drawings, and photos of new community plans and replanning of older urban centers from around the globe.

As we wait and do our part to work for these developments, the

Figure 18. Education in Art History—a Museum-Cover Design by Paul Rand. (From Catalogue, "20th Century Art, Arensburg Collection," Art Institute of Chicago, 1949.)

Figure 19. Fourth-Grade Child's Work in Linoleum Block. (Endpapers from Natalie Robinson Cole, "The Arts in the Classroom," John Day, 1940.)

268

museum will still be maintaining its status as educator of the American public. The range of art interests toward which Dana contributed so excellent an introducton will continue to be reflected in museum calendars. Comprehensive developmental exhibits may increase and become even more thorough in treatment of industrial-design fields. A subject certain to be treated is the technical progression of printing and the new design forms it has given birth to. Such themes as the forms of standard furniture pieces, or the evolution of several decades of clothing design, have already been used on the basis of certain special design approaches, and can be expanded to inclusive and educational surveys of entire fields of characteristic production. Exhibits like these have been done well, but they can be more widely organized and circulated. Just as important to the nation at large, they ought to be accompanied by well-printed catalogues and books.

Recently, large exhibits of the work of amateurs have been shown. Some museum will one day reap enormous prestige by presenting the first national exhibit, thoughtfully and representatively organized, of the art work of American children. Projected, as it ought to be, by a professional staff, the show can be as revealing, though perhaps not as violently greeted, as the Armory Show. Children's art work, shown as a major exhibit, might well be displayed anonymously. Should this drastic approach not seem feasible, then all the other undesirable aspects of contemporary professional exhibits ought to be eliminated. There should be no prizes and no competitive selection.

The value of a child-art exhibition would be in its aim to make the work better understood among parents and the interested public, and to present a cross section of the emotional-intellectual expression of the day as it came from a cross section of America's children.

Another exhibition which could perform a great service to the public would be one on the visual and plastic arts produced all over the country by adult amateurs, with particular emphasis on the three-dimensional media known as crafts. Merely to gather together the several hundred objects necessary to form an exhibit group would serve little purpose, no matter how excellent the individual pieces might be. The real job a museum could do superlatively well would be that of showing clearly the difference in aesthetic values between a cute little ash tray, modeled in the form of a shiny green leaf, and a similar tray employing clay form and surface glaze in a manner best adapted to the media of clay craft. American "hobby" activity is of great significance, more than important enough for a major art museum to treat as a subject for display and helpful aesthetic analysis.

Museums have been expanding educational functions other than the exhibits they organize. The museum child and adult classes continue to grow where they are established, and are being started in small museums. The nature of these classes changes from community to community, but most of them are valuable additions to the cities' facilities. If there is evident any one trend in development, it is the healthy one of broadening the classes offered to include more three-dimensional work in sculptural and craft media.

Finally, museums are taking a lead in education for better motion-picture products. Few of even the smallest museums fail to schedule series of important films, European, Asiatic, and American. Since most of these are the non-Hollywood make, the result of the programs is to make an audience more sensitive to film values and more eager to welcome fresh approaches to film art. While the Museum of Modern Art's Film Library is still drawn upon heavily for this nation-wide trend, there is also an increasingly large number of agencies, private and institutional, making unusual film available. A small but lively activity in independent short-film producing has the encouragement of the museum exhibitors. Television, too, may be influenced by this phase of museum education.

The museums will continue to interpret, to make available to us, the main outlines of our attitudes toward the arts. As usual, the artists will frequently speak out as opposed to certain practices, and in so doing they will affect direction and policy. Teachers of art, often more remote from museums, might well adopt a more interested critical surveillance of their chief regional galleries. For the sake of art education beyond the museum, we may hope that more institutions can publish permanent illustrated records with their major efforts; and that all museums will find more productive forms of sponsoring the contemporary art forms, particularly painting, sculpture, and the graphic arts, than those which have prevailed in the last decade.

ANTICIPATION: THE ART SCHOOL—INDEPENDENT, COLLEGE, AND UNIVERSITY

The art school or art department of today is professional, and it is impressively technical in the eyes of lay visitors. It would seem impossible for these schools not to produce in the next quarter century a flood of students who will radically alter the practice and the public acceptance of the arts.

Only a small fraction of the art graduates can hope to be employed full-time in art vocations, but that fact does not act as a deterrent to continued high enrollment across the nation. Art courses are being taken by many students in the same frame of mind once found only among students in the general-humanities courses. Particularly does this apply to college women, who find a background including a good general-humanities course, and a general design, drawing, and art-history preparation with a special arts or crafts interest, just as valuable and more individualized than an academic four-year curriculum in the college of letters and science. Vocationally, art preparation for women does not yet open for them many opportunities in design and commercial art, but it does make possible careers in teaching and in many parts of the business of retail merchandising. Men in the numbers now enrolled in art schools are aware of the likelihood that many will find themselves in jobs sometimes remotely related to the arts, but there is an often-expressed conviction on the part of students that creative art work on the college level gives them an assurance that they can find a spot where their abilities can be used. For men graduates, teaching as well as jobs in varied design fields present opportunities. As with colleges of engineering and commerce, the sidelines entered by art graduates are numerous but not unbelievable. Sales work, insurance writing, personnel work, general office work, mostly in firms connected with design or advertising, are jobs often occupied by men and women who have had a considerable art background.

The increase in the proportion of art-trained persons to the rest of the population is bound to make itself felt, and will be absorbed easily and with value into American communities. Our cities and towns will find that art training, as it is now widely practiced, is one which insists upon a broad experience with tools. This training, if it is faulty, puts greater value upon a familiarity with many tools than upon a mastery of any. The result is that art students have a refreshing willingness to try almost anything, from designing for a mimeographed publication to landscape architecture. All that stops many art graduates from designing in any field is the coldness of union and other professional groups to letting them get started.

Alert art faculties are in process of constant revision of first-year or "basic" studio courses. They are currently overeager to make our required sequences of courses too close in spirit and administration to those of the technical schools. No tears need be shed for the dilettante, low-productivity days through which art schools have passed; but it is not wholly reassuring to see the large number of men and women students fleeing American schools for Mexico or France so that they can "just paint." Granted that is not the only attraction, and that there is something healthy in travel for anyone in the arts, the possibility still exists that the American art school may have been pushing too hard on rigid requirements.

After all, "just painting" is one of the most independent of art disciplines. Our best generation of designers, those of the thirties and forties, was as often as not the product of "just painting" in art schools. College, university, and art-school departments are all guilty of providing too little time for the third-, fourth-, or fifth-year student simply to paint or make pots or work in the design shops. Out of such thoughtful concentration have come hundreds of excellent artists, sometimes leaders in work quite remote from that which occupied their time as undergraduates. It is the philosophical and technical independence of the older student which is stunted in today's art school.

No other means of combining some academic classes, an adequate technical art preparation, and some mature growth as an artist—no means of securing all three of these aims, in addition to some professional work in education—is visible except that of making five years the minimum time needed for a first arts degree, with one or more additional years for the second degree.

Artist-teachers predominantly agree with Lester Longman's attitude toward the doctoral degree for teachers of "practical" art, as distinguished from teachers of the history of art. He contends that the doctorate is the license of the scholar, and is not designed to meet the needs of growth for a strong creator in the visual and plastic arts. For additional work on the second degree, there is no doubt that the majority of artists in teaching situations would prefer graduate work that offered more studio work, with scholarly work available in education and art history.

Two viewpoints collide head on. Artists and art teachers do not want to carry the scholarly work necessary to a Ph. D. degree. They do so only to meet arbitrary requirements. But many schools continue emphasis upon degrees as the primary indication of excellence, colleges being the greatest sinners in this regard. By their fixed policy, many colleges will have to select unknown young people with doctoral degrees in preference to an excellent and experienced teacher who is also a widely known craftsman or artist in his field. The fact that continued growth in an artist's creative work is worth more to him as a person and as a teacher than formal academic study in no way seems to influence the selection of faculty or the standards for promotion in many colleges. The university departments and the independent art schools have not succumbed to this fascination for the degree in the art fields; and since the universities are in most instances the graduate schools of their region, it is within their power to influence the practice.

The graduate schools should themselves lead in creating an advanced framework of study, not merely meeting the customary scholarly requirements, but demanding of their students an equally rigorous regime in general and specialized art areas, together with such associated academic studies as seem valuable to the artist and artist-teacher.

ANTICIPATION: ART IN THE ELEMENTARY CURRICULUM

In elementary schools today, there is too great a difference in art education. The majority of rural schools have teachers whose art preparation has been slight to nonexistent, and few rural areas have art consultants, itinerant teachers, or supervisors. The same situation prevails in many village and small-town schools. For the larger cities, some art is taught in most systems, and the classroom teachers average more background in art, at least to the extent of one or two college classes in art or art-education methods. Most of the larger cities have some full-time art-staff members assigned to the elementary schools, but this is a most variable element. Cities of a million or more population may have as few as four to eight supervisors for all the elementary schools, while many suburban and smaller-city schools have a full-time art teacher or teachers in every elementary-school building.

There is general approval of a strong art program in elementary education. The factors that make for strength are twofold: first, classroom elementary teachers with a good general background, some art experience in college, and a flexible outlook, able to work with and learn from a good art consultant. The second of these factors, the art consultant, requires certain conditions under which his work will reach maximum effectiveness. He ought to be able to spend not less than a half hour to forty-five minutes in each classroom twice a month or, better yet, weekly. The art consultant needs to be able to adjust his time freely, spending more time in one school one week, and less another, depending upon the progress of work going forward. Regarding the physical plant, new elementary-school construction ought to include a general art and project room where all art classes can share special tools and work space not available in the ordinary classroom.

The goals of our American scheme of education will not be reached until the quality of education everywhere is as good as the best anywhere. For that reason, the extension of art education depends heavily upon the plans for school aid from state and federal government, upon reorganization plans making possible larger and better-equipped school plants, and upon local plans to equalize school facilities for all children, suburban, urban, and rural, of all races and in all areas of the country. The predominance of good elementary-school art work in suburban and urban areas is not the choice of the rural and sparsely settled regions. With their inadequately planned districts and consequent dearth of tax moneys, they cannot afford a thorough school program without some outside assistance.

Assuming progress in the equalization and democratization of opportunities, what qualitative developments should elementary-school art education offer, and how will they be achieved?

First in importance is the broadening and improving of the art courses offered the elementary teacher in his college preparation. Art teachers must give their college students an understanding of the arts as literally a visual and plastic education, an alerting of the sensuous equipment to respond to the environment. The college student of elementary education must successfully express himself in paint, clay, paper, with crayon, brush, and hand tools of various sorts. He must see his fellow students working in diverse ways and being encouraged to continue in their diversity. The college teachers of this group do incalculable harm when they impose arbitrary semi-professional standards of aesthetic achievement. At no other time and with no other group of students is there more need for using instructional approaches to bring out a gamut of creative work in every medium that is used.

What needs to be the approach of this group to contemporary art? In industrial design, commercial art, the motion picture, and television, the college art teacher need do no more than give students a feeling for an intelligent, open-minded attitude toward these arts. What is the design used for; does it achieve its purpose; is the established purpose worth-while; how does it make use of the materials involved? Questions like these serve to create an environment where all things are accepted as worthy of attention and where aesthetic criticism is soundly based upon observable relationships. Cars, washing machines, and textbooks can be looked at in such terms by any college group without feeling any pain, without requiring agreement with the art teacher unless it is through understanding.

About contemporary painting and sculpture, the teacher of general art is not as well informed nor as confident, and the students in elementary education find the question of meaning in contemporary pictorial arts much more puzzling. A thousand miles from New York City and two hours' drive from the nearest art colleague, an art teacher is not encouraged to argue the point that a reproduction of a Jackson Pollock painting and the latest spatter-paint design for linoleum are remarkably alike. The layman who does observe a similarity is likely to be more interested in aesthetic qualities than are many of his fellow citizens. In this instance the art teacher inevitably identifies himself with his own community, and finds as time passes that his fellow townsmen are closer to his sympathies than are unknown artists in New York or in other countries.

The art teacher of prospective elementary teachers needs, as much as any art professional, to be aquainted with the visual experiments that the twentieth century has produced. The convention that all pictures must be visualized pleasantly as decorating an over-mantel space need no longer be agreed with, even with students who have had little time in art class. But since time is pressing, the art teacher will have to be selective, presenting some examples of cubist and probably of surrealist painting accompanied by examples of the use of surrealist and cubist devices in current advertising, or motion picture or television. To attempt an extremely brief run-through of many contemporary pictorial approaches is usually not possible. It is better to demonstrate more slowly a rational, inquiring frame of mind in regard to a few difficult works.

Emphasis is put upon the art training of the elementary teacher because the excellence of his background will determine how much progress can be made by art-supervising teachers in the elementary grades. Whether there is a great deal of art in an elementary room or very little, the creative experience is qualified or enhanced by the sympathies and understanding of the grade teacher. The quality of art class offered in our elementary-education college curriculum is a key element in the improvement of art education.

ANTICIPATION: THE ART-EDUCATION ASSOCIATIONS

Since 1947, the teacher of art has had the opportunity of participation in larger, more active, and more influential associations for art education than ever before. In that year, intermittent efforts to revive and make more significant the art department of the National Education Association culminated in the formation of a National Art Education Association firmly tied financially and politically to the four regional groups: Eastern Arts, Southeastern Arts, Western Arts, and Pacific Arts. Each of these associations gained in membership strength, continued their meetings and publications, and to their activity was added a national activity not before attempted, at least on so ambitious a scale.

Simultaneously, state associations in existence seemed to be encouraged to fresh efforts, and additional groups were formed in states where there had been none. An effort to tie in the state associations with the national-regional structure has succeeded on a policy, good-will basis, but not very widely on a related financial basis. Probably the importance of local autonomy will cancel out financial coördination between state and national units.

Meanwhile, the Museum of Modern Art has continued to sponsor its Committee on Art Education. This group has been smaller, more independent of geography, of less-widespread membership. Its activities and policies have in some ways been more specific, and it has tried to set a higher qualitative standard, than seems possible to the larger associations. With its New York City location and the museum building as its annual meeting place, it has emphasized the relationship of the work of contemporary artists to art education. It has sought a uniformly high standard of art work in the schools. More vigorously than any other group, it has questioned the educational value of the contest idea in art education. To a great extent, it has been a study group. If the national, regional, and state setup discourages such independent agencies, it will be an absolute loss in art education.

The questions arise: What values do the organizations have for the art teacher? What influence will they have on art teaching in Biloxi or Rhinelander? What may be expected of the art-education associations?

Their elaborate organizational schemes require faculty members in various schools who can and will sacrifice much of their time to carrying on operations. Edwin Ziegfeld, Italo de Francesco, and Victor D'Amico in the national association and in the Museum Committee on Art Education have given leadership in both organizational and policy direction. Their work, with the assistance of a hundred or

277

more persons, has created our instruments for mutual improvement in an organized form.

The past fifty years present a picture of art-education meetings attended primarily by art administrators and college teachers, in addition to the public-school personnel in the vicinity of the city where the meeting is being held. The policies, the philosophy, and the practical processes discussed at conventions have, so to speak, filtered down to the classroom from on high. The present strengthening of state art-education associations might tend to fasten the pattern more securely than ever. The heads go to the regional and national meetings and pass on the word at the state meetings.

If it does happen that way, may not the adequacy of the system be questioned? Should not classroom teachers more frequently represent their city or their county at special field meetings? For that matter, would not their teaching be improved and the morale of the staff lifted if their professional competence were thus recognized? Classroom teachers need to be sought out for vocal and written contributions to the association, not merely for their membership dues.

Immediately a problem arises which has seldom been acknowledged. If the average art teacher is to be encouraged to make contributions to the association in the form of writing, speaking, and exhibiting, the spread between currently dominant philosophies and methods and the work of the classroom teacher will often be startlingly evident. But if the association really wants to reach the persons who are doing the teaching it must provide forum opportunities for the work of representative teachers, not only for unusual, gifted, and progressive teachers. Too often, as organizational affairs are now conducted, the bulk of activity consists of writing and talking about general qualities in student art work. The understanding of a given philosophical approach, or the failure to understand it, is quickly revealed in the student work from any teacher's class, but analytical sessions based on the observation of student pieces are much too infrequent.

The most valuable recent trend in art-education meetings has been the effort to bring persons from related fields of interest as guest speakers, most often to speak on their own work as they see its relationship to the arts and art education. The impulse to broaden liberal background brings more worth-while content to the meetings than a narrow interpretation of professional interest.

There is an overweening desire on the part of some art educators to employ association strength politically, to advance art education by stiffening requirements in teacher certification, by increasing art-curriculum requirements as qualifications for state aid, by urging the inclusion of paid personnel on state department staffs, and by pushing any other means of recognizing and providing for art education in the school systems.

A fine line may be drawn here, but there are many who feel that administrative compulsions or regulations favoring the spread of art education should be enacted when art has become a desirable, indispensable part of the curriculum in the minds of school people and interested citizens. Following this line of thought, art-education associations could accomplish most by enlarging upon and demonstrating the value of art in the school. The exploitation of politico-administrative devices should be kept in its place as a means to an end, and ought not to divert the profession away from the arts or education.

If some art educators, after years spent in various forms of lobbying and political activities, find themselves unhappily at cross-purposes with their colleagues more active in the arts, they need to question whether or not the things they did have actually brought creative experiences to a larger proportion of people. If the answer is clearly affirmative, there need be no self-reproach; the failure to have time or to take time to do art work of their own, and hence their comparative lack of rapport with producing artists, is a burden they must expect. They may wish that artists and artist-teachers appreciated more the eventual worth of political, organizational effort, but it is unrealistic to expect that they will. The creative nature of the organizer's work is perhaps too remote from the kind of work which engrosses most of the artist's time.

The art producer will contend that more and better art will solve the problems of art in any society. The art-educated person who has a flair for working in the complex pattern of social groupings will feel impatiently that "something" must be done to make art count for more in the community.

The art teachers' associations can improve art opportunities in education by a judicious balancing of the labors of both kinds of teachers. There will always be a tendency for the organizers to dominate the scene simply because they have performed the miracle of keeping an organization alive, but they need the productive artist-teacher's contribution if their own activity is to attain full significance.

WHAT TO EXPECT OF ART TEACHERS?

American schools do not begin to expect enough from the art teachers they employ. To state the converse, graduates of the professional art courses are prepared to do far more work for their adopted communities than they are permitted.

As new members of a faculty group, art teachers are usually welcome and there is always plenty of activity waiting for them. They have a full quota of classes or a combination schedule of high-school classes and classes in the elementary schools, where they teach or serve as consultants to the classroom teacher. In addition to their basic school assignments, as is the case with nearly all school people these days, they are expected to assume other duties. Among these may be the supervision of corridors and cafeteria, the direction of a homeroom group, occasional duties in the community campaigns which legitimately reach into the school, and, looming largest of all in time consumed and demands upon the teacher, the junior- and senior-high-school "extracurricular" program.

Obviously, set design and construction and costuming for drama may well fall to an art teacher. Equally probable is the assignment to faculty supervision of the annual. And the nearly always disorganized and time-consuming tasks of party decoration and publicity campaigns for everything from athletics to Keep Our School Clean have, more than any other single factor, caused disruption and dismay to young teachers trying to get a worth-while art curriculum set up.

Most of these demands and involvements are natural and must be met. There should be more aid from administrative officers than is usually the case. The new art-faculty member, experienced or inexperienced, has at least one busy year to put in getting his studio, materials, and equipment organized for his teaching. For art is individual in its organization, and a good art teacher should bring a distinctive quality to the community. If he does, some reorganization of the physical plant will be essential, no matter how excellent the predecessor may have been. Consequently, administrators can help by carefully advising against too many commitments to the numerous perfectly appropriate activities which may be suggested. A capable teacher will be more ready to offer his abilities to school and community enterprises where they could be used, and to carry through with helpful work, if he is not pushed beyond hope of rescue in his first few months in a new place.

As yet, we have not reached the nub of the argument that most communities are not getting full value from their art faculty. They assuredly are not, and the failure is found in the fact that the art teacher's preparation as artist *and* teacher is almost universally overlooked or ignored.

The graduates of all good schools today are on the way to becoming mature artists in one or more media. Most of them are interested in one or two or three fields, which may be print making, ceramics, painting, metalcrafts, theater design, sculpture, or design in materials like wood, leather, or textiles. As a preparation for their teaching and because artists realize that their special skill is enriched by working in other materials, the art teacher is able to work in most of the other media. Oftentimes a lively artist-teacher will teach himself and his students some one of the media for which he did not have time as a professional student.

It is the teacher's professional advancement and progress as an artist which the schools have not recognized as one of the values an art teacher can bring to the school. The failure to insist upon this development, to provide for it, and to expect the advantages it could produce has been the largest cause for art teachers' relative impermanence in all but the largest cities. This failure has been the cause of uncounted cases of art teachers who have become, not the most active and creative members of a faculty, but the most difficult, who develop crotchety habits accounted for by their colleagues as "artistic temperament." I would not wish to imply that large cities do take steps to benefit by their art teachers' continued growth as artists, for they do no better than their smaller neighbors. Larger salaries are attractive to teachers, but more than that is the attraction for art teachers of the galleries, the larger music and theater program, and the encouragement of other persons interested in art. Even if the metropolitan schools show little concern for the creative product of their teachers, there are other teachers, artists, and designers with whom the teacher has something in common, and who impel him to continue his own work.

The smaller school systems could, however, take advantage of their greater administrative flexibility by venturing to create art departments of more importance and value than is now common.

What proposals, exactly, are to be made in thus trying to realize fully on the presence of an art staff? Is the art member to be relieved of a large part of his responsibilities to the students, perhaps by subtracting from his class load, or from homeroom or hall supervision, or maybe most of the extracurricular chores ordinarily shunted to the art room? Certainly the time must be found, and it must be subtracted from other things. Social life needs to be maintained by the single teacher in various personal and community interests; it is a little more confined to the home in the case of married teachers. But the creative work of an independent artist-craftsman can steal time from what most people use for recreation. To work at a silk-screen print of one's own is recreational after the teacher has been working with students doing screen prints in class. Time must be taken somewhat from the school program, too, not only from the teacher's recreation hours. But here it need not be counted as lost to the school, for, properly spent, the teacher's creative hours will yield a fine return in student interest and classwork.

In return for being relieved of some fringe activity, best determined by administrator and teacher on the basis of the local situation, the art teacher can be prevailed upon with little or no resistance to set up and keep in operation a personal studio; that is, to use the school's art facilities, with an adjoining office workshop if it be available, as a place to work regularly.

Ideally, the work on personal projects ought to move forward during at least three or four two-hour stints each school week. In some communities, a habit of long standing may be advanced as making such a proposal impossible. In these communities, school buildings are locked at five in the afternoon and all day Saturday and Sunday, being open to students and faculty alike only during the daylight hours five days weekly.

If there is any one factor making the high school and elementary teacher feel less of a scholar and a responsible agent to the community employing him than does the college teacher, it is the lack of confidence in faculty and students which this policy toward informal after-class activities infers.

The art teacher who is encouraged to look upon the studio facilities as creative tools for himself as well as his students would, in ninety-nine cases out of a hundred, make full use of them during afternoon hours that could be spared, in the evenings, and on week ends. Since no activity is more pleasant than that which is shared, and since class activities would be stimulated by teacher-and-student work associations outside of class, the art teacher would inevitably invite students to work with him occasionally. In this kind of work and relationship there are problems that would have to be foreseen and forestalled. The young teacher would especially have to be reminded of the wisdom of making such work privileges available on a fair-distribution pattern, and not always to favorite or talented students.

A school which is not customarily open in out-of-school hours, or for which faculty members do not have keys, would face the problem on the basis of all or none. Naturally, no such privilege could be granted only to an art teacher. Obviously, if one teacher returns to the building at night, others will follow. There is sometimes projected a dismal picture of the weary teacher alone at her desk, eyes smarting late at night, thanklessly completing her labors. As any teacher who does have access to his building at all hours knows, there are innumerable instances when he would rather go home or about personal business at once after the last class hour, so that he can return in the evening to work out a problem where material is handy and at a time when he is less rushed, more able to concentrate. The classrooms and offices of colleges, universities, and professional schools are never altogether unoccupied.

It is this need to use the most complete laboratory equipment available for hours at a time that the present-day artist-teacher realizes so strongly, and that is least provided for when he takes a teaching job. Administrators who are making it easy for the teacher to do his creative work are aware that they have a teacher whose contribution to the school is multiplied. His influence with students, faculty colleagues, and parents is much more constructive than would be possible if he had renounced altogether, or seriously curtailed, his creative output.

As a last word on this theme, it may be desirable to indicate the range of interest possible to artists on a school faculty. Mistakenly, it is sometimes assumed that art activity is confined to picture making or at most to a craft. And part of the public believes that only the artist who produces to exhibit publicly is really good. Neither of these requirements are essential to the teacher. He may well be the most creative influence in his school; he may have a greater range of personal work going on all the time, all of it of good quality; and he may not paint and he may not be exhibiting. He might, for instance, be designing and helping some students to make new display cases and racks for the school corridor or lobby. He might be spending a year or more experimenting for the first time in that school with ceramics prior to introducing it in classes. He might be working occasionally on an extra-fee basis doing some typographical design or display designs for local merchants in a town not large enough to support a commercial-art or design firm. Just as with the teacher who likes to paint independently, activities like these, where the teacher is continuing to work in the arts for himself, are the essential fact for an artist-teacher who is never going to fall behind in his work. The school that wants a good art program must look for such teachers and provide them with every incentive to keep up their status as creative artists.

WHAT MAY THE ART STUDENT EXPECT?

Education in the arts cannot bring on a happy existence uninterrupted by the chills and fevers of our society. But the continuation and improvement of our present approach to art education constitute one guarantee that our democratic society has not closed up shop, and that it is not succumbing to the fears and hates dominating a Nazi, Fascist, or Communist state.

At the close of this work dealing with some of the backgrounds of art education, the influences that have shaped it, and its important present practices, let us dwell upon what men, women, and children can expect, what they ought to expect, from education in the arts.

When children go to school for the first time, their parents should anticipate that they will each day have some work with art materials. They should learn, as parents, to want their children's work to be freely done, and they should regret anything said by themselves or by a teacher which compares their work unfavorably with that of another child. What they should be privileged to observe is that their child is becoming accustomed to using paints and clay and paper, possibly other materials, and that he is developing ideas which he is eager to try out each time the art period comes around.

As his teacher does not expect him to achieve by imitation the voice quality of Laurence Olivier, so, too, she will not expect him to attain the pictorial powers of a magazine illustrator by copying. The passage of time and constant professional urging by art teachers should begin to make clear the harm done by the lackadaisical, copy-cat pages of the workbooks. It has never been too early to start education for independent thinking; we can expect elementary teachers, as their training improves or as their consulting teacher in art helps them with the problem of art activity, to note the connection between unwholesomely timid art work and the quantity of picture copy material that has been used.

New elementary schools are everywhere needed. New secondary schools will shortly be just as necessary. The elementary school needs an activity art room or a plan for each classroom which includes generous work spaces on the floor, a sink, and some large work tables. Many more schools will have full-time or part-time art teachers in the elementary grades; elementary teachers will themselves have an improved art background; and where the consultant art teacher is favored over the departmental teacher, the consultant will find much more and much better art activity possible.

In the elementary grades, however the staff problem is solved, the better space is needed not only for what is now thought of as art work but also for the multitude of other design and craft activities such as model making, map drawing and modeling, poster making, hobby displays, drama settings, and so on. And to repeat, the art teacher or consultant should have an interest in the creative possibilities, the skills, that could be developed in the school day, not alone in what takes place in the art period.

City and country children alike still lack more than they ought the opportunity to design, to handle and shape materials. Peaceful industry will replace the nervous disorder in many classrooms when more manual experiences with tools and materials are made possible. The most significant advance that can be planned for in this area is to increase the scope of craft work and to cast it in the creative pattern of art education, whether its end product is the individual form of painting or in the group enterprise of a model village suggested by a unit in the social studies.

Secondary students in the junior- and senior-high division look upon art as a minor class in which is enrolled a small number of students. Summarizing several issues already discussed at greater length will best outline what seems to me part of the future in secondary-school art education.

The art teacher in the secondary schools is now most often a producing craftsman-artist. He is more awake than ever to the forms of contemporary art, and he welcomes the inquiry into relationships of the arts to other studies. He is frequently a faculty leader in formal and informal curriculum integration. This caliber of teacher can provide the basis for a more extensive program in art education.

Guidance counselors should welcome a good art department, and often they do, but many persons now in this guidance position cherish misconceptions about the role of the arts in secondary schools. Their prejudice is in the direction of forcing academically gifted children out of the arts, and of virtually forcing the less able academic student into art work. So long as art work is an elective, neither of these compulsions is good. The intelligent student with some art interests needs the work. Our professional schools in law, medicine, engineering, commerce, the humanities, and education are filled with students who are aesthetic illiterates in all but the art of literature, partly because "guidance" has assumed that to know and work with art materials is a dubious venture for anyone with an I.Q. over 120 and aged over fourteen.

286

The reverse of this, the secondary student of less than average gifts in academic work, may well expect a fine experience in art class. Sometimes, since he is less inhibited by fear of failure, by the expectation to excel, he expresses himself more freely and successfully than his more brilliant classmates. However, it is just as likely that he may not belong in art class, but in shop or music or drama. Guidance personnel needs not only to know that creative experience is valuable for such a student, but that the kind of creative experience is of equal concern in course planning.

Beyond the confines of the general art course for all interested students, we may expect to see in the future an expansion of special craft classes in the medium-sized and larger high schools. Semester courses in commercial art, ceramics, metalcraft, stagecraft, and others reflect the popularity of the crafts fields and also the special crafts background of the faculty. The practice of requiring a general art course before entering the special craft work is often more of a device to prevent a stampede enrollment than it is the necessity for background in design. There is evident a nation-wide desire for more art craftwork on the part of high-school students, which has for some years been deliberately held down because of lack of space and because administration is reluctant to face the realignment of faculty which any pronounced shift in student preferences causes.

One aspect of the problem of the arts in high school is certainly that the high-school student still needs some activity learning other than what he gets in the gym. The day devoted entirely to academic learning is not in balance for young people of that age. Another face of the matter is that secondary-school faculties have not come to believe that their liberal-education goal must include direct experience with some fine-arts expression. Simply because choral groups, art classes, shop groups, and drama classes or clubs are not concerned primarily with the printed or written word should no longer imply that these activities are essentially technical or manual, and hence not truly liberal. American high schools do not graduate many students ready to express themselves as thoughtful citizens. Direct expression in the arts can be one of the most helpful disciplines for the student whose experience is mostly that of a learner from books.

The remaining category of general students of the arts, the adult, is somewhat better off, where there is any arts instruction, than is the high-school student. The vocational school, the opportunity school, the evening university extension, the museum classes, and the myriad other agencies sponsoring art and craft classes offer whatever they can that has been in demand.

The adult student wishing to advance his art education is free of requirements and is able to study whatever his community resources and the available teaching staff make possible. This often causes some curious lists of class offerings in situations where a teacher can be employed to teach relatively minor or sometimes outdated work, for example, photo tinting or china painting; but in communities where the vocational school is reasonably large, there is a good roster of art classes. Rural areas, as usual, are lacking in adult-education facilities, and in the majority of places have not moved to avail themselves of the use of schools in the nearby towns.

Where it does exist, adult education provides an extension of work in the arts begun earlier, or, for a large group, it provides creative design and the learning of skills in crafts for persons whose art work has not progressed beyond the lower grades. The wide spread of vocational interests possessed by members of adult arts and crafts classes is especially significant, including, as it does, large numbers of professional people, office workers, and factory personnel—in fact, the people whose means of livelihood does not provide much of the satisfaction of making a complete object from their own design. In the work of the adult class, as at other age levels and in other kinds of educational organization, we are closer to the start than to the full realization of the arts in education.

IN CONCLUSION

Attempts at broad-scale definitions may seem out of place at the end of a book instead of the beginning. Each new phase of art education, as it was considered, might have been prefaced by definitions of art or by revisions of the preceding definition. This was not explicitly performed in most instances because it seemed that what was taught in the schools, the way it was taught, and the emphases selected gave the clues needed to understand what was defined as art.

Because the art expression of our time seems to be more than ordinarily confusing, it will be of value to identify some of the larger qualities of contemporary art. Many will have noticed the frequent references to the current enigmas of art. Newspapers and magazines feature pictures of prize-winning paintings which bewilder many people and infuriate others. Dangerous efforts are often launched to make artists paint pictures more acceptable to the general public. Occasional fights are reported, some ending in physical brawls, over exhibition prizes and rejections. The terms degenerate and decadent are popular with the critics of modern arts who do not understand what they are seeing and hearing.

In view of a situation so thick with misunderstanding and bitterness, it is important to propose some generalizations supporting the place of the visual and plastic arts, and as a buttress to one's plea for strengthening education in the arts. Visual and plastic arts of our day, those that are independently produced, are done in search of a truth. The use of the word suggests a moral implication, an implication which it is meant should be made and which contemporary art justifies. People who have reacted violently to contemporary art, who are placing on it and the artist some of the aggression and fear reactions for which they seek an outlet, will say that the artist's truth must be an ugly one.

It may be. But note that I have written contemporary art is in search of *a* truth, not *the* truth. Honestly created art, like democratic society, is always in search of truth, of relative truths, not of absolute dogmas. The individual artist is as various as the individual taxpayer, a fact to be observed in any exhibition of art from those of the New York galleries to a showing of amateur painters in a rural village. The truth sought is that to be seen by each artist afresh. The abstract and near-abstract paintings of some of our most advanced painters have a far more complex reason for existence than a more naturalistic picture. But even if an abstract painting is done as an exercise by a student and is consequently not the most profoundly serious of works, it possesses, willy-nilly, a truth of its own, which is the product of the student's own inimitable handling of paint and shapes.

The truth of the uniqueness of the individual is the greatest gift of the arts today, and only democracy will tolerate this gift. Not all of the art of our society is of this category. The largest volume of art work permits relatively little individuality; that is the work done for advertising and magazine and billboard illustration. But even here, the best-known artists are recognized for some unique quality in their work. It is in the museums rather than in pictorial publications that we see the frankly experimental efforts of the painter whose work was done independently of any precommissioned plan, and this is the work which rouses great enmity. It is the right to explore, sometimes in dark places, which we must preserve for the artist, just as we must preserve freedom of speech and press for political and social ideas.

The expression of that which any individual feels most deeply is perhaps the greatest strength of our society, and it is the easiest to endanger. When we encounter a strongly held conviction running counter to our own certainties, we are all eagerness to correct the error in our neighbor's thinking. The extent of our democracy can be judged by the fact that in most instances of our experience where ideas clash head on, we try to compromise, or we give up with the reflection that we all have a right to our own beliefs. Only when we permit one man to silence another by force or intimidation are we imitating the police state of fascism and communism.

The older we grow as a country, the more complex living becomes for individuals and for the nation, and the more various, subtle, and tragic will true expression in the arts become. Not all of life is lived at the level of a ten-year-old boy's love of a Fourth of July parade.

I inject the symbol of a parade here because it makes an excellent case study of the varied impact a single event has had and might have on different people, and how differently it has been used as a subject for painting. Childe Hassam, in the year of America's entry into the First World War, did several paintings in his impressionist manner of parades, of the flags decorating the office window ledges along Fifth Avenue in New York City. All was color and vivacity and a love of the big city in the mood of patriotic fervor. War had come, but in Hassam's painting it had brought only ticker-tape hysteria, brilliantly clad marching bands, and bright-eyed girls cheering the line of march.

Many years later, John Steuart Curry painted a parade; the subject of soldiers dominated the space, the line of men filled three quarters of the canvas, buildings were only a background. Uniforms were bright and meticulous, a girl's figure clutches at a soldier's sleeve, flags wave, and streamers descend. And all the soldiers' faces are painted not as ordinary faces but as if they had begun to assume the aspect of skulls, eyes sightless, cheeks fallen.

Still another artist, Lee Gatch, has often painted the subject of marching men in close to a totally abstract pattern and has caught the rhythmic beat of forms in procession, the flash of the rifle's thin length against the larger body of its bearer, the rattle of drumsticks against the drumhead. Again we feel the heart-stirring lift of color, step, music, that in its simplest forms we like in a parade, a parade we need not think of as a prelude to death or grief. Strange things happen to paintings as time recedes from the day of their completion. The Hassam now has a pallid melancholy made more intense by the really few spots of bright color in the prevailing muted grays. What was meant to portray light and life and the setting for tumult now pales perceptibly before the more intense organized color impact of Gatch's abstraction. Hassam creates a nostalgia in us with his painting of a city and an event that have passed. Gatch creates no city at all, but the patent leather, the shiny badges, sun glint, the linear crisscross of identical arms swinging, and helmets in wavelike undulation are all contained in his structure of shapes and color.

Child artists are like their professional colleagues in interpretation of experience. One of them would paint a parade as an unbroken group of bright-orange sticks with what looks like a moon on one side of the page and a monkey on a string at the other side; the subject, a band with drum major in front and the bass drum at the rear. Another child might do a painting of a huge sky with a tiny little line of buildings, people on the sidewalk, and little blue men scattered here and there—the child's visual memory of the policemen scattered in the crowd. If the child is asked why the emphasis is on the sky, he might say it was just before the thunderstorm on parade day.

Individual expression, to be strong, to be valuable in breeding independence and character, cannot be conformist. The desire to make

291

all art pleasant to look at, or "understandable," would shortly include the desire to make it say only "Americanism," and of course that in the view of the critic making the evaluation, not the artist.

The search for individual truths and for relative truths is never-ending and properly unpredictable. Both facets are necessary to the arts. Both qualities must be encouraged in arts education. The variety of arts today, which to some is aptly described as turmoil, should be cherished by the whole nation as proof of our unlikeness to any totalitarian regime.

To this point, I have been trying to clarify my thinking on the subject of the truths which the artist seeks in his interpretation of experience, and to explain the importance to him of that interpretation, and the importance to society of welcoming the artist's product.

There is another truth in the infinitely different forms of modern art, one with which the teacher is much concerned. That truth is apparent to the person who has begun to be aware, through the art work of others, of the inimitable qualities of their own experiences. This effort at projection from one's own background to the emotional life of another individual by way of art is for most people as important as the need for personal expression. An example of two altogether different works of art and their kind of challenge to the beholder may make clearer this virtue of contemporary art.

Morris Graves has painted a water color called *Blind Bird*. As a contrasting study, think of the thousands of reproductions of prints and paintings of some hunting subject, say, *Mallards Rising*. The busy but fundamentally unconcerned craftsman painting hunting scenes is turning out replicas of a commonplace symbol. Millions of men seize upon such pictures to remind them of a pleasure they know or, more remotely, a pleasure they think they ought to know. The visual stimulus of such a standardized subject could be better replaced by the smell of a coat still redolent of marsh water and powder smell. The picture itself is like a traffic light or a picture of Santa Claus, symbols we recognize automatically without expecting to examine them with care or interest. The paint quality of a hunting picture is unimportant. The use of pictorial images is so taken for granted that it is disappointing to see it changed too much: one or two people in a boat in the marsh reeds, guns raised or just being lowered, ducks flying off in middle distance, one or two hit and flut-tering to the water. The whole scene has the repetitive, ritual quality of any repeated ceremony. As a work of art, a hunting picture is more a background, a visual evidence of its owner's interest. If the owner of such a picture is not even interested in hunting, its pres-ence in his home depicts with cruel clarity the individual's reliance on familiar symbolism for his home decoration, the desire above all else for conformity in one's environment.

Graves' painting, *Blind Bird*, has to be sought out. It is a water color. A dark wash of gray has covered the tan paper first. The bird clings to a rocklike form drawn in angular brush strokes. Then a net-work of white lines, dots, and brush strokes has built up the snarly, gravelly area around and over the rock forms. The figure of the humped and blank-eyed bird has been created with variations in black and gray paint. His claws, oversize and clumsy for the bulk of the bird, cling to the rock and are covered with the mesh of lines crossing the rock. The beak is small and pointed, and the huge pointed oval shapes of the eyes are painted like opaque blue-black shells set in the head. Arching around and over the solid form of the bird is a transparent band of gray, darker than the gray wash which forms the major area of the picture.

One may see in the painting the influence of the Oriental brush drawings. The charm of the opaque linear whites against the trans-parent grays and blacks can be apprehended and recognized for its sensitivity in line and for the delicacy of the superimposition of the two diverse pigment qualities. The luminous nature of the wash background has something of the fascination we feel in the brush drawings of Rembrandt or the water colors of Cézanne.

Offhand, the sentences above can be dismissed as one more aim-less shuffle through the underbrush of critical art verbiage, another attempt to prove that the artist and those who would "appreciate" his product are sensitive fellows.

Artists must be sensitive, sensitive to life. And the primary hope for general art education is that the citizen can develop some of that sensitivity. Sensitivity that can see beyond the visual clichés of the *Mallards Rising*, and that has time and energy to spend on the *Blind Bird*, is a quality which the world can use. Seeing *Blind Bird* for the

merit of its aesthetic form, for the symbol of a living, helpless crea-
ture clinging to a fragment of solidity in a world of tangling, tripping
strings, is a form of insight to be achieved slowly. It represents an
insight indispensable for the kind of citizens and leaders of citizens
we will be needing most desperately.

This is to say that the leaders in our society, as well as numbers
of ordinary folk, must be lovers of art. The next fifty years and more
will find us in the midst of reconciling the infinitely various cultures
and subcultures of the Eastern and Western worlds. In the last hundred years it has been repeatedly acknowledged that the arts form
one of the best possible clues to understanding other cultures, and
could become instruments for coöperative, constructive ventures between peoples.

Now we need to use every instrument available for such projects
as we must initiate. An administrator of United States funds for agricultural investment abroad, a corporation lawyer, an elementary-
grade teacher, a labor-union leader—all will become more effective
in their work if they develop their capabilities for accepting and
penetrating art forms at first uninteresting or, worse than that, even
repulsive to them.

The jazz of the American Negro, the painting of the Australian
bushmen, the drama of the old Moscow Art Theater, the paintings
of Picasso, the architecture of the Near East, all are eloquent voices
needing to be understood by artists of other lands, but most of all by
citizens in all walks of life—and, through them, by their leaders.

Nothing less than politics, business, science, and commerce must
combine with art to distribute world-wide the kind of agreement
transcending differences which Wendell Willkie foresaw as "One
World."

A State Department official aware of the differences historically
and in his emotional reactions between Moslem and Hindu architecture will be able to counsel with India and Pakistan on a living
basis, not as a representative of a concrete-encased foreign power—
a file-drawer type of person knowing little and caring less for the
aesthetic values other men live for. A business leader who ponders
on the architectural dignity of some European cities, and who is not
defeated at the start in translating some of those values for the

United States, could become an indispensable aid to his local and state planning offices, and in the improvement of living conditions generally.

To accomplish the integrating acts which American and world society needs will require men and women who have learned to search the arts for wisdom: the wisdom of knowing themselves and their environment, and the wisdom of probing beyond the superficial in art and life.

The teacher of art must see his subject, the arts, as an element of human existence which has both formed and interpreted much of the positive values of earthly existence. Art not separated from science or industry, nor divorced from political or financial affairs, but rather that activity of human beings which encompasses everything from the shape of buildings to that incredible machine, television, and from the work of the lonely painter to the group production of the live theater—it is this the art teacher deals with. The citizen aged three to eighty can be helped to use art in all its forms, to express ideas from within and from outside the individual personality. All can be helped to see anew and discriminately things which prejudice, conformity, habit, and dead tradition would shield from their eyes and ears and hands and hearts.

Bibliography

Barzun, Jacques, *Teacher in America*, Doubleday, 1954.

Berkman, Aaron, *Art and Space*, Social Science, 1949.

Blake, Vernon, *Drawing for Children and Others*, Oxford, 1927 (reprinted, 1944).

Blake, Vernon, *The Art and Craft of Drawing*, Oxford, 1927 (reprinted, 1952).

Chapman, William, ed., *Films on Art*, American Federation of Arts, 1952.

Darlington Hall Trustees, *The Visual Arts: The Arts Inquiry by Political and Economic Planning* (PEP), Cumberledge, 1946.

de Francesco, Italo, *This Is Art Education 1952*, National Art Education Association, 1952.

Dudley, Louise, and Faricy, Austin, *The Humanities: Applied Aesthetics*, McGraw-Hill, 1951.

Ellsworth, Maud and Andrews, Michael F., *Growing with Art*, B. H. Sanborn, 1951.

Erdt, Margaret Hamilton, *Teaching Art in the Elementary School,* Rinehart, 1954.

Gaitskell, Charles D., *Arts and Crafts in Our School,* Ryerson, 1949.

Gaitskell, Charles D. and Margaret, *Art Education in the Kindergarten,* Bennett, 1952.

Gropius, Walter, "Design Topics," *Magazine of Art,* December, 1947, p. 298.

Happold, F. C., *Vision und Craftsmanship,* Faber and Faber, 1949.

Harrison, Elizabeth, *Self-Expression Through Art,* Gage, 1951.

Holtzman, Harry, and James, Martin, eds., *Transformations,* 3 Vols., Wittenborn Schultz, 1950–1952.

Keiler, Manfred L., *Art in the Schoolroom,* University of Nebraska, 1951.

Kepes, Gyorgy, *The Language of Vision,* Theobold, 1944.

Kuh, Katherine, *Art Has Many Faces,* Harper, 1951.

Landis, Mildred M., *Meaningful Art Education,* Bennett, 1951.

Langer, Suzanne, *Feeling and Form,* Scribners, 1953.

Langer, Suzanne, *Philosophy in a New Key,* Harvard University, 1942 (Pelican ed., 1948).

McCausland, Elizabeth; Farnum, Royal Bailey; and Vaughan, Dana P., *Art Professions in the United States,* Cooper Union, 1950.

Mendelowitz, Daniel M., *Children Are Artists,* Stanford University Press, 1953.

Nicolaides, Kimon, *The Natural Way to Draw,* Houghton Mifflin, 1941.

Ott, Richard, *The Art of Children,* Pantheon Books, 1952.

Petrie, Marie, *Art and Regeneration,* Elek, 1946.

Rand, Paul, *Some Thoughts on Design,* Wittenborn Schultz, 1947.

Rasmusen, Henry N., *Art Structure, A Textbook of Creative Design,* McGraw-Hill, 1950.

Rathbun, Mary C., and Hayes, Bartlett H., *Layman's Guide to Modern Art,* Oxford, 1949.

Riley, Olive L., *Your Art Heritage,* Harper, 1952.

Rosenthal, Rudolph, and Ratzka, Helena, *The Story of Modern Applied Art,* Harper, 1948.

Saarinen, Eliel, *Search for Form,* Reinhold, 1948.

Schaeffer-Simmern, Henry, *The Unfolding of Artistic Activity,* University of California, 1947.

Schneider, Daniel E., *The Psychoanalyst and the Artist,* Farrar, Straus, 1950.

Scott, Robert Gillam, *Design Fundamentals,* McGraw-Hill, 1951.

Sherman, Hoyt, *Drawing by Seeing: A New Development in Teaching the Visual Arts,* Hinds, Hayden, and Eldredge, 1947.

Sherman, Hoyt, *Cézanne and Visual Form,* Ohio State Visual Demonstration Center, Ohio State University, 1952.

Walker Art Center, *Everyday Art Quarterly,* Vol. I, Summer, 1946.

Young, Arthur R., ed., *This Is Art Education 1951*, National Art Education Association, 1951.

Ziegfeld, Edwin, ed., *Education and Art, A Symposium*, UNESCO (United Nations Educational, Scientific, and Cultural Organization), 1953.

Index of Names

INDEX OF NAMES

Index of Subjects

INDEX OF SUBJECTS